A [illegible]

OF MUMBAI

Vivek Tandon

SCHOLASTIC

New York Toronto London Auckland Sydney
Mexico City New Delhi Hong Kong Buenos Aires

To the memory of Rahimtulla Chinwalla (1919-2006): Novelist, Guide, Friend, Therapist, Photographer, Humanist.

Published by Scholastic India Pvt. Ltd.
A subsidiary of Scholastic Inc., New York, 10012 (USA).
Publishers since 1920, with international operations in Canada, Australia, New Zealand, the United Kingdom, Mexico, India, Argentina, and Hong Kong.

For information regarding permission, write to:
Scholastic India Pvt. Ltd.
Golf View Corporate Tower-A, 3rd Floor,
DLF Phase V, Gurgaon 122002 (India)

Typeset in Garamond

First edition: September 2008

ISBN-10: 81-8477-129-0
ISBN-13: 978-81-8477-129-9

Printed at Yash Printographics, Noida

CONTENTS

Author's Note

The details in this book are authentic to Mumbai. However, certain features will have inevitably changed, since Mumbai is a dynamic, constantly changing metropolis.

The speech patterns of different characters reflect the grammar and slang of their different native languages. India has over a hundred, and all of them leak into Mumbai!

The antiques described in the book are based on historical fact, even when they are fictional. Details of the flood in the book are authentic to the great Mumbai flood of July 2005, though it has been set a month later in the year.

The Shabby Gold Box

The three bought cold drinks and spicy chaat, sat down on the cool grass in a shady corner, and the blind man told them how it had all begun.

'It began at Queen's Necklace, only last night. My friend was selling roasted peanuts and chana-dal from a public bench. I had spread my mat on the floor behind the bench and I was playing my music. There were young couples all around me, all thinking that life was a flim, and they were the hero and heroine. They wanted to hear love songs from old old flims! I made a good pile of money last night. There was a cool breeze blowing in from the sea, and life was a dream.

'By twelve-thirty, the crowds had gone. My friend had also gone, with his peanut-roaster. There was only one couple there, and they wouldn't let me stop playing! After they left, there was nobody close by. The sea was quiet. Though I can't see, my skin could feel the cool darkness—at this time of month the moon is slender, a pure silver crescent.

'I counted the money I had made for the day and put it in my pocket. I was just beginning to get up and fold my mat when I heard a strange noise from behind me.

'There was something about the sound that made my blood stand still in my veins. I sat still, listening very carefully. Then there was another strange noise, as if a balloon was going "phusss …".

'Now, son, I pride myself on being able to understand almost any sound I hear. But this sound I couldn't make out, so I kept sitting, waiting to hear more.

'I then heard the dragging footsteps of two drunken men. They came to the stone bench, then I heard a thud, as if one drunk had clumsily sat down. Then the other man's footsteps walked away neatly from the bench, as if he had suddenly become completely sober! Even this, I could not understand.

'I waited for two minutes, but after that there was no sound from the bench. *No* sound at all, even though one man was still sitting!

'Now beta, I can even hear the breath of a newborn baby in his deepest, most peaceful sleep. But there was just *no sound at all* from that bench.

'I was beginning to wonder what I should do when the other man's footsteps came back—there was somebody with him. They both sat down on the bench. I then heard very soft slapping sounds, again and again.

'I heard one man say admiringly, "You don't have much blood on you." The other man said proudly: "I stabbed him in the other side, away from my body." The way they spoke, I knew they were goondas. One man whispered, "Do you know the police is giving a reward of one lakh rupees for this box?" The other whispered: "The box is not on Michael's body!"

'I suddenly understood, in a flash, the whole story of the strange sounds I had heard. The first strange sound had been of a knife piercing clothes and flesh. The second sound, like a balloon going "phusss ..." was the dying man's last breath. The footsteps that I had thought were of two drunk men had actually been the footsteps of the killer holding up the dead body and walking it to the bench. The thud, which I had thought was one drunk clumsily sitting down, had been when the killer seated the dead man on the bench: and now, he and another goonda were patting the body of the dead man, searching for something, going through his pockets ...'

For a moment Pappu stopped listening to what the old man was saying, and remembered how it had all begun for *him.* He could hardly believe that only this morning ...

Pappu had been waiting for the electric train on his way to school when he saw an old blind man walking his way.

He looked like a beggar. His eyes wandered about searching the sky emptily. He felt the floor before him with his cane, and at his waist was an odd, rectangular wooden case—Pappu couldn't make out what it was. Was it a shoe-polish box, or did it have cigarettes he was selling?

The blind man stopped in front of the signboard, with its dotted lights that spelt out the train timings and stations: Churchgate, Charni Road Station, Dadar, Bandra and 8.15—two of the lights had gone out in the 8.15, so there were gaps in it. It read like 3.15.

The blind man had a dyed beard and a fez, the Muslim cap. His eyes rolling like marbles chipped long ago, he spread a cloth on the grimy cement floor in front of the signboard. He sat cross-legged on it and opened his wooden case.

Pappu was really confused to see what was inside the case: it was crammed with wires and needles and what looked like buttons.

The blind man carefully laid his cane and his cloth bag to one side. He cleared his throat, and suddenly began to tug at the wires inside his wooden case so that Pappu thought he wanted to break them.

But as he plucked at the wires and pressed the buttons, like magic a beautiful tune began to flow out. It was a musical instrument!

A crowd quickly gathered around him as he played an old film song. Though he was only playing the tune, he played so well that Pappu could almost hear the sad words of the song:

Ae mere dil kahi aur chal
Ghum ki duniya se dil bhar gaya …
(O my heart, let us go somewhere else
We have had our fill of this world of sadness …)

Pappu's parents had told him never to give money to beggars.

'But he is not a beggar, he's a musician,' he thought. So he put a five-rupee note in the open lid of the musical case, where others were putting money too. Inches away, the blind man's fingers plucked the sad notes from the wires.

Pappu heard a screech behind him, and he was startled to see his train braking to a halt. The crowd around the blind man disappeared as people rushed to the train. Pappu was about to run after them when he saw the five-rupee note he had put in the box flutter in the breeze.

And that was what really started it all of course.

He bent forward, took a coin and put it on the note to weigh it down—

The beautiful, gentle tune was cruelly cut off. The blind man's fingers sprang from the wires and closed around Pappu's wrist.

'Let me go! I'll miss my train!' Pappu cried, trying to pull his hand away.

'Why?' the blind man snarled. 'Why did you put your hand in my musical case again? Why?'

With a shock, Pappu looked at the man's eyes—was he really blind? Or could he see?

But the eyes were unseeing, hard. 'Why?' the blind man's voice was rough, hard. His grimy brown fingers dug hard into Pappu's wrist, feeling like rusty iron on his flesh.

Finally, Pappu found his voice—but he found it in

pieces—he had to stammer.

'I—I kept a five-rupee note in your bo-box the first time. It was flying off in the wind, so I—I tried to keep it down with a coin.'

The blind man let go of his hand at once.

'Ae khuda! And I was suspecting you?' He spoke in an Urdu that was pleasing to the ear.

'How could you see it was me again?' Pappu asked, rubbing his wrist.

'See? Brother, though I can't use my eyes, I can use my ears, can't I? Come here!'

He turned Pappu around so that he could feel his school bag, strapped on his back. The bag had two metal buckles, and the blind man struck one against the other with a clink.

'See?' he said. 'I heard this sound when you leaned forward the first time, and I recognised it again the second time.'

'Oh!' Pappu said. 'My train is gone!'

The time and route of the next train flickered on the signboard. The blind man asked Pappu to name any tune he wanted to hear. Pappu named another old, sad song, which the blind man again played beautifully. A crowd gathered again. The old man, as he played this time, had a strange smile on his face, as if he were smiling secretly to himself.

As he finished the tune the next train drew up.

'Khuda hafiz, Chacha,' Pappu said.

'Khuda hafiz, beta.'

Pappu boarded the train. He didn't see a big burly

Maharashtrian talk to the blind man and then jump into the coach behind Pappu's. As the train rolled out Pappu looked back to see the blind man playing another tune, that strange, secret smile still on his lips.

In the second period, during the maths test, Pappu reached into his bag for the compass box.

His hand touched something strange and hard and round inside.

There was a new maths Sir—they didn't like him much. He was sitting at his table, his nose buried in a thriller. So Pappu carefully took the thing out and studied it beneath his desktop. It was a small pipe-shaped box he had never seen before in his life. It gleamed sharply where the light touched it in the desk, and it looked like it was made of gold. But it looked very old. It even smelled old. It had what looked like one or two shiny diamonds in it, puncturing the dark inside the desk with their needle-like lights.

Pappu couldn't understand it. He had reached school late, had put his bag inside his desk, and had not moved at all from his place. So it couldn't be something somebody had put in, as a joke.

The pipe-shaped box had a strange design on it. The design had some small dents on it, where there must have been more of those diamond-like stones. Pappu looked again at the shiny stones—'My God!' he thought. 'I think these are real diamonds! They must be worth lakhs of rupees!'

PHUT! Pappu felt a sharp rap on his head, and looked up to find Sir frowning down at him.

Sir's voice boomed: 'What are you doing, boy, under your desk? Show me!'

Under the desk, Pappu's hand quickly slipped the old box back in the bag. Sir raised the desk-top and, seeing his half-open bag said, 'Accha! Copying, is it?' He didn't even bother to make sure.

'No, Sir. I never copy—'

'Chupp! As punishment, you will stay back after the last period and dust all the trophies in the principal's room.'

'But Sir—'

'Quiet! Now continue your test, or I'll give you zero!'

Behind him there was a titter from Pigface Paintal. 'He's supposed to be my buddy!' Pappu thought, steaming with anger and shame.

He didn't do the test well at all. (Later he found he had failed it. But by then of course it didn't matter.) And he couldn't stop thinking of the golden pipe-shaped box with real diamonds. What could be inside it?

Pappu didn't get a chance to open the box till first recess. When he took it out Pigface Paintal pounced on him.

'He-e-ey! You robbed your grandma's jewellery box or something? Let me look!'

'I'll show you afterwards,' Pappu dodged his fat hands. Luckily someone called Paintal and he turned away.

Pappu ran to the playground and went to the corner that was hidden by wild grass from the rest of the school.

He took the golden box out of his pocket. It looked even more beautiful out here than it had in the classroom. The design seemed to be an old Mughal one. The diamonds went off in the sun like tiny firecrackers.

'My god,' he thought. 'If the *box* is so beautiful, how beautiful must what's inside be!' With trembling hands, he unscrewed the top.

There was only dust inside! Dust that was fine, and perhaps hundreds of years old, like the box itself. Pappu looked carefully, but there was nothing else.

Pappu sat on the grass, puzzled and disappointed. The box looked as if it had once belonged to some king or queen. Where had it come from? How come it was here, in his hands, right now?

'Hissssss!'

Pappu jumped. He saw the wild grass move, and he remembered the rumours about snakes in this part of the playground.

'Hissssss!'

Pappu yelped and fell, his heart beating so hard it beat all the breath out of his body so that he didn't even have the strength to breathe back in again. The grass was so tall he couldn't see the snake—so it might bite him any moment.

'Hissssss!'

'Pchew! Pchchchew! Beta!'

The voice came from the fence—Pappu saw a face peeping from above it. But he still couldn't see the snake.

'Pchew! Hisss! Pchchchew! Hisss! Pchchew!'

At last Pappu understood that the man at the fence, who was making the vulgar kissing sound to call him, was also making the hissing sound. There was no snake!

Pappu gave a whoop of joy and fell back in the grass with relief.

'Beta! Pchchew! Hisss!'

'You frightened me …' Pappu said, getting up.

And then he had another surprise. For the face above the fence was the blind man's dark face, brown fez on top, and below, his beard red with the henna dye. His lips were stained, too, with the red of paan and tobacco. They smiled secretly even now.

'Beta, come here! Pchchew!'

'You put the box in my bag!' cried Pappu.

'Box? What box? Come here!'

Pappu stood where he was. He suddenly understood why the old man's smile looked secret. It was because of the unseeing eyes above. How can a blind man smile at you when he can't see you? So when he smiles, he smiles to himself, secretly in his dark world.

'How did you get here?' Pappu asked. 'How …'

'I brought him here,' boomed a big voice, and another head rose above the fence. 'I followed you here from the station this morning, after you met him.'

The new face was big, scowling, burly—obviously a goonda, Pappu thought.

Just then a whistle sounded, and a third face showed up over the fence. It was a policeman, who smiled broadly at the goonda.

'Oh no!' groaned the goonda. The policeman waved a pair of handcuffs. The goonda's eyes gleamed dangerously, but when a second policeman's face appeared he cursed in Marathi and let them handcuff him.

The policeman eyed the blind man suspiciously.

'Who's this?' he asked Pappu in Marathi. Pappu answered, also in Marathi, 'Oh it's all right, he works for my family.'

As soon as he said it he wished he hadn't. He didn't know why he had lied—maybe because of the beautiful music in the morning.

'I owe you, son,' said the blind man when the policeman had gone. 'Otherwise they could have arrested me too. Now give me the box.'

'Why?'

'It's mine! Give it to me!'

'What's so important about the box?'

For a moment Pappu thought the blind man had become deaf as well: he didn't answer, and he was very still.

Pappu asked, 'It's empty, isn't it? So what's so special about the box?'

The blind man said heatedly, one arm holding on to the fence as the other waved blindly in the air: 'It's empty, no, so what good is it to you? Give it to me!'

'Did you steal it?'

In answer, the blind man took one of his hands away and reached deep down on the other side.

When the hand came back it had a pistol in it. And

the pistol was pointed exactly at Pappu's heart.

Pappu's heart jumped. He was very frightened, and very puzzled. Could the old man see? The fright and puzzlement got mixed up in his head, and it began to spin and ache.

'Don't move son,' the blind man growled (and when somebody growls in Urdu, it sounds very impressive.) 'I can't see you, but my ears know exactly where you are. If you move an inch, I'll hear you. And I'll shoot!'

Pappu looked at the pistol, and suddenly he felt tears creeping up in his eyes. He had liked the old man so much, he had loved his music. And now …

'It's—it's unfair!' he cried. 'I just saved you from the POLICEMAN!' He felt a choking inside him, and he blinked back the stinging moistness rising in his eyes.

The blind man lowered the pistol, and swallowed hard.

'Son, just give me the box,' he said more softly.

Pappu walked slowly towards him, his chest heaving with the anger and hurt inside.

When he gave the box over the fence, the blind man caught hold of his wrist.

Pappu cried, 'Let me go!' He looked frantically over the blind man's shoulder for the policemen, but they were nowhere in sight. The school fence faced the backs of some government houses, so there was nobody else.

'You've got to help me, son!' the blind man's voice was desperate. 'Now they've arrested Shinde, I've got to search the whole of Mumbai myself. Me, a blind man! How can I? I need your help!'

'Let me go!' Pappu struggled to pull away.

'I'm not asking you to do anything bad or unlawful! No, I'm asking you to help me recover a national treasure for the government! Help me only for one hour. You'll be a hero, and I'll … we'll get a reward!'

'You should be asking the police for help, not running away from them,' Pappu said. He twisted, trying to free his wrist.

'You're right, but the police—I went to them, but just because I'm a poor, blind man—they won't listen to me! They called me a senile old—' He was very bitter.

'Let me go!' Pappu caught hold of the gun.

'Don't!' The blind man cocked the pistol.

The barrel was now set to go off inches from Pappu's face.

Something very funny happened. Before this Pappu was terrified, and feeling very hurt. But now suddenly his head cleared. His eyes were suddenly completely dry, and he could see everything very clearly, he could hear everything clearly and he could think very clearly and coolly. He grew very still.

They stood like statues, he and the blind man, for what seemed to be a long time. Pappu felt sweat trickling down his face, and there was sweat on the blind man's face as well.

Then the blind man tried to say something. But the sound wouldn't come out, and he had to clear his throat and try again.

'Climb up the fence, son. Very slowly.'

Pappu did as he was told. The blind man never let go of his arm.

Pappu was afraid, but suddenly very calm. When he got down on the other side, he saw the blind man had a cloth bag hanging from one shoulder to his hip. He pulled out a dirty old shawl from it and flung it around Pappu's shoulders. He put the pistol in the hand that was around Pappu, so that it was hidden beneath the shawl.

He made Pappu put the golden box in the bag. He took his cane, which was leaning against the fence alongside his musical case. He made Pappu pick that up.

Then he made Pappu walk with him. No one came out of the houses facing the fence, so nobody saw the drama with the pistol, which was lucky for the blind man.

Unlucky for Pappu. Oddly in this moment, he found himself thinking that at least he wouldn't have to stay back and dust the trophies!

The lane led to the highway, which led straight to the heart of Mumbai. The traffic on it was heavy.

Pappu's eyes automatically searched for the ice-cream cart to the left, where all the students rushed during recess if they had any money.

He got a shock to see Pigface Paintal looking straight at him, curiously, as if he were something that had run out from the zoo. Pigface Paintal (or PP, as they called him for short) was sucking non-stop at an ice-lolly, its bright red spreading on his fat lips and cheeks, nose, and a little even on his fat specs. He kept poking it deep inside his mouth as if he was trying to paint every corner inside bright red—and he was succeeding!

'Stop a taxi when you see one,' the blind man said.

Pappu knew he must look odd, in the close embrace of the blind man. He made a face at PP, and gave him a little wave. PP didn't wave at him, because he didn't want Pappu to walk up to him and share his next ice-lolly. His first was almost over.

Pappu waved at him wildly, with the arm that wasn't crushed between him and the blind man.

'What are you doing?' the blind man asked crossly.

'Er ... waving at a taxi,' Pappu said. 'Taxi! Taxi!' he yelled at PP. Paintal stared at him, looking more Pigfaced than ever. He silently started slobbering over his second ice-lolly, staring at Pappu—-ice-lollies are more fun if you have a show to watch while you're licking them.

'You're waving in the wrong direction,' the blind man said suspiciously. 'We need a taxi travelling *this* way. That's why we're standing on *this* side of the road.'

So Pappu had to stop waving at PP. He turned to face the right way. When he saw a taxi, he stayed silent. But when an ordinary car went by he would wave wildly at people around him, looking hard at them and crying: 'Taxi! Taxi!' Especially he would twist around at Pigface, and look hard at *him*. He tried to mouth, 'Police. Police.' Pigface looked at his ice-lolly, looked at him, and slowly shook his head. Pigface thought

Pappu was mouthing 'Puhlease, Puhlease'—but he would never give up his ice-lolly! He'd think up some excuse later, like … he'd been starving to death or something.

People around Pappu looked at him as if he were mad. Pappu stopped waving.

There was a fisherwoman, her sari raised to her thighs and wrapped tightly around her body. In her hand was a bag of groceries she'd just bought. As she walked primly by, she looked at Pappu.

The blind man's nose twitched.

'A fisherwoman,' Pappu heard him mutter under his breath.

There was something kindly in her look to Pappu … she reminded him of his ayah. So Pappu began to signal to her.

But her kindly look disappeared at once, and she walked by without looking at Pappu again.

This puzzled Pappu. There were other passers-by, and he tried signalling to them but they too would at once look away and hurry by. 'Why don't they understand me?' Pappu thought miserably. 'Why don't they stop?'

One man quickly put a rupee coin in Pappu's hand, and Pappu at last understood.

The blind man's dirty shawl hid, almost completely, his school uniform. And Pappu had the musical case with him. To busy passers-by, he and the blind man were a couple of beggars. And in Mumbai, it was no new thing for a mad beggar to wave wildly in the air, make faces at passers-by and hail taxis that weren't there.

'Why don't they stop?' growled the blind man.

For one wild moment Pappu thought again: Can he see? Can he see me trying to stop these people? But then: 'Say something,' grumbled the blind man. 'The taxis, why aren't they stopping?'

Pappu breathed a sign of relief (he hoped the blind man didn't hear it). When the next empty taxi came, he stopped it almost gladly.

'Marine Drive,' said the blind man, anxiously.

'Do you have the money?' the driver asked. 'It'll take about Rs 200.'

'Rs 200! Y'Allah!' the blind man muttered.

As they got in, Pappu looked back and saw PP, bare ice-stick in his hand, looking towards them, stunned.

Pappu thought, 'I think he's seen the pistol!' He mouthed 'POLICE' once more before the blind man pushed him into the cab.

As the taxi began to move, he thought he glimpsed in the mirror PP jumping up and down, but he couldn't be sure.

In the back seat of the cab the blind man leaned his cane against the front seat and pulled Pappu gently towards him. But his gun was still pointed at him. He whispered in his ear: 'Son you have to help me. Khuda knows I don't want to treat you this way, but ... without you, I have no chance.' Pappu, looking at the hard face, so sad, so close to his, almost believed him.

The blind man took a sad, deep breath, and breathed out such a strong smell of tobacco that Pappu twisted and almost jumped out of the car.

The blind man reminded him of the pistol by pressing it to his ribs.

'Listen!' he whispered fiercely. 'On the western coast of Mumbai, a smuggler's launch will dock tomorrow night. He'll be coming to collect this golden pipe-shaped box I put in your bag. He wants to steal from Hindustan a great treasure …'

'But this box is empty.'

'Yes! But for hundreds of years it had something for which hundreds were killed. In fact, twenty-four hours from this moment—' The blind man stopped suddenly.

Twenty-four hours—was the blind man thinking of yesterday, or tomorrow? Pappu couldn't help looking at the pistol in his hand and shrinking from it.

The blind man felt this. He immediately pulled the pistol back.

'Oh! You don't have anything to fear from me, boy! I want to help the go'rrment recover this treasure.' His voice became almost begging. 'I need your help for only one more hour. There is no risk, khuda ki kasam—I swear I would not allow an innocent boy like you to even come near danger. Just … stay with this cursed old man for one hour longer, and after that you'll never see me again.'

Only one more hour? And after that, suppose he said, sorry, just another hour more? And then another? Why had he taken Pappu? If he wanted to help the government, he should have just gone to the police. Pappu felt a horrible chill pass through his body.

The Snow Queen

The blind man moved back from Pappu and leaned against the car door, as if he was very tired. He stayed like that for some time.

Outside the windows Pappu could see they were travelling past the prosperous suburb of Bandra; then, before Mahim, the fisherman's village with its old upturned deep brown fishing boats, its flags fluttering brightly in the wind, and its stink twice as big as the village itself; then the Muslim area of Mahim, with its big bright green mosque; past Shivaji Park, where Sunil Gavaskar, Sachin Tendulkar and many others had learnt to be great cricketers: past the long line of devotees on the roads outside Sidhi Vinayak Temple.

When they got to Breach Candy, the blind man took up his musical case and played another old tune, again sad.

When the taxi slowed at the next signal, Pappu's hand went slowly towards his door handle.

But the blind man stopped playing suddenly, and when Pappu looked the pistol was pointed at him again.

'Brother, why have you stopped?' the taxi driver asked. 'You play beautifully.'

The blind man sighed sadly, and said: 'Mia, I don't feel like it.'

The rest of the journey passed in silence. Past the beaches of Breach Candy, past Kemp's Corner flyover, speeding over the cleaner and broader roads here till they finally got to Marine Drive.

Even though it was noon, the broad six-lane road on Marine Drive was bustling with traffic. Beside it on the sun-yellow Chowpatty Beach, the stalls of ice cream, kulfi and spicy chaat were hot with bright colours. They were not as crowded as the busy road.

On the other side of the beach the blue-marine green sea sparkled right up to the horizon. Its lazy waves washed up to the beach with a giant, comforting 'Hushshsh', a sound that itself surged and fell, surged and fell, like the waves before their final crash.

Before they got out of the taxi the blind man again put the shawl around Pappu, with the pistol underneath it. They got out with difficulty.

'The man we're looking for,' the blind man said, 'is somewhere here, his address is Isnokuin, Chowpatty. I don't know what Isnokuin could be. You take me there, and then you can go. Come, let's cross the road.'

Isnokuin—where could that be? Pappu thought about it. Since this was Chowpatty, where spicy chaat and milkshakes and ice creams were sold, that could be Snow Queen. Perhaps it was simply the name of one of the stalls.

But he didn't say anything.

As they waited for a gap in the fast-moving traffic, Pappu spotted a policeman on the other side of the road.

His heart missed a beat, and he at once looked away so that the blind man could not see what he was thinking. (But then, of course, he remembered the blind man could never *see* what he was thinking.)

The policeman had a white-and-brown uniform, which meant he was a traffic policeman.

'That means,' Pappu thought, 'that he doesn't have a pistol. The blind man does.'

But then he thought, the pistol was useless to the blind man unless he had someone right next to him, like Pappu was. On this busy, noisy road, if Pappu could get even six feet away the blind man wouldn't be able to hear where he was. So he wouldn't be able to point the pistol at where he heard Pappu was.

While Pappu was thinking this the policeman suddenly turned and began to walk away from them. He was going farther and farther away …

Pappu desperately looked for a gap in the traffic. All this time the blind man had him tightly by the arm, underneath the shawl. On the other side of the road the policeman's back was growing smaller and smaller …

When it was almost too late, Pappu thought he saw a break in the traffic. But they would have to really hurry to make it.

'Let us go! Let us cross,' he tugged at the blind man. Then he tried to break away and run, but the blind man was holding on tightly, and so they just knocked against each other and moved slowly to the centre of the road.

A big white Sumo was heading straight for them at top speed—but in another second the policeman would be out of sight. So he yelled:

'Police! Police!'

'Screech! Screee …' went burning tyres on the road.

The blind man stopped where he was, on the road. At the same time Pappu saw the policeman disappear around the corner without hearing him. Pappu felt the blind man push the pistol against his ribs, and he closed his eyes.

'He's going to shoot me now,' he thought.

'Screeee …'

Time seemed to freeze. The sound of the tyres was deafening. Still with closed eyes, Pappu suddenly felt the blind man move the pistol from him, and let go of his arm.

'… eeeee …'

The sound of the Sumo's tyres passed them by. The Sumo had missed them!

Pappu opened his eyes. They were in the middle of the road, and the blind man was standing looking miserable, the pistol pointed limply at the ground.

'Take me to the police, son,' he was saying. 'I deserve it, after showing a small child like you a gun. I should be put in jail and never let out. Where's the police?' He held out his hands to be handcuffed, because he thought the policeman was walking towards him. 'Canastable sahb, put on the handcuffs and throw me in jail. I deserve whatever you do to me.'

All this while cars whizzed by at top speed on all sides. One driver slowed down to curse at them.

Pappu took the blind man's hand and the blind man followed him to the side of the road like a baby. He thought he was leading him to the policeman, and again he held out his hands.

When no one handcuffed him, he was puzzled.

'Where is this police of yours?'

Pappu wasn't sure what to answer, or do. So he took the blind man to one of the stone benches on the beach, a little way from the chaat and ice-cream stalls.

Pappu asked him to sit and he sat obediently, though he looked puzzled.

Pappu asked, 'Could I have your pistol?'

'Yes. There are no bullets in it.'

Pappu carefully checked, and it was indeed empty!

Pappu tried to put the pistol in his pocket, but it was so big that it stuck out and he had to cover it with his hand to hide it.

'Take me to the police, son,' the blind man said, in a tired voice that made Pappu feel sad for him.

Pappu wanted time to think so he said, 'Play me a tune first.'

As the blind man played, Pappu thought, I should give him up to the police. It would be the right thing to do.

But somehow he didn't want to. He couldn't.

When the tune was over Pappu asked: 'Give me the golden box.'

The blind man gave it to him, and Pappu looked at it some more. But it did not give up its secrets. It was still an old box set with little diamonds, most of which had fallen away.

'Why did you put it in my bag?'

'I'm going senile, that's why. I was frightened because at the station I thought I recognised the voice of someone who had only twenty-four hours ago—he had … spilt blood for the box.'

Pappu shivered.

'But it wasn't him. It was only a voice that resembled his.'

'What *is* this box?'

'What can I say, son. I don't know.'

Pappu was confused. 'You *don't know*?'

'No. The first time I saw that box was twenty-four hours ago, when I heard a man being killed because of it.'

'You *heard* …?'

'I was on Queen's Necklace, playing my music for the young couples who roam there. It was past midnight. I was almost alone there when I heard a strange sound behind me. Now beta, I pride myself on being able to recognise all kinds of sounds. But this sound was so strange, I couldn't recognise—'

Suddenly Pappu felt a huge hand on his hand, with which he was trying to hide the pistol in his pocket. He looked up to see a hefty goonda with a horribly colourful scarf glowering down at him. The goonda said: 'Kulfi, falooda, or salty ice cream?'

Pappu didn't know what to say. Then, after a long time, he heard the blind man reply: 'Just strawberry ice cream with salt and pepper please.'

The goonda said, 'I saw this little mosquito threaten you with the pistol. I would have walked on, thinking it was a toy. Then I recognised the golden box, and I realised something serious was happening. You,' he said to Pappu, 'be careful. I've got a big knife under my dhoti.'

He took the pistol from Pappu, and put that under his dhoti too.

'I'm Irfaan,' he said to the blind man.

'I'm Hafiz,' the blind man replied.

Irfaan took Pappu by the arm, and the blind man followed.

They went to an ice-cream stall close by, which the goonda seemed to own. In front was a signboard with 'Snow Queen' painted on it, as horribly colourful as the goonda's scarf. Below the sign was a counter from which a man served the customers, sitting on two rickety wooden benches in front of him.

Irfaan took the blind man and Pappu to the back of the stall and they went inside. It was a small room with tin walls, bare except for two big ice-cream freezers and one or two trunks.

Irfaan lifted the top of a freezer and growled at Pappu: 'What flavour do you like?'

'F-f-flavour?' Pappu said, after some time.

'WHAT FLAVOUR OF ICE CREAM DO YOU LIKE?'

'St-taw-trawberry.'

'Don't shout at the boy,' the blind man said softly.

Irfaan took out a strawberry cup, small size, and shoved it into Pappu's hands.

'You sit there and eat quietly.'

They sat down on the trunks. Irfaan gave the blind man his pistol back, and giving Pappu a sour look signalled to him to start eating.

But Pappu was so frightened he couldn't eat. In fact, it was difficult for him to even begin to swallow.

Irfaan looked at Pappu. 'EAT!' he shouted.

Pappu began trembling madly.

Irfaan said softly, 'What are we going to do with this mosquito, Hafiz? We'll have to do something.' Then even more softly: 'Is he a Mussalmaan?'

A deep fear went through Pappu, and the papercup slipped from his shaking hands. The icecream spread all over the floor.

Irfaan sprang up and roared: 'YOU …!' He hit Pappu hard, so that Pappu was sent sprawling on the floor.

Pappu waited for the next blow. But it didn't come. He waited …

After a while he heard Irfaan's voice, very gentle: 'What are you doing, Hafiz?'

Then he heard the blind man's voice, also very gentle: 'Move to the corner, Irfaan, slowly, away from the child. I can hear exactly where you are.'

Pappu looked up to see the blind man pointing his pistol at the goonda, exactly at his heart. The pistol was cocked.

It was also, Pappu knew, empty.

But Irfaan didn't know. He moved, very carefully, away from Pappu.

'Hafiz? We have to do something about this mosquito ...'

'Sit down, or ... or do you want to hear the message Ikka has sent you?'

Irfaan looked at the blind man, then looked menacingly at Pappu and sat down. The blind man put the pistol back in his cloth bag. But he kept his hand close to the top of the bag.

Irfaan said, 'Give me the message from Ikka. Have the police caught him? Ikka's smart ... police would never suspect someone who's stone-blind ... Hafiz, we have to do something about this mosquito ... How did you pick him up?'

'Arre, by accident brother. But tell me Irfaan, what is the signal? Where is the American going to dock?'

Irfaan glowered at the blind man for a while. Then he said, rudely, 'You see to your own work. Give me the message.'

'Yes, yes, I was just giving it. Ikka wants you to get the goods out—they're hidden in dabbaa number E-52. He wants you to take them tomorrow night to the American yourself, take the money from him, and keep it. Ikka says he will be out of jail, pukka, in four or five days. Whatever happens, Ikka says, he will be talking to you when he comes out.'

The goonda sat for a minute. He seemed stunned by what the blind man said.

He rushed to his feet and pounced at the blind man.

Running Homeward

The blind man had his gun out so fast, Pappu didn't even see it move. One moment it wasn't there, the next moment it was.

The goonda sprang back, for the gun was pointed at his heart.

The blind man said, 'Beta, come here near me. Move very carefully, don't pass near him.' Pappu obeyed.

When he sat next to the blind man, he could feel him relax. 'Now what's the matter, Irfaanbhai?' the blind man asked.

Irfaan was silent.

The blind man said, 'Irfaanbhai, I cannot see. I need you to talk to me. If you don't, a blind man like me has no hope. I'm desperate. I am cornered. I'll have to shoot you, because it's the only thing I can do.'

Irfaan hesitated. Then he said defiantly, 'There is lots of Public outside …' He used the English word 'public'.

'I don't care. I'll say you're a goonda, and I had to shoot in self-defence. Why, you're not a goonda,

Irfaanbhai? They might not believe me?'

Pappu felt the blind man hold his breath: not only were his eyes sightless, which Irfaan knew, but his gun was empty. If Irfaan decided to call his bluff, all would be over …

After some time, Irfaan swallowed and said, 'You're not from Ikka. He sends me his messages sealed with cellotape, his signature under the tape. If he can't, then he sends his messages with *two* special passwords. You didn't give the second one.'

'Accha', the blind man said, hiding his relief that Irfaan was not calling his bluff. 'And where do you shine the signal to the sea tomorrow?'

'The terrace of a building called Akash Ganga, by the shore at Breach Candy. The time …'

'The time is eleven tomorrow night,' the blind man said in an eager, dreamy voice. 'Go on.'

The goonda swallowed. 'The American's boat will be there, five-six hundred feet out in the sea. We are to shine the signal, he will shine back the answer. And on his boat the deal is to be done.'

'And the signal, Irfaan? What's the signal?' the blind man's voice was like a child asking to be told his favourite story.

Irfaan now suddenly realised that he was giving too much away—perhaps everything.

'Don't be shy Irfaanbhai. You've already said so much …' the blind man taunted.

It was the wrong thing to say. Irfaan's big chest rose and fell with humiliation. He tried to rise, as silently as he could.

The blind man's pistol rose, always pointed at his heart. Irfaan sat down again. But the blind man was rattled.

'Son,' he said, 'go round to the front of the stall and tell the man there that his boss wants some milkshake. Bring it here, and also bring a teaspoon. And son—knock five times, loudly, when you come back.'

When he was outside, Pappu's legs trembled from wanting to run. Only a stretch of sand was between him and the highway. There were three or four taxis queued up on the road. It would take him ten seconds to get into one, and be off home, back into his comfortable everyday world.

A picture came to his mind: of the blind man inside the ice-cream stall, pointing an empty pistol at Irfaan, waiting for Pappu to come back … sweating, and waiting with the empty pistol … and after some time realising that Pappu was not coming back, even though the blind man had used an empty pistol to save him … and then the blind man would have to keep the empty pistol on Irfaan, not being able to see anything, not knowing what he would do once Irfaan also understood Pappu wasn't coming back …

So, legs still trembling, Pappu went to the man at the Snow Queen counter, and asked for a milkshake for his boss.

'What flavour?' the man asked.

'St-taw-strawberry.'

As he turned to go back to the tin room, Pappu's

face came up against a fat nose that wouldn't move.

'PP!' One 'P' he whispered from fright, the second 'P' he yelled from surprise. PP was what they called Pigface when they felt okay about him. 'PP! Are the cops with you?'

'No. Where are you taking that?' PP eyed the milkshake greedily. It had ice cream and cashews, and cardamom in it. It was as horribly colourful as the Snow Queen signboard above.

'PP, are you crazy?' He remembered that the blind man was waiting for him. 'I have to take it inside. Call the police!'

He waited to see Pigface nod, but he didn't.

'PP!'

PP said, 'If we go to the police now, will we get the reward?'

'How do you know about the reward?'

PP only smiled. Pappu was so angry, the big glass shook in his hand and the milkshake spilled from it. But the blind man was waiting—he had to go in.

Inside, the two were exactly as he had left them. Both were stuck against the wall in fear.

The blind man took out of his pocket two pills, and gave them to Pappu.

'Mix them in the milkshake, son. Mix them well.'

Pappu put the pills and stirred the milkshake. The blind man asked Irfaan. 'So what is dabbaa number E-52? Where is dabbaa number E-52?'

Pappu wondered: could it be a train ka dabbaa? Or a lunch ka dabbaa? There were so many kinds of boxes in Mumbai. It could be a special guest's box at the race course. It could be something as simple as a bank locker …

Irfaan said, 'Bhaiya, I don't know what that means. I have to ask someone else.'

'Who?'

Irfaanbhai began to whine. 'Arre, how can I tell you? I have told you enough to get me killed, have a little pity on me …'

'Beta,' the blind man said to Pappu, who had almost finished stirring. 'Put the glass on the floor, in between Irfaanbhai and you. Irfaanbhai, if I hear you moving toward the child, I will shoot. Public will forgive me if by mistake I hit your heart.'

Pappu carefully, without removing his eyes from Irfaanbhai, placed the glass in the centre of the floor, and moved back to his corner.

'Irfaanbhai, just taste this milkshake, till the glass is empty. Son—make sure he drinks every drop.'

Irfaanbhai asked nervously, 'What have you put in it?'

The blind man laughed coldly. 'I am desperate, but not mad. It is not some deadly poison, Irfaanbhai. It is only a harmless medicine for sleeping.'

Irfaanbhai gingerly drank till the tall glass was empty.

'Keep the glass carefully behind you. And tell me truthfully. What do you know about the dabbaa E-52?'

But soon, the goonda was slumped on the floor, snoring loudly.

The blind man let out a big sigh of relief. He lowered his empty pistol.

'Run away, son. Go home.'

Pappu wanted to run away, but instead he stood there like a fool.

'Go!'

Pappu turned.

'But son. *Don't* tell the police! Give me time to find the treasure first.'

'How will you find it?' Pappu asked.

'I'll go to some friends and take their help. Even though some of them are not completely trustworthy,' he laughed. 'But this is no business for a young boy like you. I'll manage. Khuda hafiz, beta.'

Pappu nodded, and then ran off without knowing where he was headed. But his heart was telling him, don't run away! Don't leave the old man!

Outside, over the wide, crowded six-lane road, there was an overbridge for pedestrians to cross. He ran up its steps, and was halfway across the overbridge when Pigface caught up with him.

'Pappu! Pappu! Yaar, what happened?'

'Pigface! You moron! Why didn't you call the police?' Pappu spoke without slowing down.

It was a wonder PP's plump legs found room to get past each other as he ran. 'When the blind dude (*pant*) told you about the reward in the school playground (*pant*) I thought I overheard something about a reward, but I wasn't sure (*pant*) and I forgot about it. Then (*pant*) I saw the blind dude's pistol when you'll got into the cab, and I thought wow, that's (*pant*) cool! If I'd called the police, yaar, they'd have spoilt the fun! So I got into another cab and followed you. Almost finished my pocket money (*pant*),' PP said pitifully. He looked ridiculous, running and talking.

'You KING-SIZED MORON! So you did suspect something, but that didn't matter to you as much as the ice-lolly! Greedy as Pigface.' It was a saying in school which normally Pappu didn't use. But he was furious.

By the time they climbed down the overbridge to the other side of the road Pappu felt as ridiculous as PP, talking and running and being so frightened in broad daylight. He stopped. PP stopped too, and said: 'It was not the reward, but the adventure …'

Pappu looked at the stall on the other side of the road.

He couldn't see it clearly because of the traffic. Slowly, without realising it, his feet climbed up, step by step, back up the overbridge. PP followed.

'Pappu—'

'Shhh!'

On both sides of the overbridge were big boards advertising perfumes, shirts and company shares. Hiding behind one, Pappu could see Irfaan mia's stall.

'Pappu—'

Pappu ignored him. He couldn't take his eyes off the stall. But nothing happened.

PP said, 'I wish we had x-ray vision, no? Why don't you ask your mother to get x-ray specs from abroad next time—'

'Shhh!'

After some time, the blind man came out from the back door and locked it with a key.

He went around to the front of the stall and, to Pappu's surprise, ordered a big frothed glass of faluda with ice cream. He sat down on one of the stall's two benches and ate with great enjoyment.

When he had finished he walked to the highway. He was about to cross it when a traffic policeman stopped him.

It was the same policeman that Pappu had tried to call half an hour ago.

Pappu watched as the policeman spoke with him. The policeman looked up straight at Pappu and pointed toward him. And then he and the blind man both began to climb the steps, towards Pappu.

Then the policeman suddenly turned away and left the blind man to slowly climb the stairs, clutching at the railing.

When he reached the top, he went on walking as if he didn't know Pappu was standing close by.

He had reached the other side of the overbridge when at last Pappu couldn't stand it any more. He ran to the old man, crying out 'Chacha! Chacha!' Behind him he heard PP also say, 'Chacha! Chacha!' and he felt like hitting him.

The blind man stopped suddenly. 'Ai, *two* boys? This second boy, where did he come from? Who is he?'

Pappu asked the blind man, 'Chacha, what did the policeman say to you?'

'What police? Beta, why don't you go home?'

'The policeman who walked up the steps a little way with you!'

The blind man started guiltily. 'Was that a police? Y'Allah! Is he around now?'

'No, he went away after he spoke to you.'

The blind man relaxed. 'I didn't know he was a police. He was just helping me, he told me to use the overbridge to cross the road. Who's this other boy?'

'He's from my school. He followed us here.'

'Well now he can follow you back. It's best for both of you. When I brought you here, I thought I would let you go before I met anyone dangerous. But what happened? You're best far away from me.'

'Chacha, I want to stay with you.'

'Why?'

'I'm afraid something might happen.'

The blind man was silent for a while. Then he said, softly: 'To me or to you?'

For some reason, Pappu felt his face go hot with blood. He didn't know how to answer, so he was silent.

'Go home, silly boy. You're best rid of a goonda like me.'

The blind man turned and walked away.

After some time, Pappu began following him. He was irritated that PP followed *him*, two steps behind.

And he wanted to help the blind man. Also, he wanted him to go to the police. He thought it would be safer.

The blind man crossed the road, crossed Charni Road Station and took a double-decker bound for

Breach Candy.

In the upper storey, the conductor helped the blind man to the front seat. Pappu and PP slipped into a seat two rows behind.

The windows in the front were open. The route was mostly close to the sea and so though it was noon, and though it hadn't rained for over a week, a cool moist breeze blew in, fresh and open in their faces.

The blind man seemed more cheerful. He blissfully took out his musical case and played another old tune as if he were alone in the bus. '*Thandi thandi hawa mein dil lalchaaye* …' (In the cool, cool wind, my heart flutters with temptation …) When he finished, there was a hearty round of applause from behind. He turned his head sideways and brought his hand to his head in a salaam, as if he was quite used to this.

'Oi you two devils,' he said cheerily. 'Are you still there? Don't you have any school?'

PP said, 'Wow! How do you know it's us?'

The blind man chuckled and beckoned to them to come forward. As PP jumped up, the other passengers looked wonderingly at the unlikely combination of the blind man and the two schoolboys.

Soon they were sitting next to the blind man, the breeze in their face.

'So you gentlemen are named …?' he asked.

'Paintal.' He was sitting next to him, and Pappu couldn't help thinking that wasn't right. *He* should be sitting next to the blind man.

'Pappu.'

'So tell us, Paintal-sahb, why are you following us?'

'Well, I heard you mention a reward to Pappu. It sounded like something exciting.'

'And Pappuji you, why are you still with me? You saw what a disreputable fellow I am?'

Pappu was suddenly struck by shyness. He couldn't answer.

'Say something, Pappuji. This unfortunate can't read your eyes.'

'I want you to go to the police. Irfaanbhai might come after you.'

'He won't. For the next forty-eight hours at least, Irfaanbhai will be sleeping the sleep of the innocent.'

Pappu said, 'But after he wakes up? Once you claim the reward, he might be able to find you from the newspapers, or TV.'

The blind man sighed. 'It looks like I will not be claiming the reward. Because I don't know where the treasure is. Or even what it is. And the police, I have already tried. They wouldn't listen to me.'

'Why?'

Suddenly, the blind man's head became completely still for a few seconds. Then he said, 'Let us get down at the next stop.'

The next stop was the one before Breach Candy. Just behind the stop there was a garden, and then the huge black rocks of the sea.

They went inside the garden. They bought some cold drinks, spicy chaat, and sat down on the cool grass in a shady corner. The blind man told them the whole story.

'It began at Queen's Necklace, only last night. My friend was selling roasted peanuts and chana-dal from a public bench …'

The blind man told them of the strange sounds that he could not at first understand, until he heard the two goondas …

THE SECRET OF THE GOLDEN BOX

'Then the two men began to argue. One said, "The box! You killed Michael without finding the box!" The other said, "He had the box in his pocket! He showed it to me just five minutes ago." Then there were more soft, patting sounds. One said, "The American will be docking in his boat day after tomorrow, at eleven at night. Commander will kill us if we don't find the box by then. Commander showed the American the treasure *in* the box, and that's what he's bringing his dollars for. He won't pay without the box." The other asked, "So where is the treasure?" The first one called him something I cannot repeat, and said, "Ikka brought that to Mumbai, separately. He and Commander may be fifty-fifty partners, but their trust in each other is zero-zero." The other said, "Ikka trusted Michael more, hain?", to which the first answered, "We've just killed Ikka's right-hand man. I had a drink with Michael once, in that club of his opposite Metro Cinema." Here both men fell silent, perhaps from shame at murdering someone who was of their own brotherhood.

'Then the first man said, "All-right-all-right now there is a paper that should have a message to Irfaan mian with the password. Look for the paper, let's at least find the paper!"

'They searched some more, but they couldn't even find the paper. One said to the other, "You son of sin! Commander will kill you." Then the other said, "One minute. Is this the Irfaan who used to be a railway mechanic before he got into the business?" The other said, "That is what I have heard. He used to take bets for Ikka on the race course." The first one said, "I think maybe I know where his chawl is." The other said, "Fool, it would be no use. Shhh! Someone's coming. Let's leave the body. We'll tell Commander we have done the job, it's not our fault we couldn't find anything on the body!"

'I heard a young couple walking this way. The two men ran away.

'The couple were walking on my side of the bench. When they were close to me I heard the girl cry out, "Look!" I heard her pick up something metallic and hollow from the floor, and the next thing I knew she had pushed the golden box into my hand, saying "Baba, this is your box? It was lying on the floor." Then they walked on.

'All this was happening but I was just sitting there, too shocked to move. Now I thought of screaming, murder! Murder! Then I thought of these young hero-heroines on Queen's Necklace, and I thought why spoil their mood? I knew the area well, and I knew police had put up a wooden hut two crossings away. So I walked quickly there and said to the police, "Canastable sahb, there's been a murder only four-five minutes walk from here. If you would take the trouble of coming with me then …" The two police seemed to find what I said funny, but one of them came with me.

'I led him to the bench where I had been sitting and said, "There on the bench." "Where?" he said, rudely. I said, "Canastable sahb, right there, in front of your eyes!" He shouted at me, called me senile old man, and went away.

'For quite a few seconds I stood there in shock, wondering if I had taken leave of my senses, or if he had. Then I came and felt the bench, but the body had gone!

'But my hand became wet, and I could feel it was blood. The police hadn't seen it maybe because it was dark. I tried to follow the police and show him the blood on my hands, but he ignored me. "Huth! I'm going back to sleep, don't wake me up this time!" And some other names he called me, after which I stopped. I washed my hands at a tap close by. Without the body, what could I do? My heart felt heavy, and so did the box in my pocket. But I hadn't had my dinner and it was one-thirty. So I went straight to a nearby dhaba.

'I normally enjoy their kabab, but bhaiya today, when I thought of meat it reminded me … I had a vegetarian dinner, yes, like a pukka Hindu, and I was happy with it. I met Shinde there, I knew him from before. He is a pickpocket but not such a bad man, and I told him my story.

'After the meal, I felt in the box, and I found only this sealed envelope, and paper. Shinde read it out for me.'

He took out an opened envelope, and showed it to Pappu. On it was written, in Hindi: 'Irfaan mia—Snokiun, Chowpatty. Strawberry ice cream with salt and pepper.' Inside the envelope was a piece of paper on which was written: 'Irfaan: take the goods from dabbaa number E-52. I will contact you by tomorrow, but if I don't, take the goods to the docking point and give to the American yourself. Tell him he'll get the other goods later, when I'm out of jail within four-five days (don't tell the police, they don't know that yet)! I will collect the money from you. I trust you Irfaan, you are the only one I have told about the dabbaa. Whatever happens, I will be in touch with you when I get out. Ikka.'

PP read this over Pappu's shoulder and said, 'What could they be talking about? What treasure?'

Pappu said, 'We *must* go to the police.'

The blind man began to shake his head.

'Chacha …'

'All right, all right. But only because you say so.'

Pappu jumped up. For some reason, he felt like shouting with joy, but instead he only jumped and took the hand of the blind man and pulled.

The blind man laughed. 'Pappuji do you think you can pull me all the way?'

The police station was one of those splendid, solid

buildings built a hundred years ago by the British, entirely of large smooth cobblestones. Most of these were slate-grey, but around the arches and windows white stone had been used, looking like giant sugar cubes strung together. It had high ceilings and fans that hung low and were slow. But they moved faster than the wheels of government.

In a verandah, on a wooden bench, two havaldars lounged against each other. Pappu asked them in Marathi, 'We want to lodge a complaint. Where should we go?'

One of the havaldars stretched an arm and yawned, and then stretched his arm again with finger pointing at right angles to the arm, meaning they should go into the corridor that led inside.

So they went, Pappu leading the way, and the blind man holding his arm and tapping the floor with his cane. Not to be left out, PP caught the blind man's arm and followed.

As they went inside, the corridor widened towards the right in a room-shaped bulge. In this room-shaped bulge was a table, on which rested Inspector Stanley Coelho's feet in smart, gleaming boots. The rest of the Inspector was on a chair some way from the table, dressed in perhaps the smartest police uniform in Mumbai. He was very dark and knew he was very handsome, but he didn't know why this didn't have any effect on his darling Rita. He was speaking with her over the phone right now.

'Sweetheart, see, I *never* would argue in front of your

friends if *you* didn't first argue. When *you* argue in front of all, then how *I'm* to know you'll mind when *I* argue in front? … Tche? … Think, no?'

Next to Stanley stood Havaldar Samrat Singh, who came from Bihar. He stood at attention, as stiff and *straight* as his flared police shorts were stiff (with starch) and *round*. He stood at attention partly from duty, but mainly from shock at hearing an unmarried Hindu girl (Rita Jaisanghani) phone a young Christian man (Stanley). He took out his indignation by violently chewing on tobacco.

He was so busy chewing that it took him some time to notice the blind man, Pappu, and Pigface. Inspector Stanley didn't notice because Rita was so busy giving *him* a real chewing.

'Okay, okay, I'll say sorry … No no, I'm *really* sorry, or else why I should say, no? … How many times you want me to say? I've *said* sorry, it's enough, no?'

The blind man whispered to Pappu, 'See? They're all too busy to do their job. It is a tradition here to show rank by making you wait.'

But Inspector Coelho was made of better stuff. He noticed the three and he tried to wind up.

'Okay bye, I've got public here … Rita, of course every time you want to talk, I got public. Arre job is such na, police job is to serve public. So if you phone me in office public is bound to come, no?'

'Yes?' At last the phone was down, and even his feet were down from the table, and Inspector Coelho politely asked them to sit on the bench that was on the other side of his table.

Pappu helped the blind man to the bench, and then he said, in English, 'Well …'

'Innispector sahb,' the blind man said in Urdu, 'we want to lodge a complaint.' Then he waited for the policeman to say something rude.

But Inspector Coelho prided himself on never being rude to anybody—okay, he was now and then rude to Rita, but that was different.

He asked them in Mumbaiya, Mumbai's mixed language everyone understands:

'Do you want to lodge FIR? Is it a criminal … hey!' He looked at the blind man. 'Aren't you the man who sings at Queen's Necklace? I tell you men, your singing is too good! My girlfriend Rita, she's always in a better mood when she hears you!'

The blind man giggled like a baby. 'Sahb, you come there? You come there, in the evenings?' Suddenly he was deeply moved. 'Sahb, it is people like you, people who respect my music, who … sahb, why only me, my whole family, back home in the village, we are grateful to decent people like you who treat a human being like a human being.'

The Inspector waved it away hurriedly—things were getting too 'senti' for him. 'No, no. All right, men, what can I do for you?'

The blind man thought. 'Did you go to Queen's Necklace yesterday, sahb?'

'Yesterday? Not yesterday. Why?'

'Yesterday night, at Queen's Necklace, I found this.'

Here the blind man took out the old golden box and put it on the table.

The Inspector's jaw dropped almost to the table. He looked at the box stupidly for a minute, as if it had hit him senseless. Then he grabbed its top and unscrewed it hurriedly.

Fingers trembling with excitement, he took out the paper inside it.

When he had read it, he turned to the blind man. 'Where did you find this box?'

The blind man told him his story. When he mentioned that the murderers called their victim Michael, Stanley gave a start of recognition. When he came to the part where he took Pappu from his school, Pappu interrupted (because he knew that the truth would get the blind man in prison) and said that *he* had left the school of his own will. The blind man smiled his secret smile.

When he came to the part about how Pappu and he had put Irfaan mia to sleep, Inspector Coelho patted Pappu on the back. 'Brave boy,' he said admiringly. Pappu felt his face become hot.

The Inspector turned to the blind man. 'Will he still be there?'

'He should be, sahb.'

'Samrat! Get my motorbike—no! Get a jeep, these people have to come along too!'

While Samrat got the jeep, the Inspector made a call to his boss, Commissioner Talwar.

'Sir, we found the little box that Ikka sent out ... no

sir, they are not inside … it was taken from a dead body by a blind man, sir … yessir, a blind man, he's with me. He is just taking me to a gang member he has drugged to sleep, sir … I'll tell you the whole story when I come back sir, I thought you should know we have got the box …'

The Inspector kept the phone down and looked around for Samrat, but he hadn't come.

When Samrat finally came, the Inspector asked, 'What took you so long?' Samrat gave some long answer about bureaucratic delay, and the Inspector gave him a long, suspicious look.

The Inspector insisted both Samrat and he change into civilian clothes, and at last they were speeding in the jeep towards Queen's Necklace, all of them in the back except Samrat, who sat in front with the driver.

The Inspector asked the blind man, 'Do you know what that box is?'

'No, Innispector sahb. All I know is that people are murdering for it. And there is a big reward for it.'

'Hmm. Well, people have been murdering for it for centuries. This box had inside—'

'Diamonds?' the blind man interrupted excitedly. 'Royal rubies?'

The Inspector laughed. 'This box had papers inside, men.'

'Papers?' the blind man was puzzled and disappointed.

The Inspector turned solemn. 'Papers. Love letters of Emperor Shah Jahan and Mumtaz Mahal.'

The blind man gasped.

Pappu said, 'You mean, the emperor who built the Taj Mahal ...'

The Inspector nodded. 'In memory of his queen, Mumtaz Mahal.'

'Y'Allah!'

PP said, 'Wow! How much are they worth in the black market?' Everybody ignored him.

The Inspector said, 'In late seventeenth century, they were popular with Mughal lords because Mughal princes believed the Taj letters—as they called them—spelled out the secrets of love. Some believed they spelled out the secrets of power. Fifty years later, people were killing to get them, then for hundred years they disappeared—I think they were hidden, buried somewhere. Then they were found again about a year ago, and went to the National Museum in New Delhi. But they were stolen again within a week. The museum caretaker—only man to read them in one hundred years—was killed in the robbery. So nobody even knows what is in the letters.'

The blind man murmured softly to himself, 'Bhai, what are pearls and diamonds compared to this?'

'Two gangs had got together to do the robbery—Battleship gang, headed by Commander, and Ikka gang, headed by man who called himself Ikka. The two gangs fought. Somebody in one gang betrayed somebody in the other gang, then that somebody betrayed back the first gang and so on, and that is how we were able to arrest Commander three days back. Day after that, we arrested Ikka.'

'Oh no!' PP said, hitting his forehead with his hand.

Inspector asked, 'What is it?'

PP said nothing, just looked hot and red.

'What is it? You sad that we arrested Ikka or what? What is it, tell me now, don't fool, tell the truth.'

PP, looking hotter and redder, said: 'If you arrested him, then he'll tell you where the treasure is hidden. Then … we won't have any chance of the … reward.'

'No, men, he can't tell us. Just today morning Ikka was shot dead trying to escape.'

They rode the rest of the way in silence.

The World-Famous Art Dealer

In the history of crime, Irfaan's arrest was perhaps the most comfortable ever: he snored contentedly throughout. No one else noticed either: the Inspector and Samrat walked out of Snow Queen holding Irfaan up between them, looking in their civilian clothes like three slightly drunk goondas heading towards another drink.

At the police station, the police doctor injected into Irfaan some antidote to sleeping pills. The blind man told the doctor that it wouldn't work before forty-eight hours, but soon Irfaan mia woke up in a daze, in a prison cell.

'Hwaa …' he said.

The Inspector went straight to the point: 'Men, where's dabbaa number E-52?'

Irfaan's eyes were crossed, and his fat tongue lay crossed against his teeth as he tried to speak: 'O there, lunch ka dabbaa? Lunch box?'

The Inspector said in a ringing, confident voice: 'Ikka said you have to get the goods. How? How are you going to go to dabbaa number E-52?'

Irfaan's eyes rolled, and his arms waved in the air as if he was trying to point at something with all his fingers, hands and legs. 'Go. Go … station, catch train … rubbish!'

After this, Irfaan mia, with a final wave of his huge arms, went to sleep again. The Inspector looked at the doctor, who shook his head.

'He's not going to wake again for forty-eight hours. The effect of the potion will wear off only then.'

The Inspector shook his head gloomily. 'I'm sure he'll never tell where the dabbaa is. He would rather spend ten years in jail and then come out and enjoy the loot …'

Later, in uniform at his desk, the Inspector took down the blind man's story on official paper. When the blind man came to the part where he found the paper in the shabby gold box, Pappu asked: 'I don't understand, why should a message for Irfaan be sent in the gold box? I mean, shouldn't the gold box be hidden wherever the Taj letter is, with the letter inside?'

Inspector shook his head. 'Life is never so straight men—especially life of crime. Like, suppose Ikka is being chased, so he hides Taj letter somewhere on the way and keeps gold box to fool person chasing … then later, suppose he wants to send message to Irfaan real quick so he just puts his message conveniently in gold box without thinking much—'

'Inspector Coelho?' boomed a large, polished voice. They looked up to see a large, polished businessman-type, wearing a posh, striped three-piece suit and gold-rimmed spectacles with tinted glasses. He was swabbing his large, fair face with a large, clean handkerchief. 'Inspector Coelho,' the large man boomed. 'We have met before, of course.'

'Eh? Then why I don't know you?'

'Uh, that must be because I meant, er, we have met, er met … metaphorically speaking. Uh, *telephonically* speaking! I'm Keki Screwvala, the World-famous Art Dealer.' The booming stopped and suddenly there was an impish grin: 'We chatted on the phone, remember?' Back to the boom: 'I hear you have finally got the gold box in police custody?' Behind Screwvala stood a small man who looked like his secretary.

The Inspector looked puzzled. 'How did you hear …?'

'Ah Inspector, I'm a man of ways, I'm a man of means—Ha! Ha! Ha! Ha!' He turned to the blind man and the children. 'Ah, is this the brave trio who got the box for you?'

The Inspector suddenly looked at Samrat, who immediately coughed and, in trying to act natural—as he would act in his home-village—turned to a corner to spit out the chewed tobacco of his paan.

'Not to do that!' the Inspector shouted angrily and Samrat nervously swallowed the tobacco instead.

Screwvala was bending forward and shaking smooth hands with the children and the blind man. 'What a pleasure it is to meet you! Oh! It's the little people who I … who I … like, I mean, like … uh, yes, LIKE! How wonderful! With children like you, who can say that

India's future is not bright! Bright as GOLD. Hehehe …' His small secretary fluttered around behind him, making small 'Yes, Yes' sounds, like a bird twittering around its tree.

The Inspector turned angrily to Screwvala: 'Mister, I told you, keep out! When we find the treasure it goes back to National Museum. What good is it then to you?'

Screwvala cheerfully leaned his face into the Inspector's: 'You're very frank. I like that. Frankness is a good thing. But remember, you can have too much of a good thing for your own, uh, good …'

The Inspector, who was scowling into Screwvala's face so close to his, slapped his desk loudly and laughed. He turned to the kids: 'Ai, men, what's he saying men? You know?'

Screwvala moved his face closer to the Inspector's, who turned back to him and said: 'What is treasure to you unless you have some shady plan?'

At the word 'shady', Screwvala suddenly straightened up. 'How dare you use the word shady about me?' he said tightly.

The Inspector looked closely at him. 'Hey men? You getting even shadier when I say shady? Hey?' Awkwardly for Screwvala, his pink skin had begun growing dark with anger.

The Inspector kept looking at Screwvala. Screwvala tried hard not to become shadier. Pappu and PP went 'Purrp! Purrpp! Purrp!' from trying not to laugh. Screwvala went 'Purrpp! Purrpp! Phurrp!' from trying not to explode.

'Eh, what's he trying to say men?' the Inspector asked the kids. 'Purrp? Purrp? Oh thanks! I get it! Purrp … purrple, he's trying to say Purrple!'

This made the kids finally explode with laughter, because that was exactly Screwvala's latest shade!

'Inspector Coelho,' Screwvala boomed, 'I am a World-famous Art Dealer, and a member of the Zoroastrian community—famous throughout India for our honesty. A man of my standing is not affected by someone of your standing sitting there trying to, uh, trying to … to sit on *my* laurels!' The Inspector scratched his head, so Screwvala clarified without the boom: 'I mean, don't think you can affect a man of my standing, hm?' He turned angrily—then he remembered, and turned back.

With his large, clean hanky, he wiped the anger off his face, and with an angelic smile that forgave their giggling, said in a gentle voice, 'Goodbye, kids. Till we meet again. Uh, Al wida, Mr Hafiz.' His secretary scurried after him as he left.

The Inspector shook his head, then looked at Samrat, who cleared his throat nervously and looked somewhere else. Inspector said, still looking at Samrat, 'I wish someone will report to Screwvala that if he fools with these kids, I will personally break his legs.' He turned to the children: 'Ai men! You don't have school or what? You should go.'

Pappu said, 'By the time we reach, it will be over.'

'Go home then. You had lunch, men?'

Pigface answered in a weak meek voice: 'No, sir, we

were too freaked to even think of it. We're only children, and now we'll have to wait at least two hours to get home and eat. We live in the suburbs …'

'No no, men, you'll have lunch with me—and uncle too. I'll take you to a very special place … just give me two minutes to finish this paperwork …'

Near the garden that came before Breach Candy was something that was almost a stall, and almost a restaurant. It was a concrete patch with one room, in front of which were a few tables fixed in the ground, like mushrooms, and plastic seats. The Inspector helped the blind man to a seat and ordered some pizza, some colas, and ice creams.

'After this you men go straight home, to your parents.'

Pigface said, 'I can't. This morning, my father-mother went to visit relatives in Pune—it's Janmashtmi tomorrow, you know, and they're going to celebrate together.'

'Why you didn't go?'

'Because I had school today, holiday's only tomorrow. So I'm supposed to go home to my best friend's house, two floors below mine.'

The Inspector said, 'So go straight there. They will be waiting for you.'

Pappu said sadly, 'At least your father-mother are coming back in a day. Mine won't be back for a week. They've gone to London.' Pappu's parents had a roaring international business in fashionable clothes, with boutiques in London, Paris and New York.

The Inspector said, 'So where you putting up, man?'

'At home, with my ayah.'

'Okay. So you go straight *there*.'

The food came. The pizza and the sauce made a terrific combination with the colas. Pigface showed that he was Pigstomach as well!

Then the Inspector cancelled the ice creams—he took them to the softy shop close by, opposite Breach Candy Hospital, for some of the most delicious softies in India. Here even Pappu made a pig of himself. Pigface heaped mountains—no, mountain *ranges* of ice cream on his plate, and then made them disappear. The Inspector said: 'Eat man, eat. Government of India is paying. Small reward for you people for helping to catch Irfaanbhai.'

The blind man enjoyed himself too, Pappu could tell. He sat and ate quietly, carefully, not talking much, listening to the boys enjoy themselves.

When they had almost finished, the Inspector said, 'Stop!'

All three stopped at once. 'Not you, uncle, you carry on. But these two boys, I just remembered. Shouldn't you boys be fasting today, the day before Janmashtmi?'

Pappu said, 'Fasting? But that only traditional people do. Traditional people and mothers.'

The Inspector laughed loudly, slapping his smartly creased trousers. 'Accha, do modern people and sons play handi on Janmashtmi day?'

Pappu nodded, biting deeper into his softy. The Inspector sighed. 'For you people tomorrow is great fun, but for us poor policemen, I swear! The whole city is full of tolis of boys going around in huge huge trucks! Before I joined police I also used to do it, with Hindu friends. But now I feel like an old gardener who's chasing boys doing mischief to garden!'

At the end, the Inspector gave them all his cell number. 'But not to worry, none of the gang has seen you—only Irfaan mia, and he will be safe with us for a long time. But Screwvala has seen you. He won't do violence, but he will try other tricks you can be sure. He's a very powerful man, very rich. So don't talk to any strangers, be careful. If you have any problems, phone me. Uncle we'll try to talk to Irfaan mia, and see if we can get some clues about the treasure.' He turned gloomy. 'Though I don't think he'll tell us anything.'

He was in the jeep before Pappu remembered: 'You said you'll take us to a very special place for lunch? What was special?'

'The last lead that police got about the gold box, before you fellows came, was from here.'

'Oh?'

The Inspector pointed at a twenty-storey building about a furlong away. 'See that building, with the blue top? That's Akash Ganga.'

The blind man perked up. 'The building from where they'll shine the signal to the American …'

'Correct. If—'

'But now that Irfaan is with you, no one might come!' Pappu said.

'Correct, men. Now if you look at the distance between that building and this spot—' Just then his walkie-talkie crackled. 'Hello?' His expression changed. 'Yessir! … Yessir … yes … At once!' He did not bother to finish with 'sir', just threw the walkie-talkie on the seat next to him and started the ignition.

'Emergency-robbery-at-Kenilworth,' he dashed off to the kids. Kenilworth was a building half a kilometre away, on Peddar Road.

'What's been stolen?' asked Pappu.

He thought he heard, as the jeep sped away: 'Nuclear reactor parts.'

An Exciting Discovery in a Garbage Box

Pappu stood there: had he heard correctly? 'Did you hear what the Inspector said just now?' he asked PP. PP said the Inspector said nothing.

The blind man's face turned toward the sky. 'Khuda hafiz, children. It is time for you to go back.'

'What about tomorrow night?' PP asked. 'The American is going to come from the sea!'

The blind man was silent. Then he repeated, softly, 'It is time for you to go back.'

Pappu helped him change the subject. He groaned: 'Go back! To a big empty bungalow with only ayah and a TV.'

The blind man sighed. 'Beta, a big empty bungalow is no bad thing. Look at me, I can't even go back to my little chawl tonight. I'll have to find a different place to sleep tonight.'

'Why?' Pappu asked.

'Innispector says no one has seen me except Irfaanbhai. But what if Irfaan's man, who was selling his ice cream, saw me? Now that Irfaanbhai has been arrested, what if they search for the blind man he was last seen with?'

A thought struck Pappu. 'Why don't you come to *my* bungalow today? You can sleep *there*, and nobody would ever find you.'

The blind man said, 'No no. You have already spent too much time involved with this dangerous matter. Anyway, your ayah will not let someone like me in the house, and she would be correct, because your parents are not home.'

'Oh, I can persuade Ayah. No problem. And PP, I'll even tell her to phone your best friend's parents, and tell them you're staying with me tonight. When they hear an adult talking, they won't have any problems.'

PP nodded excitedly, and Pappu kept telling the blind man that it was the safest thing for him to do. But the blind man shook his head.

They were standing on the pavement outside the softy shop when suddenly the blind man said, 'Screwvala sahb! He must have had us followed.'

And indeed there he was, getting off from a big air-conditioned car on the other side of the road, his voice booming instructions at his driver.

At the same time the blind man's nostrils quivered. 'Kabaadiwalla,' he said. He could smell a ragpicker.

'Hurry up, hurry up,' the ragpicker called to someone across the road. 'We have to fill the hand-cart. Have you done dabbaa number 52?'

The three friends gasped.

The ragpicker was a little urchin wearing torn dirty

clothes, except for a bright red scarf like the filmstar Govinda. His skin was black with sunburn, and he carried over his shoulder a torn, half-full jute sack. He was talking to a man who was at the steering wheel of a blue tempo parked on the other side of the road. The man answered, 'No. Let's just do 52, and then go to clear the goods!'

'Y'Allah!' the blind man exclaimed. 'Remember, Innispector had said that this spot was where they found the last clue … What do you see, beta?'

Pappu described the tempo to him —it seemed to be a kind of makeshift garbage truck. Not garbage actually, just kabaadi, or junk.

The urchin was standing on their side of the road, waiting for the tempo which was turning around to pick him.

Screwvala had crossed the road by this time. 'Adawarz hai, mian,' he said to the blind man in a most polished Luckhnawi accent. 'Hello, hello, hello—'

'Hello! Taxi! Hello taxi! Hello taxi!' Pappu called out. As the taxi stopped between them and Screwvala, the blind man said: 'Good boy! Khuda hafiz sahb!' he said to the open-mouthed Screwvala, and he and the boys hastily piled into the cab.

Screwvala bent down, so his face was close to Pigface's window. From his open mouth came: 'Ba … ba …'

'Black sheep!' Pigface said, and wound up the glass in his face.

The blind man said, 'We can follow them and see where they're going. Though … what dabbaa number

52 could they be talking about?'

Pigface said to the driver, like a hero in a detective film: 'Quick! *Follow that car*!'

The driver said aggressively, 'What car-var? I can't see any car.'

'The blue tempo,' Pappu said.

Pigface said, 'Quick! *Follow that tempo*!'

As they took off after the tempo Pappu looked behind, to see Screwvala's huge posh car had made a u-turn, and he was getting into it and pointing at them.

'Screwvala's coming in his car after us. I wonder if he heard about dabbaa number? He must have, Samrat must have told him.'

'Samrat?' The blind man didn't understand, so Pappu told him about the look Inspector had given Samrat when Screwvala had come in.

The tempo was going rather fast, and they followed closely. Pappu stared at the painted back, wondering what this 'dabbaa number 52' could be.

The back of the tempo had a painting of sunrise on it, in colours that were vulgar but, realised Pappu, that would have been stunning if they had actually been in a real sky. The part of the painted sunrise that was clear blue sky blended in neatly with the cheap blue of the rest of the tempo. Below the painting were the large, roughly painted words in English, 'OK. TATA'. Pappu's eyes went straight from these words to the inside front of his cab, where above the windscreen were two lines in Hindi, in small roughly stroked letters:

The world drinks, just as bees will ever hover.

But when a driver drinks, he will loose his lover.

'Keep a little distance, so that they don't see us,' Pappu told the driver.

The blind man nodded. 'Good thinking. So that they don't see us, and we can't smell them.'

'Screwvala's white Mercedes is still on our tail. What a car!' Pigface said.

Soon—they were still at Breach Candy—the tempo stopped near a huge, yellow box of garbage. It was the kind that can be slotted into a garbage truck to become its back.

'Chacha, this is perhaps the cleanest garbage box I have seen in India,' Pappu whispered to the blind man. 'On its side is painted, Number 52.'

'Not E-52?' the blind man asked.

'No.'

'Hm. But we are close to the spot where police found the last big clue. And this is the area where the American is coming … And remember what Irfaan mumbled to Inspector? "Go. Go … station, catch train … rubbish." Remember?'

Behind them, Pappu saw the white Mercedes stop. From inside its tinted windows, he thought he could see Screwvala staring, dumbstruck, at the Number 52 lettering.

In front of them, the urchin had jumped out of the tempo and disappeared into the garbage box with his sack, which was now empty. Pappu described to the blind man how he came out with a sack that was full.

'Aha!' said Pigface. 'What could be *inside* it?'

'Rubbish?' the blind man said.

'That's strange,' Pappu said.

'Strange, ask *me* what's strange,' the driver muttered. They pretended not to hear, but Pappu could see the driver was pleased he had the chance to make that crack. His idea of heaven was carrying passengers who gave him many chances to make cracks at them.

The urchin hopped back into the tempo with his sack, and off they went again.

Pigface was looking in the rear window: 'Look at that car move!'

'Where could they be going?' Pappu wondered.

'Dharavi, I think,' the blind man said.

'Dharavi?' Pappu had never been to Dharavi, though he had heard of it. It was the biggest slum in Asia, perhaps in the world. He had sometimes passed through it, quickly, in his parents' car. It was a shanty town, not very clean …

'Beta, Dharavi is a little like … that big Amrican city, Nioo Yark. It is the Nioo Yark of the world's slums. It is such a big collection of hovels, but not just that. It also has businesses worth crores of rupees, done from buildings that are themselves made of kabaadi. And its biggest business *is* the kabaadi business. That is what I think our friends in front are doing.'

'*What* are they doing?' Pappu asked.

'Beta, they have selected certain things from the garbage dumps. Now they will take them to Nayak Nagar—that's the area in Dharavi where most of the kabaadi businesses are.'

'Pigface, stop sitting backward to admire Screwvala's Mercedes. Doesn't it embarrass you?'

'Look!' Pigface said. Pappu turned around and saw that the Mercedes was cut off from them by a traffic signal. From past the stream of traffic they could see Screwvala open the door, stand on the dusty road and wave desperately to them!

'Good! Screwvala won't hassle us any more,' Pappu said. But he hadn't counted on Screwvala's cunning.

They travelled for about fifteen minutes. A few scattered clouds came pleasantly before the sun, and by the time they came to the sprawling mini-city of tin and cardboard shacks that was Dharavi, there was a slight drizzle.

The tempo went to Nayak Nagar—a long line of shacks, much higher than the others. They were godowns.

The tempo stopped in front of a godown, and the urchin and the driver went inside.

The taxi stopped a little way off.

'Maybe I should walk up there and see what's happening,' Pappu said.

'It seems to me that I know what you'll find,' the blind man said. 'But go ahead.'

'Me too,' Pigface got up to go but the blind man held him back.

'Let Pappu go,' he said.

Pappu walked past the tempo, and casually looked into the godown the urchin had gone into.

In front of the godown there was a kind of small room, with a table and two stools and with no door separating it from the road. It was shadowy inside, and Pappu went into this front room, a square light shadow set amongst the deeper shadows. He knew that even if someone saw him there, he could say he was sheltering from the drizzle.

Deeper inside, behind a door that was now open there was a kind of large hall—the actual godown. It was as high as a double-decker, and much much broader, he could only see part of its broadness. In the dim light of a neon he could see a man sitting on the floor, surrounded by sacks and thousands of little glass bottles, which he seemed to be sorting. All around him were shelves made of wire netting, on which there were hundreds upon hundreds of sacks of kabaadi. Behind these shelves gleamed (at least close to the neon light) walls that were patchworks of rusted metal sheet, wood, or wire netting, all lashed or sometimes welded together. The roof was made of bamboo poles, above which were plastic sheets and thick cardboard taken from cartons, interlacing each other like tiles. And he could see deeper inside there were more rooms divided by metal sheets or grilles, with more endless piles of kabaadiwalla sacks. He could even hear the sound of a phone ringing, and he marvelled that you could get a landline in such a temporary shack.

The bottles around the man were of so many different shapes and colours, and Pappu remembered what the blind man had told him in the taxi: 'In Nayak Nagar the kabaadi is separated into four items—glass, plastic, metal and paper. Each business specialises in one item. Each business cleans what comes in, sorts it out, and then sends it to the big-big companies. Like the glass is sent to Coca Cola, the paper is sent to paper companies, and they get brand new glass or paper made from it. The glass is also sorted according to colour, so the amber glass is sent to medicine companies, the white glass to the cold drink companies …' He could see that the bottles were in five groups—white, amber, green, red and blue … they were in a hundred designs, fancy ones from Paris, quaint ones from the village, plain medicine bottles and others with complicated, delicate twists …

It was like entering a different world, and Pappu was so fascinated he quite forgot the danger until a short man with a big tilak on his forehead, and chewing paan ferociously, suddenly came out from the godown and caught him by the neck.

The urchin appeared next to him. 'Yes, that's the boy! They followed us from Breach Candy in a car!'

'What are you doing here?' the short man asked threateningly. 'Eh? What? Who sent you? But you look like a boy from a decent family?'

'Arre bhai,' came the blind man's voice from the light drizzle outside. 'He *is* a decent boy. He is just doing a school project on poor people, like you and me.' The blind man entered, hand on Pigface's shoulder. His beautiful Urdu immediately softened the short man, who let go of Pappu at once.

He said, 'Forgive me, mia, I'm a little shaken nowadays. The gang that controls this area wants me to pay more hafta, and they have been playing all kinds of tricks.'

Then he and the blind man had a friendly conversation—it turned out they were both from the same part of Uttar Pradesh, and they parted with cordial promises of being in touch.

As they came out, Pigface saw Screwvala a little way off—his white Mercedes was parked behind their taxi.

Pappu suddenly slapped his forehead. 'Quick!' he cried out to the blind man and Pigface. 'We must get to dabbaa number 52 at once! I'm sure we'll find our answer in it! In the bottom right-hand corner, you'll see!'

'But …' the blind man said.

'I think Screwvala heard you just now. How did he get here?' Pigface wondered.

Pappu said, 'Quick! I'll explain in the taxi!' He and Pigface walked to the taxi as fast as they could, holding the blind man's hand. Screwvala hurriedly got back into his car. By the time their taxi started the Mercedes had already leapt forward and speeded far ahead.

'Wow! That Mercedes's going to get there before us!' Pigface said.

'Though how he got here …' Pappu wondered. 'We left him far behind …'

The blind man said, 'He made a clever guess. After all, where would a tempo full of kabaadi go to if not to the kabaadi centre of Mumbai? And don't forget, his name is Screwvala. His family was in the screws and hardware business, and they know. Now Pappuji, why are we rushing back to the dabbaa number 52? In the bottom right-hand corner, what will we find there? Could it be what I suspect, a piece of … twisted metal?'

'The Mercedes's disappeared. Absolutely out of sight. What are you people talking about? Somebody tell me, no?' Pigface was cross.

But the other two refused to explain to him. 'Ask Pappuji,' the blind man said.

Pappu said, 'Just wait till you get to dabbaa number 52.'

'This is not fair!' Pigface snapped. 'I'm going to get off unless you people tell me! Driver!'

'Hainh?' the driver grunted.

'Driver!'

'Hainh? Grhainh?'

Pigface looked at Pappu and the blind man. 'Um, driver, can't you go a little faster?'

The driver sighed sadly and looked upward. And while he looked up, the cab almost banged into another car.

'Son of sin! Budmash!' their driver yelled out to the other. 'Trying to hit me when I'm not looking, hainh?'

The Mercedes was parked a little distance from dabbaa number 52, but Screwvala was not in it.

'Where is Screwvala?' Pigface asked. The other two burst out laughing.

Pigface was puzzled. 'What's funny?'

'In the bottom right-hand corner of the …' Pappu couldn't finish, he was laughing so hard.

'Mia, you should be in flims, what wonderful acting,'

the blind man said. And Pigface realised that Pappu had purposely cried out about finding the answer in the bottom right-hand corner of dabbaa number 52 so that Screwvala could hear him.

Pigface looked at the garbage box—there were sounds coming from inside it, thumping and scraping sounds.

Suddenly, there was a cry from inside, and then a jumping sound, and then Keki Screwvala emerged, suited and booted—and sooted! He looked angrily at where the laughing was coming from. He had a dirty hand blocking his nose, and his expensive suit, expensive watch and expensive spectacles were all covered in filth. When he saw them, he let out an enraged trumpeting sound, like an elephant's.

'Driver! Go!' Pappu said, and they went off, trailing clouds of laughter. Pappu described the scene to the blind man, whose ears had already informed him of much of what had happened.

'Who knows where-where they come from?' the driver muttered glumly to himself. But he drove them to Pappu's bungalow, which was all they wanted from him.

THE LATE-NIGHT KNOCK

It was around five when they reached Carter Road, where Pappu's parents' huge bungalow stood about a little way from Otter's Club, facing the sea. Even the taxi-driver was impressed as he stopped outside the massive iron gates. Pappu rang a bell at the gate, and they waited for the guard to come and open it.

'That bungalow belongs to Anubhav Khanna, the film star,' he pointed at a bungalow close by.

Pigface looked. On the road, a few feet from the bungalow a dark, oily brahmin sat in the shadow of an umbrella, looking intently at them.

He was sitting cross-legged on a small cloth spread on the grass, with the stem of his umbrella planted behind him. He was a tall, lanky fellow with a white turban, white dhoti, bright yellow shirt and black coat. Across his wide dark forehead were stripes in sandal-paste and coloured powder. On the bridge of his nose were two bindis, of yellow and red. His big white eyes had a squint, his sharp chin had a pepper stubble and on his face was a keen, somewhat sullen watchfulness.

In his lap was a sleek electronic planner, on his fingers were many heavy rings, and by his side were arranged many charts and manuals, and his sandals.

He raised his hand and beckoned. They looked behind them to see who he was beckoning, and he beckoned again and again.

'An astrologer,' the blind man said when Pappu described him.

'I don't believe in astrology,' Pappu said.

'I don't also,' said Pigface. 'Unless it's true.'

'You, thin boy,' the brahmin pointed at Pappu. 'You aren't breathing right. Breath is the only sacred thread we have, at least in this life. It is the chord that attaches you to heaven and earth. Nourish it. Don't neglect it. If you let it go to waste, it will let you go to hell.'

What nonsense, Pappu thought. But the blind man was walking toward the brahmin slowly, feeling his way with his stick. 'Chacha—' Pappu protested. But the blind man said, 'I'm a Sufi, I know what he's saying is true.'

'Baba,' he stretched out his hand. 'Baba …'

The brahmin reached out and taking his hand, guided him down to his level. He took a magnifying glass and studied the hand.

'Which time of the year were you born, mia?'

'14 September.'

The astrologer frowned thoughtfully, made a solemn noise, spread out a chart in front and did some quick calculations on the planner.

'You have come to Mumbai from U.P.?'

'Yes! Yes, baba!'

'Anyone can tell by his accent,' said Pappu. The astrologer ignored him.

'You have come to Mumbai to earn for your family in the village?'

'Yes baba! Yes!'

'Is he married?' Pappu asked the brahmin.

'I cannot answer that,' the brahmin said haughtily. 'If I answer that, I would be speaking to your lack of faith. And I only speak to faith. You,' he turned to the blind man, 'know that the mystery you're getting into is deeper than you think, and leave these children out of it.'

'I've tried to but they won't listen.'

The brahmin turned to Pappu, and was about to say something but then shook his head. He turned back to the blind man.

'And do not get too desperate for money. Or you might do something … against the country. Something that might get you in trouble with the police.'

The blind man drew his hand back as if stung.

'There,' the astrologer said, pointing at the blind man's hand. 'There's proof that what I said is true. Gift a holy man fifty rupees, and I'll gift you my blessings to save you from trouble.'

The blind man gave the money numbly. Fifty rupees was a lot for him.

The guard had come to open the gates, and the two children led the blind man in. He seemed quieter, slower and sadder.

As the gate shut behind them, they heard the brahmin

cry out: 'Mia, have your food with them and then go!'

Pappu's ayah welcomed them in the big hall.

Ayah wore a frock. She was very dark, tall and powerfully built—she was from the fishing village close by. She gave Pappu a hug—but she was looking questioningly at the blind man. She was not used to welcoming people of his class in this home.

'Ayah, this is Hafiz Chacha. He … er, he is a friend,' Pappu said.

'He is *your* friend?' Ayah said doubtfully, in her Marathi-flavoured Mumbaiya. Then she saw the blind man's musical instrument. 'Oh, on Marine Drive, *you* are fellow who plays all those beautiful old Hindi film tunes …'

'Yes indeed, I am that same nobody.' The blind man bowed as he voiced the modest Urdu phrase.

'Oh, your music even made me cry once, uncle. You play from the heart! Come uncle, sit down,' she guided him to a sofa.

Pigface had been to Pappu's house before, and he said weakly, as if he was oh *such* a delicate thing, 'Ayah, we haven't had lunch.' And he was right of course, mountains of ice cream can't be called lunch! She rubbed Pappu on the head softly and said, 'Chotu, I'll right now get you something!'

Before they knew it they were drinking cold nimbu-pani and eating salted tikis and she was in the kitchen preparing a lunch of Fresh Rabbit, as she called it.

Ayah might not be able to pronounce it right but she could make Welsh rarebit as well as anyone in the world. They ate with more sauce than Pappu's mother ever allowed, and also more Thums Up-Pepsi-Coca Cola! The perfect combination! The drawing room was filled with sounds of munching, licking and silent eating.

The blind man had never eaten such food before. Sitting cross-legged on the chair, he would sometimes say, 'Mian, what wonderful flavours!' and then 'Mian, what strange flavours!' He shifted in his chair and said, 'I don't know how you people can sit, balanced on this little platform, for a whole day!' Then a little later he said, 'What soft soft cushions.' Ayah watched the blind man's reactions in fascination.

As Pigface fingered the gadgets the drawing room was filled with, Pappu phoned Inspector Coelho on the speaker-phone so they could all hear him.

Pappu told the Inspector of what had happened after he had left them. When he told him about Mr Screwvala in the garbage box, the drawing room filled with the Inspector's roar of laughter. Ayah rushed into the drawing room in alarm.

'Pappu-man, Pappu-man, you deserve a medal. Thank you, for doing to that Screwvala chap something I can only dream of!'

After speaking to the Inspector, Pappu enjoyed his meal twice as much. It was one of the best meals of his life!

After their food, as Ayah was clearing the table Pappu told her that Pigface wanted to stay the night here, and could she just talk to his 'uncle' and tell him he was safe here?

Ayah immediately adopted Pigface. She dropped the duster in her hand, rushed to him and gave him a big hug. 'Of course baba, Pappu will be so happy to have a friend with him.' She phoned Pigface's best friend's parents, and talked to them. Pappu also talked to them. They took Pappu's number and it was agreed Pigface would stay at Pappu's that night.

Ayah agreed about the blind man too, saying, 'Chacha I'll be straight, Pappu's parents would not like. But if Inspector knows you are here'—he had spoken to Inspector Coelho on the speaker-phone too—'then I know it is okay.'

She paused awkwardly, though the blind man gave a gracious nod. She continued: 'You children-people, you can sleep in Chotu's room. I'll lay out another bed. And you Chacha, you will sleep in the guest room.'

'Aunty, don't worry about me. I will just sleep in a corner outside, in the veranda … '

'Nako, nako, what you say? Certainly not.' She ignored his protests and showed him a guest room at the end of the corridor from Pappu's. It had a bed, a phone, a table and chair, and the blind man, when he felt these with his hands, was even more uncomfortable. But in the end he had to agree.

While Ayah was showing the blind man his room (he was specially awed by the attached bathroom), Pappu showed Pigface his room.

It was a big room with a TV, a small fridge in a corner, and posters of his heroes Rahul Dravid, Sachin Tendulkar, Aamir Khan and Vishy Anand. One side of it let out on a small veranda, with a lovely colourful Rajasthani swing.

They sat at the opposite ends of the swing—it was three-people wide. Outside, the day was beginning to fade. The birds in the garden were chattering as if they were having a big, loud party. They could hear Ayah and the blind man talking in the other room.

Softly, Pigface asked him, 'Why was Chacha so hassled with the brahmin's prediction?'

'Why? What do you mean?'

Pigface leaned toward him and whispered: 'You don't believe in astrology?'

'No.'

'Then how did the brahmin know that we're involved in some mystery with Chacha? And why did Chacha draw his hand back so guiltily, when the brahmin said that bit to him about doing something against the country? You listen to me, Pappu, this Chacha of yours is not so simple. We've got to be careful—'

Pappu felt his face burn with a strange anger. 'Just shut up! Say one more word and you can sleep at your best friend's house!'

Pigface became silent, and they just swung the swing for a while. Pappu didn't want to admit it, but there was something to what Pigface said. If it wasn't astrology what was it? How *did* the brahmin know enough to warn the blind man about the children? How *did* he know enough to make the blind man snatch his hand away so guiltily? Was he some sort of spy? Perhaps for Screwvala ... were they being followed? But then why should he even talk to them? Pappu had a chilling feeling that forces much larger than them were coming down on them. When he heard that Ayah had left the blind man in the guest room, he went to him.

The blind man was sitting on the bed. He was feeling a photograph of Pappu's parents that had been lying on a shelf by the bed, and his face had a look of secret sorrow. Pappu stood awkwardly before him. When he realised the blind man couldn't see how awkwardly he stood, for some reason his body became even more awkward. The blind man patted the bed beside him, and Pappu sat.

'These ... these are your parents, right?' Pappu nodded. The blind man felt the photo frame some more, then put it back on the shelf. 'Beta, the brahmin spoke correctly. In the morning, I must leave you.'

Pappu didn't know what to say. After a while, the blind man said: 'Your parents, they leave you alone quite a lot?'

Pappu again nodded. In the middle of his second nod, the blind man suddenly put his hand on his head and he stopped nodding. The blind man patted him on the head.

'They have given you many things. But—there again the brahmin was right—they have not helped you breathe easy.'

'What did the brahmin mean, Chacha? I didn't understand what he said.'

'I understood, because I am a Sufi Muslim. He said that your breath is the thread that attaches you to heaven and earth. If you don't relax, if you don't allow yourself … the room, the ease to breathe your fill—you will lose everything you ever have or win in life. Take care of yourself, learn to breathe easy, that is the most important thing in life.'

Pappu thought. 'More important than doing the right thing?'

'Your breath will tell you to do the right thing. Beta, your parents love you. But they can't take care of you every minute of every day. Only you can. Only you can find that happiness which waits for you, within yourself. Only you can ease your mind, and feed your breath. You must stop setting your breath running after your parents, or after the world—or even, running after me. The love that you want, the God we all look for, that God is inside you. Find Him, and be comforted.'

They sat there for some time, talking. Pappu didn't understand exactly in what way the blind man understood him, but he found comfort in what the blind man said. But all the while, he also found it unreal, dreamlike, because he knew that the blind man was talking to him about something that a strange brahmin had first mentioned.

'Can you write in Hindi?' the blind man suddenly asked him.

'Yes,' Pappu said.

'Beta, could you write a letter for me? I will speak, and you write, for my family in my mulk.'

The blind man was unmarried, but in Moradabad, a small town in Uttar Pradesh, he had his sister's family, and his brother's. His sister's family was poor, and he was in Mumbai to earn for them.

'Dear sister,' Pappu wrote for the blind man. 'I hope all is well. In this grey city it is the memory of you, little Bano and little Salim that keeps my heart green … Once, I remember,' the blind man popped out of his message to tell Pappu, 'when my brother's elder Hassan was twelve, and little Salim was five, Hassan was playing gilli-danda with his friends in the aangan. Now Hassan was little Salim's hero. I was eating food with my sister and little Salim, when suddenly Salim hopped up from the mat and toddled out of the hut to the aangan where his hero was doing his heropanti. In a few minutes he came running back, bawling bitterly. His mother asked him, with too much annoyance I thought: "What happened?" "Bhaijaan won't let me play!" "Why not?" Little Salim's bawling changed into breathless sniffs while he thought and answered: "Because … because I don't know the rules!" And he began bawling again. Then he stopped bawling again, thought some more, and added: "I also … also don't know how to hit the gilli!" And then continued bawling, very bitterly.'

The blind man laughed and laughed at the memory, and his eyes became moist. 'Look beta, I could be sad that I'm far from the little ones, and my breathing would be short from the hunger of missing them. But no, I fill my heart with the memory, and my breath is full with their loving memories.'

With a sigh he continued his letter to his sister. Towards the end of the letter he dictated, 'Our nephew is of course enjoying his comfort here in Mumbai.'

'Your nephew is in Mumbai? Oh, he must know you're here?' Pappu asked. The blind man continued the letter without answering.

In the evening when Pappu looked in, the blind man was on a prayer mat he had spread in the room. Later, when Pappu asked: 'I saw you praying on your mat, Chacha?' the blind man said, 'Yes beta, I was doing my ibaadat. But I am a Sufi Muslim, and we try to be with Khuda not only when we pray. I try to reach Khuda through all that I do, eat, dream, think—especially music!'

Pappu thought. 'And in every breath?'

The blind man laughed. 'Yes … and beta, even breath has a music. A music that is closest to the divine music of silence.'

At night, Ayah prepared a special dinner for them, 'In honour of Chotu's friends,' as she said. She wouldn't tell them what she was making—she wanted to surprise them. Their table was laid on the veranda of Pappu's room, where a cool sea-wind was blowing through the garden trees.

As they waited for the food, the blind man sat in the middle of the Rajasthani swing and pushed himself with his stick slowly, to and fro, to and fro.

'Dabbaa. Box. Think boys, what type of box

could it be?'

'What about the American coming tomorrow?' PP whispered to Pappu. Pappu shook his head: he too wanted to talk about that, but he had told PP not to mention it.

'Maybe it really was in that kachre ka dabbaa, that rubbish box,' Pappu said.

'Ah no. Rubbish!' Pigface said, pleased with his joke.

'Pappuji, I also think that must be impossible. Why should anyone hide anything valuable in a garbage box when the box itself might disappear any day? And anyway, so much is taken out of the box every day, and put in, it would be a most unsafe place. What other dabbaas does Mumbai have?'

Pigface brightened. 'Lunch ka dabbaa!'

'Pigface try to think of something that's not food!'

The old man just shook his head. 'Why are you joking?'

Just then Ayah came in with plates of samosas, kachories, sowntth and colas and jalebis—all the food, Pappu thought, that his parents had forbidden her to make. But Pappu wasn't complaining.

This time the blind man didn't have any doubts. 'Wah! Wah! This is the food for kings. Aunty, I will remember this food till my dying day!'

Ayah was pleased. She was sitting in a cane chair and eating, and then she suddenly started. 'Oh Pappu! You should be fasting. Both you boys should be fasting! Tomorrow is Janmashtmi!'

Pigface grunted, Pappu quoted the Hindi saying, 'It's

the sinner-stomach that is to blame,' and they downed samosas and colas even faster than before.

'Khuda!' the blind man said. 'Janmashtmi! Even if I want to search Mumbai, will I be able to tomorrow? All the young men will be out wild on the streets—'

Pappu noticed his use of the word 'I' instead of 'we'.

'What will you search for?' asked Ayah.

'For something in a box,' Pappu said. 'We know that what we're looking for is in some kind of box. But we have no idea what kind of box. What're all the boxes in Mumbai, can you think?'

'Beta, *we* are not looking for any box,' the blind man's Urdu sounded very sharp. '*I* am looking for a box.' At this, Pappu wanted to badly ask him what he was going to do about tomorrow night. But he held his tongue.

'Uncle,' Ayah asked the blind man, 'how you move around in Mumbai? How you know where you're going.'

The blind man gave his most secret smile, and Pappu suddenly saw that the blind man was shyer in front of Ayah.

'Aunty,' he said, 'I can't see where I'm going, but I can hear where I'm going. I can smell where I'm going.'

Ayah's eyes became round. She said to Pigface, 'So wonderful, no? He uses sound to know other things around him, like we use light.'

The blind man sighed. 'Sound, aunty, sound is an enemy, and it is a friend.'

Ayah offered a samosa to Pigface, who took two, and Pappu, who took one. 'How?' she said to the blind man. 'How?'

'See, because I have to make out almost everything by sound, it is a friend. But for the same reason, any loud sound is an enemy, because it drowns out other sounds. Like the sound of a train or even shouting, make me even blinder than I am otherwise. Because then I can't hear the little sounds that tell me—that right now, you are holding the plate in front of my face. What is in it? Samosa?'

Ayah gasped. She had just held out the plate. 'How you know? Samosas, if you want.'

The blind man carefully picked up a samosa. He said, 'I heard a very small sound, the skin of your hand rubbing against the plate. But—' A plane passed overhead drowning his words. He pointed up. 'If that had passed us a moment ago, you could have hit me with the plate and I wouldn't have been able to stop you.'

Ayah put her hand on her heart. 'Why should I hit you?'

'When I walk on the road, I know by the smell whether there are vegetable-sellers close by. And I know when I pass a petrol pump by the smell, and the stop-go sound of cars in a queue. When I reach a big crossing of roads, I know by the smell of open air I am at a crossing. Then Mumbai has many other less pleasant smells. It is with such landmarks that I recognise where I am, and where I'm going: from one crossing to petrol pump, then left until I reach the vegetable-sellers, then straight from there and the first right till I reach, maybe, a garbage dump.'

Ayah shook her head in sad wonder. Then she brightened: 'Chacha, can you play for me *"Pankh hote toh udh aati re"*?

Later, when Ayah had gone to sleep, the blind man told them the story behind the Taj Mahal, and the love of Shah Jahan and Mumtaz Mahal. 'Shah Jahan was of course the emperor. But they say that when he married Mumtaz Mahal she became the king, and he became her vizier. He spent more time with her than all his other wives put together. When she died he had Taj Mahal built.'

'He must have loved her very much.'

The blind man chuckled. 'It took twenty years to build Taj Mahal. Some say that the architect who designed Taj Mahal had his hands cut off by the king so he could never build anything that would equal it in beauty. Others say that many thousand people, labourers—people like me—died in building Taj. And yet, when you look at it today, it is the most beautiful thing in the world. Khuda, whoever could understand you?'

When the doorbell rang, they were fast asleep, the blind man in his room and Pigface with Pappu in his room, wearing one of his nightsuits.

Pigface heard it, but Pappu said, 'Don't worry, Ayah will see,' and they both went back to sleep again.

But soon Ayah was shaking them awake. 'It's the policeman,' she said. 'They've come to arrest the blind man.'

Lord Krishna to the Rescue!

They jumped out of bed. The clock showed it was eleven. The blind man was standing in the corridor with a worried frown.

'Have you opened the door?' Pappu asked Ayah.

'No baba. How do we know it's really police? So late. But the watchman says it really is the police.'

They all gathered around the door.

Pigface said, 'Who is it?'

'Insp'ctor M'lhotra,' said a very Punjabi voice in very Punjabi English. 'Open the door please.' KNOCK KNOCK KNOCK!

'How do we know you really are police?' Pappu asked.

'Open the door and you vill find out please.'

'Sahb,' a smaller voice came from behind the big voice. 'He is truly police. I recognise him.'

'Does he really know?' Pigface whispered to Pappu, who whispered back, 'Gopal is the best watchman we've ever had.'

Pigface, Ayah and Pappu looked at each other,

confused. The blind man was even more confused, as he couldn't look at them. Pappu looked at him.

'Chacha, what do they want to arrest you for?'

The blind man was so shaken, he could not speak. He just shook his trembling head.

'OPEN THE DOOR NOW CHILDREN, I ORDER YOU! Y'all are nice, adjucated children. Nothing will happen t'you. Lat the p'lice do its work.'

Ayah was impressed, and even Pappu wanted for a moment to open the door. Pigface, looking at them, reached for the handle. Pappu looked at the blind man standing there, his head tilted upward toward the voice behind the door, dumb and helpless.

Pappu put out a hand to stop Pigface's hand. He desperately tried to think of something adult to say, something that would impress the policeman back.

But though he racked his brains, he could only say, 'Why do you want to arrest the blind man?'

'Child, he has done something 'gainst the law. You won't understand.'

Pappu felt defeated. He wanted to keep the man outside away from the blind man. And he *felt*, fiercely, that what was happening was wrong. But he felt trapped, helpless to save the blind man.

Ayah, looking at both of them, finally reached out to open the door.

An idea suddenly came to Pappu. He again held out a hand, to stop Ayah's hand. 'Inspector! On what charge do you want to arrest the blind man? Do you have an arrest warrant?'

They waited breathless for an answer from the other side of the door, but there was a long silence this time.

Then, very sweetly: 'I am glad you asked that question, son. Very bright child you are. Yes, I have an 'rrest warrant.'

'On what charge do you want to arrest him?'

There was another long silence, and then an embarrassed clearing of the throat. Then a full-throated: 'He has been c'nducting unLAAHful business on M'rine Drive!'

'What is he saying?' the blind man at last asked. He couldn't really follow the English.

Pappu asked, 'What, um, is the *nature* of this unlawful business?'

'Err …' There was another long silence. 'Playing music …'

The blind man understood that. 'Arre bhai, is mujick a crime?'

Here Ayah burst out in anger in Mumbaiya. 'SOUNDING MUSIC? You're arresting somebody for SOUNDING MUSIC! Thousands people sell smuggler-things on footpaths at Flora Fountain, people make stalls on *roads* and you come here AT ELEVEN O'CLOCK AT NIGHT to arrest this poor man for sounding music? You wake us up at eleven o'clock? You wait till Pappu's father comes back from England—'

'That is all illegal, M'rine Drive or Flora Fountain. I arder you to open the door. I have a warrant for his arrest, woman! Open the door or you will be standing in the way of the LAAH!'

There was just nothing that could be done! They looked at each other and Ayah reluctantly reached for the door handle.

Pappu had another idea, and stopped her again. 'Okay, we'll open the door, but on one condition only!'

'Oi, WHAT!?' Inspector Malhotra was quite tired by now.

'We will go with him to wherever you take him.'

Pause. 'Okay.'

Ayah turned to Pappu, alarmed. 'What you say? I can't allow!'

Pappu said, 'Don't worry, Ayah, we have a friend in the police—'

Ayah almost screamed out: 'Your parents will kill me! Especially your aai! You want me dead, just go with the police!' Pappu was silent.

KNOCK KNOCK KNOCK! 'OPEN THE DOOR!'

'Promise I can come with the blind man?' Pappu called out.

'Promise. Now just OPEN THE DOOR!'

Pappu reached out to open the door.

Outside, there was quite a police party. With Inspector Malhotra were three other policemen.

This made Ayah even more disgusted. 'You ...You ... you come to arrest dangerous criminal or blind musician?'

Inspector Malhotra was a plump sardar, with small round eyes that looked beyond Ayah and saw the blind man.

Soon Inspector Malhotra had taken a cowering Hafiz

in his arms, and left a screaming Ayah behind. Pappu followed him, Pigface too followed him. Ayah tried to call Pappu back but Inspector Malhotra said to her, 'Don't worry about the children bai, I will bring them back *mai*-self.'

'Pappu, I would come with you but your aai told not to leave the house till she came back!' Ayah was torn.

The blind man said, 'Innispector, how can you take these children—'

'Oh you shut up!' snapped the Inspector.

'But Innispector—'

Inspector Malhotra ignored him and talked to his colleagues. They reached the gate and, as they waited, the sardar holding the blind man tight as if he were a bird just caught, the police jeep came up. The sardar bundled the blind man into its back.

'Look,' Pigface whispered in Pappu's ear. Pappu looked where he was pointing and saw, in the dark to their left, a shadow—the shadow of the astrologer.

As they climbed hurriedly into the open back of the jeep the dark spoke with the astrologer's voice. 'Beware children. You are going to be attacked. Beware Inspector—'

'Oi shutup!' the Inspector snapped, and the jeep was off.

They heard Ayah shout, 'Gopal tells me from which police station Inspector you've come! Anything happens to my Pappu I send you to hell!'

The police jeep was an open one. As it drove off, the cool air of the night streamed in and their nightclothes flapped around. The light from the street lamps too streamed in and out, in and out. One minute Pappu could see clearly the Inspector and the blind man sitting next to each other, tight, and the next it was completely dark.

Then they reached a part of the road where there was some kind of power failure, and the street lights were all off. The jeep became pitch-dark—

There was a bang! The jeep screeched to a halt. Pappu craned his neck to see somebody standing with a torch in front of the jeep, on the road.

'Inspector!' A loud gruff voice from behind the jeep, and Pappu turned to see, a few feet from him on the road, a huge man standing with another torch turned on, and a gun. 'Inspector, if you want your health give me the blind man!'

The Inspector threw his hands up at once and cried, 'Okay, okay, just don't hurt anyone. Especially not the children—'

'The children come with me.'

The Inspector's jaw fell. His hands also came down a little. 'But … but … you had said … how can I let the children …'

'Don't worry, Inspector. Nothing will happen to the children. I will take them back home myself.' Another man appeared next to the huge man—he, too, had a gun. Both the men helped the children and the blind man down, while the Inspector sat helpless making gulping sounds.

On the road, Pappu found they were surrounded by

five or six goondas and the criss-cross of their torches. Almost all of them had guns, not small ones but big guns.

The goondas stood around the police jeep as the huge man bundled them into the back of a tempo, waiting on one side. The back of the tempo was covered with a canvas roof.

There, amongst boxes packed in jute cloth, the blind man and the children sat huddled in the innermost corner, their backs to the driver's cabin. The huge man and two other goondas sat at the rear, at the open end of the tempo. The other goondas got into the front of the tempo and soon they were off.

As the tempo vroomed through silent side streets they, too, were silent at first. Now and then they would hear the singing of bhajans by a group of devotees in a maidan, or on a terrace. All over Mumbai groups of the devout must be putting statues of Lord Krishna in cradles, to celebrate his birth thousands of years ago.

Finally, Pappu said to Pigface: 'There's something weird about all this.'

After a while, the blind man said, 'There is some big fish who wants to eat the American's money.'

'How?' Pigface asked.

'Beta,' he said—they spoke in low tones, but anyway in the noise of the tempo the goondas could not hear their words. 'Think: at late night they come to Pappu's house, to arrest me. How do they know I am there? And what do they arrest me for? For playing music on Marine Drive? Crores of people in Mumbai do business on the roads, who is bothered? They *come* to your house for *me*! Then they take us, and, just by chance, the *lights* are out on the road. And on the same road somebody just by chance is waiting, and kidnaps us! There is somebody big who knows about the letters, about the money, and he wants to know from us whatever we know—'

They were silent for a while, thinking about this, when the blind man said: 'We are on Tulsi Pipe road.'

'How do you know?' Pappu asked him, surprised.

'No other long straight road in Mumbai has so many hutments lined on one side for so long. I can smell them. I also heard a train on the other side of them. Tell me, do you feel the wind?'

'What wind?'

'The wind that's coming in from a crack in the corner of this tempo, on our right-hand corner.'

Pigface was sitting closest to that corner. 'The canvas that covers us is not properly buckled at the corner, so there's an opening.'

The blind man grunted. 'This swelling up of the road that I feel—we're climbing the bridge of Lower Parel Station.'

They could hear bhajans being sung somewhere near the station. As they grew nearer it seemed to be a party of people, walking and singing.

The tempo slowed down. The singing grew louder as the tempo grew slower, till finally the tempo was crawling and was filled with the loud sounds of cymbals and drums and song. They were in the middle of the bhajan party.

Pigface sat on a box so that his body was between the crack and the goondas, who were sitting with their backs to them, facing the open air and the crowd of people milling on the road. They were of all ages, the younger ones dressed in shorts and chappals, some older ones looking as if they were going to their offices for work with their neatly rolled umbrellas. A few of them had huge gas lamps on their heads, the type used in wedding processions, and these threw some yellow light on the blind man and the boys, deep inside the tempo. They sang, '*Shyam teri bansi pukaare Radha naam* …' (Lord, your flute calls out Radha's name …')

Pigface slowly widened the crack.

The blind man whispered, 'Jump out, son. Pappuji, too. Slowly.'

The tempo was crawling in starts and stops. Pigface looked slyly toward the three goondas. They had put down their guns at their feet, so the crowd wouldn't see them. They were clapping and singing with the crowd.

Pigface disappeared through the crack.

'Pappuji, quick, you too.'

'How can I leave you alone—'

'Pappuji, please help me. Help me with this burden I have, this burden on my mind of putting two children like you into such a situation.'

Pappu was sitting on the box next to where Pigface had been sitting. Keeping his eyes on the goondas, he slowly shifted to the box where Pigface had been sitting.

The goondas seemed to be *really* getting devotional,

with the singing of the crowd.

As Pappu was about to jump out, he had an idea. His fingers began to feel around the canvas.

'Pappuji, what are you doing? Pappuji?'

Pappu felt one—he felt two—three—four. And only then, quickly, he opened all four bolts.

He looked at the goondas—they were still singing with the crowd: '*Radha ka bhi shyam ho to Mira ka bhi Shyam.*' (The lord is Radha's, and he is Mira's too). So he felt for the fifth and sixth bolts, and opened them as well.

Then he jumped and threw back the canvas roof, and a quarter of the tempo was suddenly open. Pappu quickly scampered over the boxes, and opened a few more bolts.

The goondas were amazed to find that suddenly half the tempo's back was uncovered. They were out in the open, in a crowd of devotees singing and swaying with statues of Lord Krishna. Pigface was right next to the edge of the tempo, and he jumped up in excitement and waved. Pappu also jumped up and began to sing. He caught hold of the blind man's hand, and forced him to his feet. The three goondas stopped singing—they forgot god again. One of them reached down to his gun lying on the floor, but the huge goonda stopped him.

Pappu stepped into the crowd, and arms reached out and helped him down. Then he and Pigface, still singing, helped the blind man down.

'Let us go to the station,' Pappu said. 'Quick.'

'No!' the blind man said. 'Let us stay with the crowd.'

The three goondas were climbing down from the tempo.

'They're coming,' Pigface said.

'Without their big guns,' Pappu said.

'They may have little ones in their pockets,' the blind man said. He was between the two boys, both holding a hand. The goondas made their way to them.

In the crush the huge one put a pistol to the blind man's side. He said in his ear: 'Get back or—'

The blind man said, 'You will shoot me? Your boss will be very angry with you. He wants to know what I know.'

The huge goonda stepped back a little, surprised. 'You know him?'

'Of course I know him, sir. Who doesn't know such a big man?'

Suddenly, the blind man pointed to the huge goonda's hand and shouted: 'A gun!'

In the sounds of the bhajan, nobody heard the word but the goonda's jaw fell. He looked guiltily at the gun in his hand.

Pappu and Pigface pushed backward into the crowd, to make a small empty space between them and the goonda. 'Look! A gun! A gun!'

People around them stopped singing—they could hear somebody was shouting, but they couldn't hear the words that were being shouted.

As the noise around them subsided, Pappu shouted, 'A gun! In the middle of prayer, a gun!'

Somebody else heard that. 'A gun! This man has a gun!'

The huge goonda lowered the gun, and guiltily tried to hide it behind his back. Then he put it in his pocket and began to back out. His toadies too began backing out. More and more people stopped singing. 'A gun? Who has a gun?'

The three goondas were soon out of the group of singers and back in the tempo. As more and more people stopped to look, and stopped singing, the tempo drove off, and the devotees took up their singing and walking again.

The blind man and the boys now headed for the station. Inside the station, they did not stop to buy tickets —they didn't have any money anyway, they were dressed in their nightsuits.

They walked down the stairs on to the platform, where an electrical sign said: Bandra: 12.25.

The train soon came and they climbed into the second-class compartment. At this time of night, of course, it was quite empty.

Where should they go? The train was going back to Bandra but should they go back to Pappu's house? Was that safe?

They got off the train at Bandra and the blind man said, 'Let us phone Inspector Coelho. I am quite sure he is not involved in any of this.' The boys were quite glad to hear this idea.

Stanley Coelho was sleeping when they phoned him, from the call box at Bandra Station. He gave a sleepy grunt, but when he heard Pappu's voice he was immediately wide awake. He realised something must be wrong for Pappu to phone him at this time of night.

When he heard Pappu's story he cursed, 'That Samrat! Where are you? Bandra Station? Wait there, I'll be there in ten minutes.'

Soon he was with them, wearing jeans, a loose T-shirt, and a sleepy look.

'I'm sleepy!' were Pappu's first words to him. 'But is it safe to go back home?'

'Innispector sahb, if you don't mind, may I say one thing? If you were to come back with us to the bungalow, then we can get a night's sleep, and this boy's ayah can stop worrying also.'

Inspector Coelho nodded sleepily. He immediately made arrangements to leave his police motorbike at the station, and they took a cab back to Pappu's cottage.

Ayah opened the door.

The Inspector said to her very politely: 'Ma'am, I'm Inspector Stanley Coelho—'

'You police people are what kind of people? You don't get ashamed to arrest children and blind man? I am dying here of worry—'

The Inspector was taken aback. Pappu said, 'No, no Ayah, this is a *good* policeman. He is with us to save us from the others. He's going to sleep in the bungalow, with us.'

Ayah looked suspiciously at the Inspector. But when both the others reassured her, she finally relaxed.

'I tried to phone your mummy in England,' she said

to Pappu. 'I couldn't get to talk to them. Where shall the Inspector sleep? Pappu, tonight I sleep in your room.'

And so the Inspector slept in the same room as the blind man, and Ayah slept with the children in Pappu's room.

Inspector Malhotra did not come back for them, and they slept soundly in the knowledge that Inspector Coelho was under the same roof with them.

The Distrustful Daughter

It was still quite dark when the Inspector was shaken awake.

He opened his eyes to see a sinister, shadowy figure above him. He gasped—then he realised that it was only Pigface.

'Pigface—I mean PP!' he scolded-groaned. 'What the hell—'

Then he heard the blind man's chuckle, and they put the light on. The blind man was behind Pigface, smiling secretly. Behind him was Pappu, who had voted against waking up the Inspector so early, but his face too shone with excitement.

'Innispector sahb, are you up? When Pappuji was sleeping, he had idea! He suddenly remembered that the men on Queen's Necklace said that Irfaan used to bet on the race course for Ikka. The race course! You understand?'

Stanley rubbed his eyes groggily, and made an unmusical sound.

Pigface jumped in English: 'Don't you get it? Don't

you get it, Inspector? Race course and—'

The blind man continued, 'Box. The box of race course! A box where people sit, at the race course! That's where he must have hidden it! Let us go there now.'

'Nnnww …?'

It was five o'clock. They were still singing bhajans outside, though they couldn't make them out, the sound from two separate groups was mingling. The Inspector felt suddenly, pleasantly awake. All this excitement was like cold water, without the unpleasant shock.

'Come on Pappu,' he said, 'let's get ready and try out a box at the race course!'

'I'll ask Ayah to wake up the driver,' Pappu answered. The driver was going for the festival to his hometown in the afternoon, but before that he would drop them in the Honda Accord.

The two boys brushed, Pigface using toothpaste and a finger. They quickly showered and changed, Pigface wearing something that belonged to Pappu but that Ayah said was too loose for him. The Inspector had washed his face, which gleamed crisp black and cheerful, and the blind man too had a sparkling ready look about his face.

Outside, it was still dark. They were so excited that it was only when they were in the car that they remembered what had happened late last night. Then their excitement lessened a little. But by then the air-conditioned Accord was swishing fast through empty streets.

The blind man realised that he had intended to leave

the children behind this morning. But it was Pappu's idea, how could he have left him behind? He consoled himself with the thought that at least Inspector Coelho was with them now. He would leave the children later.

The children were sitting with the Inspector in the back while the blind man sat in the front. He felt the smooth dashboard in front of him, the smooth seat he was sitting on. The driver looked at him and and laughed in a superior manner. The blind man said, 'Is this a car or aeroplane? It does not make any noise only. It feels like one is flying over the streets of Mumbai.'

Pappu suddenly remembered, and asked the Inspector: 'Oh! Was it really nuclear reactor parts that were stolen from Kenilworth? Have you'll solved the case?'

The Inspector looked at him oddly. 'What you talking men? Nuclear reactor in Kenilworth, what nonsense —I think men you're under too much strain now. Your imagination is running wild.'

'But didn't you ...' Pappu paused. Was he sure he actually heard nuclear reactor? The Inspector shook his head in disbelief. He saw Pappu's hurt look, and patted him. 'Ai Pappu men, just too much strain on you in last twenty-four hours. Relax, enjoy the festive atmosphere. I'm just talking to friends in department, I'll see nobody harasses you again like last night.'

He got onto his cell phone, and Pappu had to admire how low and smooth his voice was: 'Paluskar? Sorry to disturb you so early men, but you heard about Malhotra arresting blind man and *kids* last night? This is crazy, cannot happen again … hm, I think also must be Samrat … hm … okay …'

There were not many people on the roads as yet. But quite a few maidans and gardens had small crowds sitting on carpets, singing bhajans and chanting mantras. Lucky for them it wasn't raining.

As it began to light up a little, in some buildings Pappu saw the people of the building gathered to string up the dahi handi, or clay pot of curd and butter, suspended by a rope from two facing balconies on the third floor, or even the fifth floor. The handi was usually decorated with rupee-notes tied around it, and coins. The teams of boys for whom they were being put up had not started out yet, of course. They were probably getting drunk on bhang and encouraging each other for great feats in the day ahead.

Pappu went to sleep again, and the next thing he knew was that the driver was waking him and Pigface. To the left of the road was the sea and the sky fresh with the day's first light, and to the right was the race course.

The Accord dropped them in the carpark.

'Okay, chottu baba,' the driver said to Pappu. 'We will meet again in a week's time.'

Pappu waved goodbye, and the Accord turned around, back to the bungalow. Stanley was on his cell, pacing up and down the grass quietly but urgently.

After a few minutes he put his cell away and came to them: 'Men, it was Samrat who leaked information and I think it must be that Screwvala behind it all—maybe he wanted to talk to you in place where you would be forced to answer all his questions. I didn't know he was *so* shady … But don't worry, it won't happen again. I've taken care with my friends in department …'

They led the blind man across the inner track, where some joggers were making the rounds. Some rich kids —*seriously* rich kids, much richer than Pappu's parents, were gathered with their horses at one end of the inner track. Even from far you could see that their bright riding clothes were of the top international brands.

A brisk fresh wind raced around the race course, filling it with the scent of well-kept grass. The grounds underfoot were as deep green as the sky overhead was deep blue.

They cut across through a gap in the fence to the outer track, which was used only for the real races. Pappu had been to the races a few times, so he knew where the stalls were, and where the members' boxes were. 'Maybe the members' boxes will be numbered.' By now, the Inspector was following them, so quiet that they almost forgot him.

They walked past Gallops, the race-course restaurant, to where the stalls were.

'There are the members' boxes,' Pigface pointed.

The members' boxes were in a giant stand, different from the stand for the public or the smaller gamblers. Though they were called boxes, they were actually just open rows of seats. There was a lot of old carved wood, maybe from British times—or maybe it only looked that way. It was painted a thick white.

'What are you doing here? Only members allowed.'

They looked around to see an old watchman, in khaki uniform, looking crossly at them.

'I'm Inspector Coelho'—in Mumbaiya. 'How is the numbering of these boxes?'

'The boxes have names.'

'What kind of names?'

'Members' names. Each box belongs to a member.'

'But baba they must have numbers also!'

'Why?'

Inspector didn't know what to say to this. He realised that even if they did have numbers, the old watchman might not be able to tell him.

There was the sound of horses, and Inspector turned around to see two kids on their horses riding toward them on the inner track of the course. The outer track was closed, of course. It was only ever open for actual races, and this was off-season.

'Hey kids!' The Inspector called out across the outer track. 'Could you tell me if these boxes are numbered or what?'

The riders were a boy and a girl, both quite fair, both a little older than Pappu—about fifteen or sixteen. They looked quite posh and snobbish in their fancy riding clothes. They slowed down. From the top of their horses they looked down their noses at the Inspector.

'I'm Inspector Stanley Coelho. Could you tell me if these boxes have any numbers?'

The girl said, 'Oh you *obviously* don't know about the boxes here. They're just given names according to which member they belong to.'

'I obviously don't know, that is *obviously* why I am asking you, girl!' the Inspector said sharply. 'Is there any numbering?'

The boy next to her said, 'She's already told you there are names.'

'I'm talking to her, boy! Girl, is there any numbering also?'

The girl turned up her nose. 'I've already told you there are names.'

Another rider was coming up from behind them. He was a grown-up, but he was dressed as brightly as the kids plus he had on a funny bright yellow cap, and fancy sunglasses.

'Papa!' the girl cried out. 'This Inspector is asking some odd questions. Maybe you should talk to him.'

'What kind of questions, my dikra?'

'He wants to know if there are any numbers given to the members' boxes. I told him the boxes have members' names, but he keeps asking the same question.'

Her father came cantering up to them. His jaw hung open as he looked at Inspector Coelho. Inspector looked back at him and his jaw too fell.

'Mr Screwvala!'

Screwvala's daughter said, 'I keep telling him …'

'Dikra!' Screwvala roared. 'With the names they also have a system of—' he stopped short.

'But Papa, why—'

'Quiet, dikra!' Screwvala snapped. He suddenly spurred his horse and galloped toward the gathering of horses near the entrance of the race course.

The Inspector shouted: 'Mr Screwvala! Stop, Mr Screwvala! This is a police matter—' Screwvala ignored him.

The Inspector shook his head. 'You kids stay here.' He took a very deep breath and ran after Screwvala's horse.

As Screwvala's daughter looked at all this with astonishment, Pigface turned to Pappu: 'I'll go with him,' and he was off too. The two children on the horses also galloped off after Inspector, and Pappu and the blind man stood, with the old watchman in khaki.

'Pappuji,' the blind man whispered to him. 'Is there any place to sit close by?'

The old watchman said, 'Yes, you can sit at the stands here for some time. Only for some time, hain? Only because you're with the Inspector.'

'Then Pappuji, I'll sit here. You run along, I know you must be dying to go after them.'

Pappu was so grateful. In fact, his legs had been trembling from wanting to run after them.

'And Pappuji, remember—what can be done, do, but if you make a mistake don't punish yourself by blocking your breath.'

Pappu couldn't quite understand him. 'I'll be back just now,' he said, and he was off.

By the time he got to the Inspector and Screwvala, they were arguing loudly: 'Mr Screwvala, if you don't tell me about these box numbers just now, I'll take you to the police station.'

Screwvala snorted. 'Inspector, do you know the

people I know above you? They're so high, you won't see them even when they hit you.'

His daughter was shocked. 'Papa!'

'Quiet, dikra! That's the only language a uniform understands in this country.'

He turned to another rider who was listening nearby and whose clothes were khaki—he looked like an official. 'Pendse, as chairman of the Royal Western Indian Turf Club committee I order you to tell this man to leave club premises and only come back when he has a warrant!'

The Inspector shot back: 'Mr Pendse, as Inspector of police I order you to tell me about numbering of members' boxes!'

'Don't, Pendse, I order you not to!'

Poor Mr Pendse looked at both of them glaring at him. Everybody was frozen. The only sounds that could be heard were faraway sounds of the cars on the roads.

Then in a small meek voice, Pappu said: 'Had a nice time in the box yesterday, Mr Screwvala?'

There was a moment's silence as Screwvala turned, saw Pappu, and went red. Then he went berserk. He jumped in his saddle and his horse reared up into the air.

'Papa! What happened?' his daughter cried out, shocked. But Screwvala controlled his horse—and then aimed it at Pappu!

As the horse came toward Pappu, Pappu easily ducked under the nearest fence, where the horse couldn't follow. Seeing him safe, the Inspector took out a badge and showed it to Pendse, saying in Marathi: 'Last warning Pendse. Or I'll put you in.'

By this time Screwvala managed to control his temper, and he reined his horse in and turned back to the Inspector.

Pendse was saying, 'The boxes have members' names, but there are also numbers. In the first row you have —'

'Pendse! Stop!' Screwvala turned his horse and spurred it toward the members' boxes.

'Mr Screwvala!' the Inspector shouted, but Screwvala just rode on.

The Inspector was wearing only his T-shirt and jeans, so Pappu couldn't understand where he pulled out a pistol from. He fired into the air, and the gunshot was deafening in the silence of the race course. Screwvala reined in his horse and stopped.

But where the Inspector was standing the opposite happened! There were about a dozen horses around them, and they all neighed and squealed in terror, rearing up and down, up and down, as if the whole mass of horses was boiling. Pappu was on the other side of the fence but even he started back as if the boiling might hit him. Pigface, who was close to the horses, was as terrified by the horses' movement as the horses had been by the shot, and he ran back, stumbled and ran and ran without stopping.

As the owners tried to control the horses, most of them calmed down. But some were uncontrollable and the Inspector went to them and helped them.

Pappu realised that even though he was out of the way, even though it wasn't his fault, he *was* blocking his breath. He took a deep breath and calmed himself: then another: then another.

Only then did he see that Screwvala's daughter's mount was the most terrified of all. Its neigh was becoming more and more high-pitched. Sometimes it would rear up, sometimes it would just snort and toss its head in the air. The girl's fear was clearly writ on her face.

Pappu took a deep breath, ducked below the fence and back into the track. He was ready to step away again if the front hooves flew too close to him, but luckily the horse's angle turned away from him. Pappu moved backwards a little, and then caught hold of the reins that had fallen from the girl's hands. But he wasn't sure what to do with them! He didn't want to make the situation even worse than it was, so he held them very loosely. Just then the Inspector stepped up behind him and took the reins, holding them loosely but firmly, so that every time the horse moved suddenly the reins hurt it just a little.

In this way, gradually the horse reared up less and less, and grew calmer until the Inspector could ask the girl to hop down. She took Pappu's hand and did so.

Screwvala had ridden back, and the girl flew into her father's arms. Her face was tight and white, and she buried it in his chest.

'You idiot, you could have killed her!' Screwvala hissed at the Inspector.

'Mr Screwvala, *you* forced me to fire the shot.' But Stanley knew that, because he was not used to the race course, he had made a mistake by firing with horses around.

Screwvala's daughter said, her voice muffled against his chest: 'Papa, they saved me.'

Screwvala took off his sunglasses, and wiped his wet eyes with his sleeves. He didn't say anything for a few minutes. Then he said to Pappu: 'When I rode the horse at you, it was just to scare you. You understand?' Pappu nodded, though he wasn't completely sure.

'Inspector, go to that stall and look. That stall to the left, in that row,' he pointed. 'Go.'

The Inspector left Screwvala with his daughter there. Pappu followed him, and after some time he realised that Pigface was with him too.

When they reached the blind man, he asked them what had happened, and they told him.

They walked up to the stall in the row Screwvala had pointed at. It was numbered, 'E-5 (two seats).' Was that E-52? Pappu didn't think so …

The 'box' was basically a row of seats with a long desk —rather like a bench-and-desk in a classroom, but extra long. They looked in the ledge below the desk, there was nothing. The blind man kept making suggestions like: 'Is there any hollow part?' Or, 'Have you looked under the seat?'

They looked, but they realised this was not the 'dabbaa' they were looking for. At the same moment the three gave up and sat down, tired.

'Hey!' The old watchman shouted from below. 'Only members can sit in the members' boxes!'

'Shheh!' Inspector Stanley said to him, and he 'shheh'-ed. The blind man felt his way to the bench, and joined them.

Screwvala was riding slowly toward them.

'Look! Mr Screwvala—' Pappu said excitedly, but the Inspector shushed him.

They watched in silence as Mr Screwvala sorrowfully heaved himself off the horse, and then heaved himself up the slope of stalls to join them.

He heaved himself into their box, and sat looking at the race course silently for a few minutes.

Then Screwvala said, 'You know, I would stop looking for the letters if it were only you, Inspector. But someone else is also looking for them, high-up, *inside* the government. And if you find them, he will get them in the end and sell them abroad. So why should I stop looking for them?'

Inspector said, 'So of course you had nothing to do with midnight police circus in Pappu's house?'

Screwvala looked at Stanley with an expressionless face, for some time. 'What on earth are you talking about, Inspector?'

The Inspector didn't answer, but his jaw worked angrily. He turned away and said: 'Okay Chacha, children, today is Janmashtmi, very heavy day for us policemen. Before we started from Bandra I phoned a sub-inspector, told to meet here. He will stay with you as bodyguard—he is honest cop!' He glared at

Screwvala, who continued looking expressionlessly, almost curiously, at him. 'Ah, I think that's him coming …'

A uniform was entering the gate of the race course, a brown speck in the green of the grass. Subedaar (Sub-inspector) Naik was a short, experienced forty-five-year-old with greying hair and a gun in a holster by his side.

The Inspector introduced them and was off. Subedaar Naik stationed himself outside the box, to one side.

Screwvala turned to Pappu and cheerfully wagged his finger at him, 'You, you're a *very* naughty knotty boy.' He slapped him on the back. 'But dikra, you be careful. There are men who are interested in this gold box, not nice men like me. If you tangle with them they can be dangerous. Savage.' He then took out of his pocket a card. 'Any time you have any trouble—only *serious* trouble, mind—phone me. This is my special private cell number.' Pappu was confused, but he reached for the card. But Screwvala snatched it back. 'But this is provided to you provided you provide me with provisions, uh, assurances, that you won't provide it to, er, that nutty inimitable Inspector of yours?' Pappu nodded his head, and he got the card. 'Good. Don't phone me for ordinary trouble, hnh? Ordinary trouble *I'll* be making for you, so phoning won't help you.' He thought a little, then said, 'It might help me though.' He laughed at his own joke. Was last night the kind of thing he called a joke? Pappu wondered.

'I'm still going to go for those letters,' Screwvala continued. 'Don't forget.'

'Papa,' Screwvala's daughter was standing by the box, looking at Pappu. 'I want to go home.'

'Ah! Dikra, you look all right … and so, all is right with all the world.' Screwvala climbed out of the box, much more cheerful than when he had come.

She stretched out her hand to Pappu: 'Thank you.' Pappu stumbled and rose quickly, and shook her hand. There was a piece of paper in her palm, which she passed into his, then turned and followed her father to their car.

Pappu looked around guiltily: Subedaar Naik was looking at his hand with suspicious curiosity, but no one else had noticed. Later, when he opened the paper in private, he read in clear, open handwriting: 'Don't trust my father—Scherezade.' Below that was her cell number.

The Man on Top of the Human Pyramid

'Beta, what happened in this English-English, someone tell me in our language also,' the blind man said. Pappu told him everything except Scherezade's message. He was thinking, what did her message mean? Could he—could they trust her to help them maybe ?

'So what now?' asked Pigface.

The blind man said grimly. 'Beta, I have thought a lot. Last night's arrest was very worrying. Your Innispector sahb is honest, but who else is? There is someone very high-up and powerful after us. How long will Innispector sahb save us? If his boss calls away Subedaar Naik tomorrow, what can Innispector sahb do? We need to go to someone high-up who we can trust, to protect us.'

'Who?' asked Pappu.

'I know an MLA from Mumbai who is honest, just like Innispector sahb.'

'How do you know he is reliable?' asked Pigface.

The blind man didn't answer. 'And he is easier to meet today than other days.'

'Why?' asked Pappu.

'Beta, at Janmashtmi, all the parties try to win popularity by paying for the fat-fat rupee-garlands tied to the handis. Today, the MLA will be in the neighbourhood where his party is sponsoring the prize money, it is in Worli.'

It was seven-thirty. Screwvala had left instructions for them to be fed, so they first had a quick breakfast at Gallops.

As they came out of the race course they saw there was little traffic on the roads. But there were quite a few trucks, their backs packed with tall, lanky, teenage boys.

Subedaar Naik looked at them approvingly. 'My son is also in one of these trucks, having fun. He's a tall one, so all the teams in the neighbourhood wanted him. I remember I, too, had so much fun when I was young, even though I was not very tall … '

They crossed the road to the other side, by the sea, where the traffic ran towards Bandra. They stood on the wide footpath, trying to decide what to do for the day.

'What's going to happen tonight?' PP whispered to Pappu fiercely. 'The American … '

Pappu remembered about tonight for the first time since he'd woken up.

'What are you boys doing ghusar-phusar about?' asked the blind man amusedly.

Naik was looking at the trucks wistfully. 'My son is in our basti's team. His truck should be passing here in a little while.' He surprised them by sighing heavily. 'If today had been a holiday for me I would have gone with them … '

Pigface suddenly jumped. 'If it passes this way, Subedaar sahb, we would love to go with it.'

Naik's face became bright-greedy with hope. Pappu also jumped.

'It would be so much fun … but Chacha had some plans … ?'

All three looked at the blind man. 'Hmm … Subedaar sahb, has your son's team decided yet which handi they'll try for? Could you persuade them to go to Worli chawls to try their luck?'

Now Naik too jumped, like Pigface had. 'Of course I can, I'm the Subedaar of the neighbourhood.'

'Then bhai, Pappuji, yes. We go with Subedaar's son.'

'All right, brothers!' the Subedaar whooped with joy. 'Just be patient a little, his truck comes and we take a lift.'

Soon Naik stepped out on the road and, jumping and waving, stopped a large old Tata truck, painted a strong red.

Seeing the uniform, the driver stopped, and climbed out of the truck with a cloud on his face. 'Subedaar dada, what have I done? Today let me go, look at all these eager boys in the back … '

'Bapu!' A tall boy, wearing grey shorts, jumped out of the back of the truck and ran towards the Subedaar. 'Bapu! What are you …'

Naik began to laugh, his mouth so wide open that

the only sound of laughing that came was a squeaking from the back of his throat. 'Arre beta, I don't want to book you, I want to join you! If you have space for four people … '

'Subedaar dada,' the driver shouted in joy, 'It will be an honour! We've got a very good team, they've been practicing for a month.'

The team had not yet made up its mind where to try their luck, and so Subedaar Naik had no trouble persuading them to go to the Worli chawls: 'Bhai, they've put up a big handi on the terrace there!

The boys in the back cheered. 'Subedaar dada is Anant's father. We're going with him to Worli chawls! He's coming with us!'

The driver had the people sitting next to him move to the back, and the sub-inspector and the boys climbed into the front of the truck with him. Naik's face was happy-guilty. Here he had been expecting a day's boring duty, and now he was going to be an honoured guest at the festival of his boyhood dreams.

The blind man didn't climb in with them. It was pretty tight next to the driver already.

'Chacha, come on, we'll squeeze and make space,' Pappu said.

'No, Pappuji, even if there was plenty of space I still would prefer to go to the back.' He turned to the men who had just got off and who were making for the back: 'Oi, brothers, take me also to the back with you.'

They came and took him, and Pappu leaned out and

saw them helping him into the back of the truck, and they started.

Soon they heard the blind man singing in the back:

Bada nuthhuh-khuttuh hai re, Krishanuh-Kanhaee-e-eiyaa,
Ka kare Yashodha maee-e-iyaa, maiya re!
(Very naughty is Lord Krishan,
What does mother Yashodha do? Mother, oh!)

The crowd of teenagers roared joyfully along with him, and many passing trucks looked enviously at this unusual sight of a blind Muslim leading a crowd of delirious teenagers in singing filmi bhajans.

Pappu heard shouts from the back: 'Brother, pass Chacha that Luckhnawia bhang!'

And the blind man reply, 'Arre wah! Amrit from my mulk! Pass it here, pass it here quick, if anybody has a right to it I do!'

'Mia, should you be drinking bhang as a Mussulman?'

'Bhai we are not supposed to drink alcohol. And who said bhang is alcohol, tell me?'

There was a shout of laughter, the bhang was passed … there was a pause as he took a deep swig, and then he began another song from a Hindi film—in the film, too, it was sung by two people high on gentle bhang:

O Jai-Jai Shivuh-Shankarr, kaanta lage na kankar,
ke pyala tere
Na~A~a~A~mm ka piyah!

(O hail Shiv-Shankar,
May neither thorn nor stone hurt you
For I have drunk from a goblet in your name.)

And then the rest of the crowd took up the woman's voice, in hysterical falsetto:

O O gir jaoongi, main mar jaoongi,
jo tune mujhe thaam na liya,
oh sau rubbuh-di!
OOOOOHH, SAU RUBBUH-DIII!
(Oh, I would have stumbled
I would have died
If you had not held me
… I swear by god!)

The truck began to shake as the entire crowd swayed with their dancing, and Naik slapped himself on the thigh with glee. 'There is going to be an accident, ha-ha!'

They sang: *'Ek ke do, do ke char, mujh ko to, dikhte hai.'*
The blind man: *'Aisa hi, hota hai, jab do dil, milte hai.'*

(One is two, two is four, if you go, by what I see.
This is what, happens when two hearts happen to-o meet.)

The truck careened as the driver twisted around to shout through the little window in the back of the drivers' cabin: 'Brothers, you will topple the truck with your dancing!'

They retorted joyfully: 'Brother, you will topple the truck with your driving!' and laughed hysterically, just like they do in the film. The truck shook some more.

Sub-inspector Naik turned around. 'And give us some of the bhang too! What do you think, us men in uniform don't enjoy the good things in life?' And the cry went up behind them, 'The Subedaar wants the bhang!' 'The subedaar wants the bhang, pass it quick!' And soon the milky-white bottle came through the little window.

As Naik was about to put it to his lips, Pappu (was it simply out of some kind of jealousy?) said: 'Subedaar sahb, would the Inspector think it right that you drink bhang on the day our lives are in your hands?'

Subedaar sahb sighed, and passed the milky white bhang back through the window, lovingly caressing the bottle as it left his hands.

So, with bangs, and bhangs, and jumps and thumps and film-songs (they seemed to have lost the bhajans for a while) they finally made it to Worli chawl. Subedaar got off, but he was a bit cranky by now.

Two other trucks too stopped with them, filled with the other boys of their team—each truck, it turned out, had at least one person with a cell phone to communicate with the others.

It was nine by now, and when the boys spilled out of the trucks into the chawls they saw that another team was making a try for the handi, hanging high above the centre of the inner courtyard of the Worli chawls.

The Worli chawls were yellow-brown, painted with limewash. They were shaking from the film-songs blaring from the loudest loudspeakers the chawl-wallahs had been able to find. They needed to be loud, because there was so much noise from the chawl-wallahs.

The buildings were four storeys high, and they were shaped in a square around an inner courtyard. Every side of the square had about seven chawls to it. A balcony in front of each chawl overlooked the inner courtyard, and right now every man, woman and child in Worli chawls was crowding the balcony, leaning out and cheering the team on to climb toward the handi, hanging high in the sky above them. They kept throwing buckets of water on to the crowd. Every now and then loudspeakers would interrupt the music for a few snatched words, like: 'Nagesh, come to your mother in chawl fifteen.'

Pigface, Pappu and the blind man chose a corner near the gate, where the boys could search with their eyes in all directions but not get too wet.

The handi was a huge earthen pot, brightly painted in yellow and red and green. The rope around it had leaves and rupee-notes tied to it, fluttering gently in the fresh morning wind. The rope was a strong one, as thick as a baby's wrist.

There were countless tales of the child Lord Krishna's inventive mischievousness. One of his favourite antics was breaking earthen pots to steal the curds and butter inside, despite which he inspired much bitter-sweet love among the gopis of his village.

In the courtyard was a big bright-yellow board, saying in Marathi: 'Get the handi and claim Rs 1,00,000!' There was a symbol of the Social Reform Party on it. Near the board, in the centre of the courtyard fifteen boys had gathered in one large circle, all arms linked to each other up to the shoulder. On top of these fifteen hefty boys stood a circle of a dozen boys of normal build, also arm in arm.

The fifteen boys at the bottom were surrounded by a crowd of their friends and chawl-wallahs, who purposely crowded close around them so that if anyone fell from top, he would fall on soft flesh and not on the hard concrete floor.

Some people, who seemed to be part of the chawl's reception committee, gave Pappu's team—he found himself thinking of them as 'his team'—cold drinks while they watched the others try to make it to the handi.

Pappu described what was happening to the blind man. Eight boys climbed on the two levels of fifteen and twelve boys, who crouched so that the new group would not have such a height to climb. The eight were were all of light build.

From the surrounding balconies girls gleefully poured buckets of water on the boys, to make their bodies more slippery, and their job more difficult. Advice, too, rained down from all sides: 'Oi-ii! Hold on tight there, brothers, you're too fidgety for your own good!' Or 'Haven't you got powder? Oh brother, you knew the girls would throw water! Powder on your bodies would have made this mountain less slippery!'

Naik refused the cold drinks. There was plenty of bhang around. On Naik's lips was a big-big grin, and a bottle of bhang in his hand. The truck driver had sneaked it to him. Whenever Pappu looked his way, he would turn away, like a naughty schoolboy, to hide the bottle.

The third group of eight boys managed to climb on top of the two tiers of fifteen and twelve. When the next lot of six tried, they slid down the first three tiers of the human pyramid. The second time they tried, even boys from the groups of eight and twelve slid down, looking like crabs with their arms and legs spread to slow their fall.

They tried a few more times when the head of Worli chawls announced on the jarring loudspeakers, 'Brothers, they have made a good try; now let the newcomers try!'

The team cried out in protest: they wanted more time. Finally, the head of the chawls agreed to one more attempt. After two more failures, the team very reluctantly left the centre of the courtyard and stood on the side, hoping that the next team would not succeed and they would get another chance.

As the subedar's son's team moved in, many heads disappeared from the balconies. It was the girls running to fill buckets to welcome this team.

'See anything?' the blind man asked, his voice strangely shaky. Pappu and Pigface were searching everywhere for the political party's pandal, but had failed to spot it.

Below in the courtyard, seventeen hefty boys linked arms and shoulders to form the tight circle of the first tier. This had to be very carefully done. Though the spot directly below the handi was marked on the floor, if the circle was not correctly placed, there was the risk that they would make a tall tower that would reach up to the height of the handi—but some feet to the side of it.

Long loose ropes of water slapped on the boys from the buckets above. Giggling, they blinked their eyes quickly to help keep the water out. The water splashed in the glasses that everyone was drinking from. Some gave the glasses back to the reception committee, but most just laughed and drank on.

The next tier of thirteen climbed on the first circle, their feet resting on the shoulders and intertwined arms of the seventeen. Carefully they stood up, and made a second circle on top of them.

The third tier of nine boys began climbing, using the legs and arms of the earlier boys like the rungs of a ladder.

The water was coming down heavily, almost as if there were a cloudburst. The boys couldn't use their hands to clear the water that tickled their eyes because that would unsettle the others who were climbing above them! So they kept bending their heads to rub their eyes against their shoulders.

But they managed to keep steady and slowly, the

nine boys managed to climb up above the seventeen and thirteen, link up and form the third circle. There was applause from the balconies—and also laughter, and more water.

Then the boys for the fourth circle began their climb. This was more difficult. First, two boys clambered on to their companions, searching for footholds on their thighs. When they were safely on the top, arms linked, two more began the climb, and joined them, carefully linking up with them. And then there were two more and at last another, until there were seven boys in the fourth tier.

The cheering had slackened a little, as things got exciting and the chawl-wallahs got caught up in the suspense. At that moment somebody threw water from a bucket and the loudspeaker bellowed, 'Basta!' No more buckets of water, it had got serious now.

The cassette of film-songs that was playing reached the end of one side, but since everybody's eyes were glued to the rising tower of teenagers, only the hiss of the tape could be heard before it too died down.

At the bottom, the seventeen were still surrounded by a crowd of their friends. That was their insurance in case the tower fell. Out of this crowd three thin boys stood on the shoulders of the others, and began to climb. They would be the top layer—unless they turned out to be short of the handi, in which case there was an even smaller boy waiting.

A hush fell on the chawl. As the three made their way up, the boys already in the tower gingerly adjusted their bodies to give them more footholds to step on and push against. But now they had to be *very* careful in doing this, because as the tower grew taller it also grew more fragile.

A deep voice on the speaker said: 'Brothers, if these boys make it to the top, the Social Reform Party will give them the one-lakh cheque right now.' There were cheers.

Pappu felt the blind man's hand on his shoulder, so tight that it hurt.

'That's him,' the blind man said. 'That's the MLA.' His face had a strange, open look, almost as if he had suddenly regained his eyesight.

Escape from the Subedaar

It was only excitement, *great* excitement that brought that look to his eyes. Pappu could not understand it.

'Where is he sitting, tell me, Pappu!'

Before Pappu could detach himself, Pigface moved: 'I'll look.'

Above them, the three thin boys had reached the top—they were within striking distance. Each had a stone in his pocket, to break the pot. They stood on the top, locked in formation; motionless.

The whole tower was perfectly still for a moment. The whole chawl held its breath. One of the three slowly looked upward. Far below, in the second row from bottom, one boy had already begun to arch and duck this way and that, as if it was being slowly tortured. Soon his neighbours' bodies were also flexing and arching, trying to get the stiffness back into the lattice of arms and legs.

'Quick,' someone shouted, 'take it now!'

As the tower began to heave far below, three little boys raised their arms and grabbed for the pot. One of them missed completely and fell into the heaving bodies below. The second caught the rope with one hand and dangled. The third was lucky enough to find his hands suddenly full of the pot, which cracked and slapped him in the face with clay shards and a stream of white curd so that he turned away and fell with a cry of triumph on the others.

A cheer went up: the handi had been won! The dangling boy clambered towards the piece of pot left to pluck notes around it and throw them down. At the same time, the chawl-wallahs from the side began to give out the rope, so that the dangling boy was lowered to the ground.

In one corner of the courtyard, a wooden pandal was quickly set up for the award ceremony—the notes on the rope had been small currency, and the real money would now be formally awarded. The crowd was chanting: 'Jai Govinda! Jai Govinda!' Govinda was the child Lord Krishna's nickname, and also the nickname the boys of the winning team could boast for one day.

In the dancing-shouting wet chaos, two small, more serious-looking groups gathered around the pandal. From one of them, an elderly man who looked like a cheerful clerk stepped onto the pandal and, mike in hand, announced in Marathi: 'Friends, as Worli Chawl Building Society's secretary I am glad to announce that we have a very special prize for the Govindas. But before that, let the Social Reform Party hand over the cheque to the leader of the winning team.' He stepped down, and from the other group—and they looked really serious—a big tall man who looked like a Pathan stepped up. He was dressed in a pathani kurta-pajama.

'Friends,' he said in Hindustani, in a deep voice—and the blind man's hand again gripped Pappu tightly—'The heart is gladdened to see the enthusiasm and skill of these young boys. The Govindas of Mumbai are today famous all over the world—'

'That is him, the MLA we need to talk to. As soon as his speech is over … ' whispered the blind man.

The MLA had a beard, and a large, gentle grace about him which was reflected in his short, graceful speech. He presented the team leader with the cheque to wild cheering, and stepped down. The secretary of Worli chawl took the mike again, but they didn't hear him: they were making their way through the crowd to the small Social Reform Party group.

As they reached, a tall, dark man was saying loudly, in a Malyalee's Mumbaiya: 'Arre bai, let us go now. We are late for the meeding.' Pappu felt the blind man's hand on his shoulder urging him on and he was about to speak to the MLA but just then the tall man looked down at him. Pappu felt a chill that reached to his soul, there was something about those eyes, that face that made his heart beat faster … Had they met before? No, Pappu was sure they hadn't, but there was something about those eyes … Pappu stood there feeling stupid and looking up at the two tall men.

Pigface blurted out: 'We want to speak to you MLA sa'ab.' The MLA was saying something to the dark man and perhaps did not notice the little plump boy—two men from the Social Reform Party group came and shoved Pigface back. 'Talk to the MLA later, he has to leave. Sir, the car is at the gate.'

The MLA and the dark man were walking away, whispering and arm in arm, towards a man wearing a blue Pathani kurta-pajama, skull cap, and with face hidden in a thick beard and dark glasses.

The blind man called out, loudly over the speech and the cheering: 'Beta! Beta, your voice has grown so deep!'

The MLA stopped. The dark man let go of him and clasped the man whose face was hidden behind dark glasses and beard.

'Beta,' continued the blind man, 'my voice hasn't changed.'

The MLA stood still, his back to them, as if in a trance.

The dark man and the man in dark glasses were looking at the MLA: 'What happened?' the dark man asked.

'Beta? Do you recognise my voice?'

The MLA was still standing with his back to them—suddenly his hand went to his heart. He said something, to himself it seemed, but the dark man and his companion, looked shocked. The MLA ignored them, turned, ran towards the blind man, and raised his arms to hug him. 'Chachajaan? Chachajaan!'

Tears came to his eyes, and to the blind man's, too.

'Hassan! Hassan mian! How are you?'

The MLA laughed incredulously. 'How am I?' He shook his head, stepped back and looked at the blind man's ragged clothes. 'How am I? You tell me Chachajaan—why haven't you come to me before this?'

'Arre, why should I come to you? You are busy with big big things. I am busy with my … my music …'

'You should hear him play, sir, it's superb,' Pappu said in Hindi. Hassan looked at him, wondering.

'He is my friend,' the blind man said. 'Pappu.'

'Chachajaan, play something for me, let's go somewhere I can hear you- –'

'We have to go, Hassan, it is not a small matter, we are already late!' the dark man almost yelled.

Hassan started, and so did Pappu. That voice—strangely, though Pappu knew he had never heard this voice before, it touched a chord, a chilling chord …

'Chachajaan, let us meet soon. Today is—you are already seeing what today is like. Tomorrow I am going out of town … Monday-Tuesday evening?'

'Of course, then we can relax and talk. And beta, there *is* a matter for which I need your help, if you can give it—'

'Arre …' he was speechless for a while. 'Chachajaan, of course … ' He took a card out of his pocket and gave it to the blind man. 'Forgive me for rushing away, but just phone on my mobile tomorrow and we will meet.' He turned to go, then turned back, touched the blind man's feet and rushed away.

The blind man stood there for quite a while, silent, tears in his eyes. Then he turned away from the kids, and wiped his eyes. 'Come, Pappuji. Let us go …'

When Pappu told Subedaar Naik they had to leave, the Subedaar's face fell, his ramrod-straight shoulders drooped. Then the blind man had a bright idea: why didn't the Subedaar stay here for forty-five more minutes so that he could enjoy the victory celebration of his son's team? Meanwhile, the blind man and the kids would go to a tea house close by, and the Subedaar could join them later—but he must join them not more than forty-five minutes later; they had to leave for an urgent mission.

All the milky bhang that the Subedaar had drunk seemed to rush to his face, lighting it up with a madly white, delighted glow. Pappu admired the blind man's thoughtfulness. But when they reached the tea house, he got a big shock.

As soon as they had ordered the blind man took a slurpy sip of his tea and said to them, 'Excellent, now finish your ice creams and then you go home.'

Pappu, even though he knew the blind man had been thinking about this all day, recoiled from his ice cream. 'What!'

'Uncle, this is not fair!' said Pigface—but *he* didn't recoil from his ice cream.

'Pappuji, you know this is what I have been thinking the whole day. I beg you. The only way I can wash the sin I have committed of holding you at gunpoint is this. Please don't let this stain remain on my soul.'

This was such a true cry from the heart that it moved Pappu doubly: he felt the blind man's pain, yet such true pain aroused despair in his own heart because how could he fight against it, he would fail and soon have to part from the blind man.

'You … now you've found your nephew you don't need us!' he cried out before he could stop himself.

The blind man sat still, and Pappu felt his face burn with shame.

Suddenly, clumsily, the blind man got up. Pappu rushed to his feet to help him but the blind man said 'No! No, you keep sitting, Pappuji.'

'But …' Pappu watched as the blind man turned angrily and began to walk away. Then he turned back and said, 'Don't think I am angry at you, Pappuji. I am only angry at myself. Khuda hafiz, we will meet again. Khuda hafiz, Paintal beta.' And he turned and left.

Pappu watched his ice cream melt. He wished his last words to the blind man had not been so cruelly unfair. The Subedaar came after forty-five minutes and took them home. It was a quiet trip—Pappu and Pigface were glum, and the Subedaar befuddled with too much bhang.

By the time they got home, it was already four. Ayah welcomed them with a big hug for the two boys. 'You poor boys need to rest, it shows how tired you are.' She hustled them into bed, and their eyes closed: when they woke up they found it was five o' clock. The Subedaar was stretched out on a divan in the veranda—Ayah thought he was asleep but the boys knew he was knocked out with all that bhang.

Ayah now hustled them to a sumptuous snack—but Pappu wasn't able to enjoy it. He wished he could unsay the words he had said to the blind man. Ayah looked at him enquiringly, but how could he tell her his complicated story? She sighed, shook her head, kissed him on the forehead and knocked the sleeping Subedaar on the head. He popped up, ramrod straight.

'Take care of the children, I'm going to get vegetables and all,' she said. He grunted, and as the door shut behind her, toppled back into the divan.

Pappu and Pigface sat in the Rajasthani swing in the veranda. As they took turns moving it with their feet, they looked at each other. With each movement of the swing, Pigface's expression became more mischievous, and Pappu's more determined.

'Let's go,' Pigface said finally, 'We know where it is.'

'The time is 11 pm.'

'Yeah, we have lots of time before that.'

'We should get there before everyone else. If we reach after they do, they won't let us stay.'

'That's true.'

'Should we leave a letter?'

'Why?'

'So that they don't freak out?'

Pigface thought. 'There's no need.'

Pappu left a letter pinned to the Subedaar's shirt, telling Ayah they had gone to meet Inspector Stanley (it was the truth—he was sure they'd meet him at Akash Ganga), and she shouldn't worry about them.

But … shouldn't she? Pappu remembered Inspector Malhotra's midnight knock, and in his heart of hearts, though he dared not admit it, he wasn't so sure.

Akash Ganga

They took a taxi so that they could get there as fast as possible.

When they reached Akash Ganga, a huge saffron sunset sat across the sea at Breach Candy, its reflections on the wide rippling waters looking like the folds of the robes of a giant serene Buddha, sitting cross-legged across the horizon.

But they had to turn their backs on it and deal with a rude watchman.

When Pigface told him they were friends of 'Pappu, that boy who lives on the twelfth floor', the watchman screwed his face thoughtfully. 'Pappu?'

'Not twelfth floor, moron,' Pappu said to Pigface, 'Fourteenth floor.'

'Twelfth!'

'Fourteenth!'

'Twelfth!'

'Four—'

'Theek hai theek hai, go in,' the watchman said hurriedly.

They got into the lift and Pigface whispered, 'I hope it isn't locked?'

Soon they were on the terrace of the twenty-storeyed building, and when they saw in the shadows that the steel grill door *was* chained and locked, a shadow fell on their hearts, too. Except … Pappu touched the chain and it slid down with an easy clatter. Someone had carefully opened it and arranged it to look like it was locked. Pigface carefully closed the door behind them as they entered the terrace, as softly as they could. They were lucky there was no one there to hear the door creaking so loudly.

The terrace was like most others in Mumbai: everywhere your fingers touched rough half-finished shapes: squarish mounds on the concrete floor, railing-like barriers, clumsy half-doors, in one corner a knee-high stump of a flue gas stack. And yet all the roughness and grit they touched was strangely fresh, cleaned twenty-four–seven by the moist wind, and dried and baked by the sun …

There was a large rusty water tank in the corner of the terrace away from the sun. Behind it was a small platform in the floor, and they sat there and waited uncomfortably. The wind swept the terrace from this direction and that. Pigface took out a large chocolate and began eating.

Pappu didn't take any—he didn't think he'd ever enjoy anything again if he wasn't able to say sorry to the blind man. He was sure the blind man would turn up, that had been obvious from the way he had been avoiding speaking about the eleven o'clock meeting. He was sure Inspector Stanley would also turn up to try to trap the American, even though they didn't know what the signal was. He didn't know who else might turn up, but he knew the possibilities were endless … and frightening.

Behind them, they heard someone clear his throat.

His heart pounding, Pappu placed his finger on his lips and slowly turned around. In the growing dark he could only see the squat flue gas stack—but wait a minute! In the pauses between the sawing sound of the wind, he could hear someone chuckling.

'Chacha!' Pappu jumped up and ran to the little flue gas stack. He couldn't have been sure it would be the blind man—but it was! 'Forgive me for what I said in the afternoon!'

Without getting up from his crouch, the blind man reached out and hugged Pappu with one arm. 'It's all right beta, it's all right. I understand, don't worry. But you should not be here. How did … Where is Subedaar?'

'I'm sorry,' Pappu repeated.

The blind man patted him and let him go. 'Go back to your place before someone comes.'

Pappu ran back, his heart suddenly light and easy.

'How are you, Chacha?' said Pigface calling across.

'All right, beta,' the blind man said, and continued in a low voice: 'Now tell me, how did you badmashes escape the Subedaar? And how did you get in? Tell me softly—I'll hear anyone who comes long before he hears us.'

Pigface told him, and he laughed.

'How did *you* get in, Chacha?' Pigface asked the question Pappu was too embarrassed to ask.

'Oh, I thought that perhaps I would not be able to. But I played some pleasing music for the watchmen, and we became friends. Though—' He suddenly fell silent.

Pappu was about to speak again when the blind man said, 'Shhhh, someone's coming!'

Pappu strained his ears but could not hear anything. He thought the blind man had made a mistake but after a while, the metal door creaked open.

From behind the water tank, they couldn't hear anything else through the wind for some time. They didn't dare peep.

The first sound Pappu heard after the door creaking open was, faintly, a voice—no, *two* voices. He couldn't make out the words. Then he also heard what sounded like electronic crackles—the man on the terrace was talking to someone on the radio. After some time, he thought the man might be Stanley, but he couldn't be sure.

Pigface peeped out, and Pappu followed. The first thing that struck him was the sky, rumpled like dark blue velvet with gashes of purple. Against the banister they could just see the silhouette of a man, leaning over with something that was twinkling in his hands—a large pair of binoculars. He would look through them at the sea, then speak into his radio.

'Innispector sahb,' the whisper made them jump. The

blind man was standing by them.

All three strained their ears, but over the wind Pappu could not make out anything.

But slowly he could make out more and more words. From Stanley: '… boat … fisherboat … markings … radar … ' From the radio, a lilting Maharashtrian voice: 'Sir … wrong markings … report …'

But the talk was relaxed, there didn't seem to be any urgent action. The Inspector spent most of his time gazing at the sea through his binoculars. Then he seemed to get bored of it, and rested the heavy binoculars on the banister.

Suddenly he turned around. Pappu caught a glint of a gun out of his pocket. 'Hands up!' Pappu put up his hands as Stanley shone the torch at them: 'Sheh! Are you crazy men, coming here like this?'

Pappu realised that with a shock that without noticing it, the blind man and they had slowly moved forward, and were now only a few feet away from the Inspector. He must have heard them.

Stanley switched to Hindi: his voice did not have the respect it normally did when speaking to the blind man. 'What are you doing, uncle, bringing these children here?'

'Beta, I did not bring them here. I did not know they were coming here.'

There was an angry silence from behind the torch. 'Where's Subedaar?'

As they answered him, Pappu understood from the interruptions on the radio that he was talking to someone in a police boat out at sea, and someone else who was manning a radar. All were talking about the American boat's markings: they had laid a trap for it.

Suddenly, the lilting voice from the police boat began to talk faster—it almost shouted with excitement: 'Sir, we have in our sight the American's boat!'

'Are you sure?' Stanley asked, gripping the binoculars and getting lost in them.

Pappu could see that they were pointed towards the sea where he could see a small light or two—probably the police boat.

'Hundred percent sir, exact same markings—he's spotted us … he's turning away!'

Over the radio they heard the boat's engine rev up, and for the next ten minutes all they heard from the radio were ear-splitting whines of an engine at full throttle grinding through heavy water, and sometimes voices.

'Paluskar, where's the back-up boat?' Stanley asked—soon they heard an excited sing-shout. 'Sir, we have him cut off!' Then they heard on the radio the sound of another boat engine.

After a while, over the engines they heard the same policeman's lilting voice, still laid back but magnified on a megaphone: 'This is the police … Surrender or we shoot … Surrender now … Surrender please …' It sounded more like a mantra than a warning.

Some more confused sounds, then the voice to Stanley again: 'Sir, we have arrested the American … He is being conveyed to my boat and you can soon talk to him …'

'Good man!' said the Inspector as he waited eagerly. 'Ai Pappu, you want to talk to the American?' He had forgotten his anger.

'Here, sir, the American is here,' the radio crackled.

There was a pause, then from the other end an uncertain voice with an American accent: 'Hello?'

'Hello, state your name please.'

'This is Professor Dawkins.'

'I know Professor—' Stanley began, then stopped.

In the sky above the little lights of the boats, just below the clouds, there was a pink-red explosion—but instead of dissolving, the explosion solidified into a pink-red light that floated downward, clearly lighting up the three boats bobbing close to each other.

Before the light died out there was another pink-red explosion in the sky. The Inspector watched, awed. Then there was a third pink-red explosion. Then, in the clouds above the dissolving pink-red, there was a loud noise as if a ladder were being hacked and cut through the clouds down to the sea. Bright lights began to pierce the clouds from above, and then the clouds parted, like curtains opening, to reveal a helicopter which began to descend on the boats, searchlights shining on them. It was joined by a second helicopter—through the radio they heard the sounds of the 'coptors grow louder. Then they saw the three bobbing boats being joined by a new boat, twinkling with blue and red lights.

Paluskar hurriedly came on the radio and said in a

doleful sing-song, 'Stanley sir, what is happening?'

Behind him came a voice from another megaphone: 'Everybody freeze. Paluskar, don't harm the American—the case has now been handed to RAW, the central intelligence agency.'

'What men—' the Inspector gasped.

Then there was an explosion right where *they* were, above Akash Ganga, and suddenly Stanley, the children and the blind man were standing exposed on a bare terrace in harsh pink-red light.

'Inspector,' Paluskar was on the radio again, 'Inspector, they are telling the American he is free … he is going back to his boat … '

Before they could take this in, the noise from the helicopters at sea grew and grew and they seemed to have slipped straight from the sea right inside his head, churning his brains and Pappu thought he had gone mad, his very brains seemed to be bashing his skull—and then he realised the sound was from a third helicopter that was hovering right behind them, just beyond the rear terrace banister.

As the blind man trembled and cowered beneath the massive noise, Pappu saw sitting in the cockpit a policeman—again the Inspector's jaw fell, and he gasped: 'Commissioner Talwar!' The commissioner's voice suddenly came on Stanley's radio: 'Go home Stanley. RAW is debriefing me, we are handing over the case to them. It is now their case, forget about it.'

'But sir … we have got the American … they are letting him go, sir …'

'Forget it I say, Stanley. You bungled. Do you know Commander escaped prison this morning?'

Again, Stanley was stunned. But he recovered: 'But sir, how can I be responsible for that?'

'Inspector Stanley Coelho, you are suspended! Go home.'

'Sir—'

'Not one more word! Go home now! You are suspended, Coelho! I suspend you!'

The commissioner's helicopter rose to join the other two at sea, the light from the flare died, and they were left in the dark with the Inspector's disgrace, and shame.

Ayah's Surprise

It was two in the morning when Pappu rang the bell at his gate. A stony, silent Stanley Coelho had dropped them and wordlessly gone his way.

When they had started back from Akash Ganga, the blind man had asked the Stanley if Irfaan had talked in jail. Stanley had answered in a strangled voice that the first thing Irfaan mia did on waking was get into a knife fight with another prisoner, and he was now near-dead in hospital and unable to tell anybody anything. After that, the whole journey had been silent, no one daring to say anything. Even Pigface kept quiet.

Pappu's head was full of all kinds of questions: Why should RAW, India's central spy agency, get involved? Was this the end of the game for them? And, as they waited at the gate, how would Ayah greet them? She would probably be furious—and who could blame her?

The gate opened, and Ayah was with the guard. When she saw Pappu, she let out a sob and took him in her arms.

'Aunty, believe me, I did all I could to stop them

from coming,' the blind man said.

Ayah said to Pappu: 'Chotu, I died when I reached home. Since then, I have died a thousand times. But now … now I have settled everything. In the morning, all my worries will be over. Everything will be settled.'

She wouldn't say more. She looked after them, fed them, but now they found it difficult to speak in front of her. For a moment when she was in the kitchen the blind man did say, quietly, 'Bhaiya this is a very deep game someone is playing. Someone very high up—but … nothing is making sense. We'll talk in the morning,' he said hurriedly, as Ayah came back.

Ayah prepared their beds, and finally Pappu sank into a sleep full of nightmares about cloud-eating monsters and Ayah's teary-eyed silence.

The next day was Saturday, a holiday for both boys. Though they had only just woken up, they already felt low and tired. Ayah kept looking at the clock, and Pappu remembered what she'd said last night: 'In the morning, all my worries will be over.'

After a late breakfast the three of them managed a small, sad conference on the Rajasthani swing in the veranda. The blind man had missed little of what had happened last night, but there were a few details about which he had questions. When Pappu and Pigface described the three helicopters and the fourth boat, he shook his head in disbelief. 'So much of government money someone is spending … I don't understand.'

'But what should we do now?' whispered Pigface.

'What can we do? It is all quite strange. It looks like

the end of the road in this matter for us. But let us talk to my …' his voice shook 'my … to Hassan.'

'And … and I haven't told you, but maybe Scheh … uh, Scherezade, maybe she can give us some clues,' Pappu said.

'Mian, you are bringing in this name from *A Thousand and One Nights*' Tale?'

Pappu told them how Screwvala's daughter, Scherezade, had pushed a note into his hand. This was met with a dull silence.

Then the blind man said, 'Phone her, Pappu mian. If she is just acting for her father she won't even talk to you, she will think they have thrown us into the dustbin after what happened yesterday. Phone her—but do not tell her anything we have not already told Innispector Sahb.'

The blind man dialled Hassan on one phone, and Pappu called Scherezade's cell on another. It was already eleven.

'Hello?' Her voice was crisp and alert.

'Hello, is that, er … Scherezade?' He wasn't sure how to pronounce her name.

'Yes, it is.'

'Sche-shce-scheherezade, this is Pappu'—it suddenly struck him what a ridiculous nickname he had—Pappu! 'Remember with Inspector Stanley, at the race course …'

'Oh, of course!' she sounded pleased. 'Pappu. How are you?'

'A lot has happened since we met, er … Scherezade.

A lot … of unbelievable, very confusing things. Could we meet and … discuss …'

'Oh yes. Tell me, where are you speaking from?' She spoke in a clipped, precise British accent, which made her sound a little weird. *Nobody* spoke in a clipped British accent any more, the cool accent was American.

'I'm calling from my house, in Bandra.'

'Well, I'm at my friend's place in Bandra,' she said—she made it sound like Bahndrah—'I spent the night with her—but … what are you doing in half an hour?' She sounded quite eager to talk.

'Oh half an hour, it would be good to meet in half an hour …'

She took down his address. When the blind man heard she was coming he said, 'Brother, I don't think she is with her father, otherwise she wouldn't come.'

When the bell rang, Pappu was surprised to see Ayah jump eagerly and rush to the gate. She came back disappointedly with Scherezade.

Pappu shyly shook hands with her. She was taller than him, and in her white pants and yellow-white striped top, she looked to him like a Hollywood star—except for her British accent.

She took off her i-pod earphones and put them in a little white purse. 'I was just listening to Beethoven.'

'Bay … who?'

She raised her eyebrows. 'Beh-toe-vun? You know, he composed the *Fifth*?' When he still looked confused she took a deep breath and went 'Deh-deh-deh-dummmh,' the famous opening bars of the

Fifth Symphony.

'Ohhh, *Beee-thho-one,'* said Pappu, relieved that he understood—but then he felt hot with shame, he thought he saw her gritting her teeth. 'I'm sorry, that's the way I pronounce ...'

For some reason, she blushed, and said, 'Oh, never mind. Nice house.' He was too confused to answer. He was thinking, she must have pronounced it right and he had made a fool of himself. He tried to remember the way she'd pronounced it so he'd get it right next time.

'Take her to drawing room, I'll get some cold drinks,' Ayah said. Pappu stumbled over the stairs as he lead Scherezade to the drawing room. The blind man and Pigface were sitting there, and Pigface shook her hand eagerly. She returned the blind man's salaam hesitantly, saying, 'Uh, salaam, uncle.'

'You've eaten breakfast? Want something to drink?' Ayah asked in her abrupt Mumbaiya, snatching another hopeful glance at the window.

'Some cold water would be nice, thank you.'

'What cold water, baby, we got Coke, lassi, jal-jeera, nimbu-paani, watermelon juice, rose sherbet, Sprite. Apple juice. Chaas. You drink only water and you'll remain so thin-and-spindly only.'

Scherezade raised her eyebrows: 'Could you give me just cold water? Thank you.'

Ayah went off to the kitchen, muttering to herself: 'All this fashion-vashion will kill all these little girls ...'

'You look fantastic,' Pigface blurted out. Scherezade's raised eyebrows dropped a little, grimly. 'I mean, she's talking nonsense, calling you thin-and-spindly.'

Pappu realised he was blocking his breath again, and tried to remember what the blind man had said about it. Scherezade raised her head thoughtfully and turned to Pappu. 'Your parents are ...?'

'They're in London, on business.'

'Oh.'

There was a pause. The blind man said, 'Pappu beta, you carry on talking, I will try Hassan again. His number is busy ... Paintalji, could you come and help me? I am not used to these high-class phones ...'

Pigface looked disappointed as he led the blind man to the other room.

'Your parents have a business in what line?'

'They have a small chain of boutiques, in some international cities. They specialise in Indian-style clothing. They are most of the time travelling. They're almost ... never ... I live with my ayah—' He stumbled, it sounded like a stupid life. He looked down.

She was silent for a while, and he looked up. She was looking at him, thinking. Then she seemed to come to a decision. 'My mother died ten years ago. I live with my father. But he's never there.' She bent forward and mock-whispered: 'I *love* my ayah.'

She looked in his eyes and he knew she meant it. Then she smiled, and he at once felt comfortable. He smiled, too. Then he saw Ayah standing in the doorway, her eyes moist. Whispers sometimes carry more than voices, and she had heard what Scherezade said. And though she didn't understand much English, she'd seen enough Hindi films to know what 'I love' meant.

She rushed in with a large tray: four glasses of cold water and a katori of cashewnuts, a little plate of dhokla, a small bowl of wafers, chakri, laddoos and a plate of karanji. 'Now baby you drink water but don't go hungry. You all growing children need to enjoy good food, yes.' She placed the tray with a bang on the table and rushed out, brushing her eyes with her wrist.

Pappu and Scherezade looked at each other, startled, for a moment, then she said, 'You know what? I think I could love your ayah, too.'

Pappu joined in her laughter. He suddenly felt much better, yesterday's disaster seemed far away. Laughing, she took a dhokla, he took a chakri, but they couldn't eat because they were laughing.

Ayah popped back. Scherezade took a small bite of the dhokla and said, 'Umm, this dhokla is marvellous, Ayah.'

'Ayah's special recipe,' Pappu said. Ayah was staring at Pappu strangely with her still-moist eyes. 'What happened, Ayah?'

'Chotu, your daddy is coming anytime now. In minutes.'

Pappu could hardly believe his ears. 'What?'

'I phoned them, I was so worried for you! I told them everything, how you brought blind man home, the police-people coming at night, everything. Your aai is caught up in business, but your daddy came by aeroplane from London. Your daddy very, very angry.'

Something about the way she stood made Pappu get

up and look out of the window. His father was getting out of the Honda, the guard was helping the driver with the luggage.

'Pappu!' His father snapped, loudly, from where he was. 'What is this I hear!'

Pappu looked at Scherezade with horror. To think that she would be here to see his father come all the way from England to give him a tongue-lashing—there would be little else he knew, he couldn't remember his father having been this angry in a long, long time.

His father left the others with the luggage and strode into the drawing room. He was a businessman but looked splendidly like a barrister, tall and well-built. He had the ruddy face of someone who had lived a life of success and only ever breathed its cool, clean, air-conditioned air.

'Do you know what an important meeting I had to cancel —' He saw Scherezade and stopped. 'Who is the young lady?' he asked Pappu suspiciously—but more gently.

'She's a … friend, daddy, Sche-he-rezade.'

Daddy nodded to her. 'Good morning, Scherezade.' He pronounced her name perfectly.

'How d'you do, sir?' she stood up and they shook hands very properly. After that there was a little pause, as both relished the perfection of their manners. Then Daddy turned to Pappu: 'But I hear you have other friends? A blind *Muslim* beggar who has actually slept in *my* house?'

Pappu looked at Scherezade, who was looking very

uncomfortable. 'I'm sorry Scherezade,' Daddy said to her, 'but—'

'I'll wait in the next room,' she interrupted. 'If there is … if I may …'

Ayah said, 'Baby, come with me.' As she spoke, she came back for the tray and held it out to Daddy.

'Sahb, have ... er ... cold water ...'

Daddy reached for the glass in the tray—then saw it was laid out for four people. He snatched back his hand as if the glass had stung it. He snapped in Marathi, 'Bai do *not* bother me right now!'

Ayah and Scherezade fled to the next room.

Daddy took off his coat as if he had heavy work to do, and sat. Pappu remained standing, trembling at the thought that *he* was the heavy work. For the next twenty minutes his father grilled him. Starting with the most difficult question of all: what exactly had happened over the last two days?

Pappu looked at his curling toes and answered slowly (he knew he sounded stupid): The blind man had found this little box by accident, and he had met the blind man by accident, and then a … a goonda had threatened them with a gun and taken him from his school. The blind man had rescued him from the goonda—

'How!' his father asked, and Pappu said, Well, you see, you know he had an empty gun which he pretended to the goonda had bullets. Daddy put his hand on his forehead in despair, at what this stupid, stupid boy had got himself mixed with.

His father listening expressionlessly to Pappu's tale

of the goonda, the national treasure, the love letters ... This meant to Pappu that his father could be thinking just about anything.

Daddy's cell rang—it was a call from Moscow and he told them he'd call back. Pappu couldn't remember *ever* his father actually turning down a call because Pappu was talking. He continued his story ...

When he finished, there was a long silence. Daddy had learnt the power of sorrowful silence at his grandfather's knee. His grandfather had used it against the British. It was like passive resistance, it could be more powerful than violence, or angry words. But unlike his grandfather, he was using it not against the British Empire. He was using it on Pappu.

Pappu stood there and didn't know where to look. He burned with a secret feeling that he could only do wrong, a feeling which crushed him.

Finally, his father shook his head sadly and said, 'Has it entered your mind that this blind beggar really only wanted the reward? He wants only money, and he's just making a fool of you.'

Pappu didn't answer, and his father sighed heavily again. There was a pause. 'All this will end. You understand?'

Pappu slowly nodded, not meaning to or meaning it, his body was simply moving under his father's pressure.

'You will have nothing more to do with all this, it is a police matter. Understand?' Again Pappu's head nodded. 'And that blind beggar will not sleep in this house again. Never again, you understand?' Pappu's head nodded.

Daddy took out his cell and returned the Moscow call. Pappu stopped breathing and, after a minute, went out of the room.

He went to the garden, to the bench in the far corner. It was only a few minutes later that he felt the burning emptiness inside him come to his chest and throat, and choke him with a sob.

The Spies in Two Houses

As the rest of them sat in the guest room, Pigface occasionally babbling to Scherezade, the blind man stirred. He turned to Ayah.

'I will go to the garden—Aunty, can you help me ...'

'I'll come with you—' Scherezade said in passable Hindi. Firmly, the blind man held up his hand to stop her.

In the garden, he stopped and told Ayah, 'Aunty, you will take this trouble, of letting me talk to Pappu alone. You must turn back.' She started toward Pappu, but the blind man said, 'Aunty you can talk to him later, I might not be there that long. It is important.' She looked carefully at his face, then swallowed her own pain and went back to the guest room.

The blind man felt the edge of the concrete bench, and sat beside Pappu. 'Beta, I do not know what to say. I have brought trouble to you.'

Pappu was mute.

'You did not tell your father I held a pistol to you, otherwise we would not be sitting here. Even then he must have said that you were not wise to trust me. See how right he is! Without knowing what happened, he understands, he understands that I am not trustworthy. Beta, even after I gave up the gun to you I was still thinking only of the loot. It was only when you told me to go to the police, Pappuji, that I had a change of heart.'

'Really?' Pappu turned and looked at him through tearful eyes. The blind man's lips twitched oddly, but all he did was put his arm around Pappu's shoulder and then he looked away.

After some time, the blind man said, 'I think I must go.'

'Why?' asked Pappu, before he remembered that in fact his father had *ordered* him to tell the blind man to leave. The blind man seemed to read his thoughts, and chuckled sadly. 'Come beta, lead me to the gate.'

Pappu was speechless. The blind man sighed, then stroked him on the back. 'Don't worry, we'll see each other again.'

After a silence, Pappu muttered, 'When?'

The blind man sighed and thought. 'Tomorrow is a Sunday … come in the morning, ten o' clock, to the chaat seller outside. We will talk.'

'Promise?'

'I promise.'

'Your luggage—'

'It is all here.' The blind man was carrying his music case, and his little bag. 'I think this girl can be trusted, but be careful of what you say to her. And son, remember to nourish your breath. Don't let anyone steal it from you, not even for a moment, not even your father. But if they do steal it, you bring it back to life inside you, and you will win yourself again. And don't force yourself to breathe a particular way. Let your breath flow, let yourself flow, no matter how bad things are outside, let your heart breathe calmly. That is the life inside you. That is your most sacred thread, given to you by Allah. Let it flow with its natural smoothness.'

Pappu led him through the garden to the gate, and asked the guard to open the pedestrian door. When he heard it open the blind man hugged Pappu once. 'We *will* meet again.' His hands loosened, but then he hugged him again. '*Your* breath is *your* breath. Keep it smooth.' Then, feeling his way with his stick, he made his way to the little door and the guard shut it behind him.

When Pappu went back to the guest room, Ayah was standing at the door, and Scherezade was sitting on the bed. Pigface was sitting by the guest room's old, partly-working speakerphone that they kept forgetting to send for repair.

'I have to go home,' Pigface said, standing up. 'I just talked to my parents, they're back.'

Pappu saw him to the gate, too.

'Bye PP, you were a good sport.'

'What'll happen now Pappu?'

Pappu was too tired to think. He shook his head. 'We'll be in touch.'

When he returned he found that Scherezade was by

the phone and Ayah was still standing. Both were listening, shocked, to the spoilt speakerphone on which the voice of his father, from the parallel line in the next room, rang out clearly.

'Don't worry, sir, I have ordered Pappu to tell the blind man to leave and I'll keep him at home so he won't interfere again.'

His father was speaking in a mixture of English and Hindi. 'Right sir ... no, I was on my mobile, that's why you couldn't get through … haan, I have told him. I'll keep him at home, so he won't be able to interfere again … if he does anything I'll report to you at once, sir … I have ordered him to get the blind man out of the house. Right … we'll be in touch.' There was a click as the conversation ended. Scherezade put the speakerphone off.

She said to Pappu, 'I picked up the phone to make a call and this …'

Pappu slumped down on the bed, feeling dumb and drained. Ayah looked at them, Pappu and Scherezade were too shocked to answer. Ayah saw this and threw up her arms. 'I have to open Sahb's big suitcase.' She left the room scowling and muttering.

Pappu felt numb. The last twenty-four hours had been bad enough, but now … He looked at Scherezade. She was looking in her little white purse for something. What must she think of his family, of him?

She kept on looking into her purse, until he realised

that she was avoiding his eye because she didn't know what to say to him.

He got up. Would you ... er, would you like some water? She looked at the tray on the bedside table. 'I mean, cold water, fresh from the fridge?' She nodded.

The fridge was in the kitchen, next to the drawing room. He overheard Ayah, in the drawing room, angrily ask his father: 'Where is aai?'

'She's with … friends in Scotland. Doing important business.' Pappu thought Ayah snorted angrily. He could hear her unclasp the suitcase.

His father said, 'Don't unpack.'

'What?'

'Don't unpack, I only asked you to open it. Go to my cupboard and get that heavy blue overcoat. Put that in the suitcase and close it again.'

'Sahb, I don't understand …'

'I need that because I'm going to Moscow on urgent business. Ayah, we are counting on you, aai and I. We trust you to take care of Pappu.'

'But he needs you people—he needs his aai to take care of him!' Ayah said shrilly.

'His aai will come—but she can't come now. Ayah, you must take care of Pappu. Didn't you tell me you love him?'

'Yes, but—'

'I've put more money in your bank account. But Ayah, this business is very dangerous, that he's got mixed up in. You understand that, don't you?'

'What business is it? Explain it to me, sahb.'

There was a long pause. 'I can't tell you, Ayah … you must keep Pappu in the house. He must not be allowed to go out except to school. You have the guard, and driver, to help you—they know you are the boss. But I will tell them again. You are the boss, and you *must* not allow Pappu to step foot outside the house except for school.'

Pappu was not shocked any more—he just stood there numb, in the cold blast from the open fridge door.

There was more silence. 'You understand?' Daddy asked Ayah once again. More silence.

'Yes, sahb.'

'Good. Now pack that overcoat in the suitcase, I have to leave for the airport.'

'Yes sahb,' Ayah answered shortly.

'Oh—and call Pappu.'

She didn't answer. Pappu quietly took the glass of water to the guest room and gave it to Scherezade.

'Thank you. Your ayah was looking for you,' she said.

He sat, limply, on the chair next to her. Then he said, 'My father is leaving.'

'Leaving?'

'He's got a flight booked for Moscow. He has important business there.'

She thought, and turned toward him.

'You know, Pappu, you're not alone. I know what it feels like to have a father who is … I mean, your father is just inconsiderate. But my father is … is … worse.' She couldn't go on. She put the glass down.

Pappu sat there stupidly. 'Worse?' he asked.

'I mean I've always known he was a dealer of material that was not completely legitimate. Like a famous painting that appeared out of nowhere, after years of being stolen. All that has never mattered. But now, now—' she struggled to get it out but she couldn't.

Pappu was sitting there looking at her stupidly. She turned and touched him on the arm. 'Chin up, Pappu. For both of us, that's got to be our motto.'

Pappu didn't know what to do or say. 'Chotu! Your daddy is calling!' Ayah called as she passed by the door, whizzing from one chore to the other. Pappu looked at the door, then slowly got up to go.

Scherezade got up too, and shook his hand. He felt odd. She said, 'I'm ... I'm going to sit here, and wait.'

She sat down. She looked helpless and brave at the same time.

Pappu suddenly thought how wonderful it was to have her here. He moved to the door, but he didn't want to leave her without saying something. So he peeped back into the room and said, 'Thank you.'

She looked up and gave a little smile, and he went to his father with a stronger heart. He was no longer alone.

In the drawing room, his father was handling one of the crystal animals his mother collected. When Pappu entered, he put it down grimly and asked: 'Is the blind man still in the house?' He was repacked and ready to go. Ayah stood obediently in one corner.

Pappu looked at his father, and was suddenly glad that he was going so far away.

'No.'

'Good. Now listen to me, young man.'

Daddy gave Pappu a short speech. He was to behave himself. He was to keep out of this dangerous business he had got mixed up in, the law and police would take care of it. Every day he was to go only to school, nowhere else, then come straight back home. Now Ayah was his strict guardian. He must listen to her till his aai returned from Scotland.

'When?' asked Pappu, not expecting any real answer.

'In a few days,' said Daddy, proving him right.

Ayah stood by him while Daddy's car drove out of the gate. Neither waved.

'You're my family now, Ayah,' Pappu said to her sadly.

He heard a big sniff behind him. His head and shoulders were squeezed by two matronly arms.

'He wants me to be your jailor. Never, Chotu *never*. He can stop paying me, it's nothing to me! He—I stopped being their servant long ago. The only reason I still work in this house is *you*. You live and breathe as you want, Chotu! I will never be your jailor.' She turned him around, and her voice softened. 'But every day, you must tell me that you're okay. Promise?'

He looked at her—her eyes were moist. 'Promise,' he said. She looked up through the gate after his father with a fierce anger.

In the guest room, Scherezade was nibbling on a

dhokla a little awkwardly.

He sat next to her. 'Your father can't be worse,' he said. He wasn't sure she had even heard him. She didn't answer. She took a folded sheet out of her purse. 'I scanned this copy of a paper I found in the dustbin at home.' Pappu peered at the copy of a crumpled paper. Through the network of printed crinkles he could make out that it was the plan of an apartment.

'It looks like an ordinary plan of a flat to me,' he said. 'What were you looking in the dustbin for?'

'A few days ago my father met this odd man, in our drawing room. This man looked really strange—desperate, I can't remember anyone like him coming to our house ever before. He wore jeans, a kurta top, and had a big scar on his face. So I hung around outside the drawing room. There was some talk of a plan of to "quietly-quietly remove the dog from the Worthy Kennel". I knew my father had some odd business deals, but nothing like this. You know, this sounded like—' she stopped herself. 'And then, day before yesterday—I found this.'

'But Sche-scheh-sheh—'

'Call me Sherry. That's easier to pronounce.'

'But, Sheh … Sheh …' he found it almost as difficult to say Sherry, though for different reasons: 'Sherry … this could be anything. You're imagining things, this flat could be—'

She shook her head and pointed her finger at a small cross in a corner of one room. Next to the cross was written, 'sleeping dog.'

'Look at that. If you want to take out that "dog" quietly, it—I mean it can only be stealing, isn't it? Maybe a painting. I googled Sleeping Dog + Painting and there were 20,500 entries. Or it could be a painting with a completely different name, and just because it has a sleeping woman who Papa thinks is ugly, he's nicknamed it Sleeping Dog—he enjoys doing that.'

'But Sherry—'

And then Pappu stopped breathing again.

At the bottom of the diagram, barely readable through the printed crinkles, there was a small scribbled name.

Kenilworth.

The building the Inspector had rushed to after they had eaten ice creams.

THE STORY OF STANLEY'S FATHER

Or was it?

Scherezade was talking but he wasn't listening to her words. Her voice ran through his mind like a whirlpool carrying his thoughts almost aimlessly and meaninglessly.

Had he really heard the Inspector right? He remembered that Stanley had denied it. What a coincidence this was. Or was it? One thing was for sure now—Scherezade was not her father's spy.

Scherezade had taken out something else from her little purse, and was holding it in front of him: a tiny newspaper cutting headlined 'Mystery break-in at scientist's house'. Almost without reading, Pappu realised that the article was describing how the watchman at Kenilworth heard suspicious noises, called the police, the police found that a safe in the bedroom of a Mr Bose's house had been burgled. And he suddenly was jolted out of his confusion by the shock that Scherezade must have felt when she saw this article, after finding that plan in her dustbin. And suddenly he saw her face clearly and heard her words again. It was proof! Her face was twisted with sorrow.

'No, no,' Pappu said, though inside he was thinking, Yes! That must be it: her father was *more* than a common thief! But she must not know! And he grabbed her shoulders and said 'No!'

'Then how do you explain this?' she asked, her face fearful and yet hopeful.

'You—I can't explain it, but you are making stories up from nothing. Look, does this article say what was stolen? No! Why not? It could be anything, your father could be acting out of some good reason. And how many Kenilworths are there in Mumbai? There's one on Linking Road in Bandra—there must be at least a dozen—'

'He's been a dodgy art dealer all his life, and one day he starts … *stealing* for a *good* reason?'

Their voices must have become loud—Ayah looked in and said, 'Why you baby-people talk so loud-loud? You people hungry, that's why! Come, lunch is on the table.'

Pappu was so thankful to her. He was tired of thinking about his father, and hers. He looked at the clock: it was one thirty.

At the dining table, Ayah had laid none of the knives, forks and spoons that she did when Pappu's parents were eating. There were a few mats, some plates, katoris, spoons, glasses.

And most importantly, there was the food. Ayah made the finest bhakri in the world, light and soft. And when you ate it with her coconut and garlic chutneys, it was a secret heaven in your mouth! There was also rice and pithale. He knew there would be sweet surprises later.

Over lunch Pappu told Scherezade about the last few days, in a way that would take her mind off her father. He didn't mention her father in the garbage box! He told her about the glass factory in Dharavi, and the motorboats chasing the American. She listened raptly.

She even laughed when he told her how he mouthed 'Police' to Pigface, and Pigface thought he was mouthing 'Puhlease' for his ice-lolly. Yes, he thought, the talk and food was cheering her up. Or was it she who was trying to cheer *him* up? Whatever the reason, she seemed to be really enjoying herself.

When the dessert came—light shevai and divine amras—she licked her fingers and said, 'Oh, such delicious flavours, Ayah! And so healthy and *light* too, it's heavenly.' Though Ayah understood none of her words, she understood all of her enjoyment and beamed.

There was also srikhand for dessert, much better than you could get in the shops. Ayah told Scherezade she should try to flavour the last bits of bhakri left with it. Pappu thought this was weird but it was a hit with Scherezade. Pappu was amazed when Scherezade interrupted the most exciting twist in his story, when the American had been arrested, to ask Ayah to please sit down, and had a five-minute discussion with her about the *philosophy* of different foods of India.

After Ayah had got up to clear the dishes and Scherezade had insisted on helping her—as soon as she came back, at the door itself she turned to Pappu and asked: 'And then what happened?' He told her about how the helicopters suddenly showed up, the American was freed and Inspector Stanley suspended.

She sat silent while Ayah bustled around them cleaning the table.

'I liked Inspector Stanley,' she said finally.

'He was … really stunned. You should have seen his face.'

She thought. 'Why don't you call him?'

'You mean just now?'

'Yes, he must be so down. Why don't we meet him, try and cheer him up.'

'You don't have to go home?'

'I'm like you, Pappu,' she made a face. 'My father is busy with other things. He won't notice if I'm not there.'

Pappu felt awkward about it, so *she* dialled Stanley. She introduced herself, told him she'd heard the bad news from Pappu and said 'We wondered if we could come see you.'

She kept the phone down. 'We meet him at the gate of Green Park opposite St. Andrew's Church at 4.30 today.' Pappu didn't know what to say. He looked at the clock, it was three. St. Andrew's was not far away. 'He sounded okay,' she said, reading at least some of his thoughts.

St. Andrew's Church overlooks a crossing where the road becomes a narrow gali, and where a fishing village becomes a rich suburb. Behind the church the waves dodged the wind. In front of it, across the crossing, boys of all ages dodged each other in a game on the stony compound of Green Park building. Stanley Coelho was one of them. Green Park was a grey building, and looked like many little rough boxes jammed together. The flats had little balconies, with clotheslines, windows, plants and junk crammed in them.

Stanley had asked Pappu to join in the game since they had an uneven number of players. The football was intense—and no one played more intensely than Stanley. The smaller boys enjoyed slipping through the bigger boys' legs to kick the ball. This maddened the bigger guys, so when a small boy got in the way they gave him a smart little kick, and then a bigger kick at the ball. The little boys didn't seem to mind too much, dodging those smart kicks as if they were the price for being allowed to play.

Scherezade had joined a group of four girls sitting on a bench against a ground-floor balcony. Next to her was petite fair-skinned Grace. Her grey-green eyes followed Stanley fiercely, and every now and then she'd shout: 'Come on, Stanley! Go, Stanley, go!' The girls next to her giggled, a little embarrassed: but Stanley was their hero, too.

Stanley ignored the girls and played desperately, taking out his anger at the world on the football.

Suddenly Grace began to chant: 'Stanley! Stanley!' and the other girls chorused, 'Big-black-manly!' But they pronounced it 'manley,' because that was the cool way of saying it—and also it rhymed better.

Stanley! Stanley!
(chorus) Big-black-manley!
Beat all the guys
(chorus) 'n' win the prize!
No prize for guessing
Where that lies!

The last line was left for Grace to say. Maybe she had created this chant, or maybe all the girls had, but Grace was the leader.

Stanley paid no attention; he ran, scored a goal, ran. Pappu ran around like mad, not getting the ball much (like the other small boys—though he was *medium* small, he thought). He did get the ball once, and ran with it to the goalpost: Stanley was in front of him, his face dark and sweating. Pappu dodged—it was so easy to dodge those long legs with his little ones! As he dribbled the ball, Stanley lunged and Pappu was between the ball and him, and Stanley aimed a smart kick, and Pappu jumped out of the way so that Stanley was able to kick the ball away.

Pappu was shocked. He hadn't expected *Stanley* to do it. He hung back and watched Stanley, his face tight as he ran after the ball. Then he realised it must have been a mistake. But after five minutes it happened a second time.

The third time Stanley came at him he didn't clear out: and Stanley, face dark and tight, gave him a smart little kick.

'Ow!' Pappu yelped. He was shocked! He hadn't expected *Stanley* to kick him! The kick hurt a little, but not nearly as much as the thought of Stanley ... He turned away without looking where the ball was bouncing, sick at heart, and went to his field placement.

'Hey!' Stanley's sharp voice made him turn around and he saw that the game and the ball had moved on, but Stanley was bent double with hands on knees, panting angrily. 'Hey, I'm sorry, men!'

'That's all right,' Pappu said in a small voice. Stanley turned and, seeing the ball and game move away from him, cursed angrily.

'Damn!' he shouted at the rough compound ground. 'Damn! Damn! Damn!' Some of the others turned around and stopped. Then more stopped—the game stopped. Pappu moved up to Stanley, not knowing what to do.

Stanley put his hand on Pappu's shoulder and snapped at the others: 'What you looking at, men?'

'You okay, Stanley?' one of the other men asked.

'We two got to stop playing. You carry on!' The game restarted—but the boys kept sneaking looks at Stanley.

He took Pappu to the side, and leaned against the compound wall. 'Sorry men, sorry,' he said. Looking at his dark flushed face Pappu wondered if he would have kicked him that way even if yesterday hadn't happened.

He didn't know, and the thought frightened him.

Scherezade and Grace had walked up.

'Stanley?' asked Grace gently. 'Stanley, are you okay?'

'Yes, yes I'm okay, Grace.' She moved closer and he said, 'Grace, you know I already have a girlfriend.'

'That Hindu girl!' she said scornfully.

'Leave me alone!' Stanley shouted, and Grace flinched. Stuttering, she melted away. Behind them, the game had stopped.

'I'm so sorry,' said Scherezade. 'I heard what happened at Akash Ganga. It's most unfair.'

Stanley leant against the wall and wiped his sweat. 'Can't be helped,' he said. 'That's life.' His words were more cheerful than his voice.

'There's someone high-up in the department who's behind all this, isn't there?' she said.

He snorted. 'Yes, and there's nothing we can do about it.' They were silent. Still leaning against the wall, he shook his head in despair at the ground. 'Nothing.'

He remembered them again, and said: 'Game's over men, come to my house. My mum would like to meet you.' He led them up a badly lit, narrow staircase with a spindly railing, and stopped at the first floor. He turned to them.

'Remember, not a word to Mum. She doesn't know about yesterday.'

He waited till they both had nodded, then turned and rang the doorbell. When the door opened, it was as if a crisp rectangle of cleanliness and light had been cut into the musty corridor. A short chubby woman in an apron over her frock, welcomed them with a warm hug. Then she told Stanley to immediately go and wash his sweating face. He groaned but went.

They were in a small drawing room: the light was pouring in from the balcony on the other side. Though the walls of the tiny flat were not completely straight, and had bulges and hollows, and the paint looked powdery, the flat itself was clean as Christmas. There was a dining table with four chairs, a small fridge next to it, and towards the balcony there was a small orange sofa set and small glass cupboards surrounding a carpet. Small doors with curtains led into other rooms. To one side of the fridge, close to the dining table, there was a tiny kitchen.

'Sten tell me about you, Pappu, what a smart young fellow you are.' She patted a blushing Pappu on the cheek.

Just then Stanley came back, face washed, and she said: 'What you guys will drink, men?' She spoke that sweet English Mumbaiya that the Goans have invented—the only Mumbaiya dialect not based on Hindi.

Soon they were all drinking some cold, delicious chikoo milk shake.

She looked at Stanley fondly as he enjoyed the milkshake as much as the kids. 'You work too hard, Sten.' She turned to them. 'I so proud he made Inspector. You know, his father came to Mumbai with lot-other Goans looking for shelter, with only *one thing* in whole world.'

She looked at Stanley expectantly.

'Stanley, your father came to Mumbai with only *one thing* in whole world. What was that?'

'What was that, Mum?'

'You tell me what that was. I told you a thousand times.'

Stanley thought a little, then scratched his head guiltily. 'I'm sorry, Mum,' he said guiltily.

'His dabbaa,' she said, sighing.

Pappu almost choked on his chikoo milkshake.

Box E-52, Jer Mahal

As he spluttered, Mrs Coelho asked 'What happened, baba?' She gently rubbed his back and wiped his chin with her apron. He saw that Scherezade and Stanley too had pricked up their ears.

'Nothing, aunty.'

'Like all Goans who came to Mumbai and lived in Goan Coor dormitories, that dabbaa was only thing father owned in world. It *was* his whole world, men.'

'Coor dormitory?' said Scherezade in the politest tone Pappu had ever heard. 'What is that, aunty?'

' Coor was a dormitory-style club for all those Goans who came to Mumbai and couldn't afford rent for even one room. They came to Mumbai to work in ABC jobs—meaning A for ayah, B for butler, C for cook—'

'ABCD,' Stanley said.

'*ABC*, men,' Aunty said.

'ABCD. D for drunk.'

'Anyway,' Mrs Coelho continued, patting his head smartly, 'Sten's father was musician. Only sometimes he get work, in band, or for Hindi film song.' Pappu thought of the blind man—he would have loved to meet Stanley's father. 'Used to play violin, beautiful but to earn you had to be sweet-sweet to this chap in film studio, that bloke in band. Father used to be sweet only to violin. Sometimes to me.' She sighed again. 'But he was good father to Sten … but Sten, he saw father's tough life and he said, "not for me." He become winner, from when he was in his knickers. Win-win at school, win-win in playground. Work hard to win. Famous in Bandra. But I tell you, relax, Sten. Settle down, get married.'

Stanley put his glass down. 'I *want* to get married, Mum!' he said, and looked at her seriously. His mum looked away, then said tightly: 'We must all get married to our own kind, no?'

There was an awkward silence. She asked Scherezade, 'Hey er, baby, you want more chikoo shake?' Scherezade held out her glass. Mrs Coelho poured and sighed. 'When Goans first come to Mumbai it give them dignity, shelter, a living … it was all relaxed then men, all spread out and beautiful. Mumbai always given people shelter who run to it. But now … how long Mumbai can last, with dirty-builder-people and lying-politician?'

'Er, what about the dabbaa, Aunty?' Scherezade asked.

'Oh, all the poor Goans had them in the Coor dormitories—men, the Coors were all over Dhobi Talao then. Each man allowed to have only one big steel box. This dabbaa be your dining table when you eat, your bed when you sleep. It be your clothes-cupboard, your safe—everything you own you lock inside it. So you live out from your box—and on it. If extra guest come it become your guest chair.' Her voice became softer. 'In the evening, everyone gather around the Coor altar and say rosary. It was compulsory, but still it was beautiful, men.'

Pappu cleared his throat but couldn't ask what he wanted to ask: so Stanley asked the question instead: 'Mum, father's box, it, ur, it had a number? The dabbaa's had labels, or numbers or what?'

Mrs Coelho was taken aback. 'What you asking about the box, men? Forget box, think of your father, all those years with no money but he fought to educate you so today I can be proud of my Inspector son. What you going on about dabbaas, eh?' She put their glasses crossly on a tray and got up.

'Aunty, are there Coor clubs today also?' Pappu asked.

'Yes baba, some still in Jer Mahal, and near to it. Today I think they only call them not Coors, but Goan clubs.'

She went to the kitchen with the tray and the mixie. Stanley said slowly, 'Ikka's Michael was also a Goan … '

'My god!' Pappu smacked his forehead.

'What?'

Pappu was suddenly excited. 'Inspector, the blind man told me that after they killed Michael, one of the goondas said he had met Michael once in his club opposite Metro Cinema. I remember thinking that

Michael must be a rich don, if he had a club—'

'Opposite Metro Cinema!' Stanley interrupted loudly.

'What's so special about that?' asked Scherezade.

'Men, you know what is opposite Metro Cinema?' The children shook their heads. 'Jer Mahal is opposite Metro Cinema, that's what!'

'Of course, Jer Mahal opposite Metro Cinema all us Goans know!' from the kitchen came Mrs Coelho's voice amid the clatter of utensils.

Stanley lowered his voice: 'If Michael was living in a Goan club in Jer Mahal, then he would have a dabbaa. And the club could have numbered it. Maybe Michael hid something in his dabbaa, and could not get it himself because—yes! Commander's people started following him. He knew that they knew where he lived, and his gang thought the safest way to get what was in the dabbaa out was by sending someone who Commander's people would not recognise, like maybe Irfaan.'

'But wouldn't Commander's people have searched Michael's dabba?' Pappu asked.

Stanley thought. 'Could be ... but sometimes so much confusion is there ... Whatever, we got to trace where Michael lived, see if he—' But suddenly Stanley lost his eagerness. 'What use, men? Someone high-up will block whatever we do.'

'Oh,' Pappu said. 'We haven't told you about the MLA.'

'What MLA?'

'The MLA who's going to help us against the

high-up goondas.'

When Pappu met the blind man at the chaat-seller next morning, he found the blind man's attitude to him completely changed.

'Son,' the blind man said. 'I was wrong to want to end our friendship. Now that I have seen how your father is—heard his voice with you ... I won't leave you alone, don't worry.' Pappu hugged him, relieved.

For some reason he did not mention his father's phone call. But he told him about meeting Stanley and his mother. When he told the blind man how down Stanley was, the blind man to his surprise chuckled.

'I was finally able to phone my nephew Hassan. We will meet on Tuesday evening. I told him my Innispector friend had been unfairly suspended for helping me. Hassan asked me if I was sure that Innispector was honest, I said one hundred percent. Hassan asked me his name, and he said that he would tell his assistant to talk to Innispector's departmant.'

Two hours later, Pappu was surprised to hear Stanley's voice shouting into his phone. 'Pappu boy, thanks! That blind man's MLA nephew, his man talked to Commissioner Talwar. Asked him some difficult questions men, my suspension's been revoked! Tell my thanks to the blind man, hain?' Pappu was so glad to hear the old, cheerful Inspector Stanley!

'And more good news! While I was suspended, Paluskar—he's my friend—he's been trying to trace

Michael's Goan Coor club for me. He found you see in Jer Mahal there are half-dozen Goan clubs. Each Coor club has name of Goan village, with people from that village.'

'Cool!'

'Now each club has two-three halls, and in each hall dozen men sleeping on mats on floor. There are *four* Michaels in all those Jer Mahal clubs.'

'Oh!'

'But one Michael is missing for two weeks. We think that is our Michael—Michael Da Cunha, couldn't find any photos of him yet. We trying his club tomorrow evening. Want to come?'

Near Marine Lines Station, past the Mosque-in-the-middle-of-the-road, just after you reach Metro Cinema is a botched bloated intersection of six roads. In the curve between two of these roads opposite Metro rests a large grey ramshackle old building, five storeys high, sagging and spreading like the lush curves on the giant ghost of a blousy lady. This is Jer Mahal.

At 9 pm on Monday evening, a police jeep drove up to the building. It was driven by Constable Pande, next to whom sat Inspector Stanley. Behind were the blind man, Pappu, Scherezade and Paluskar. The building loomed above them with a dusty gleam, lit by the bright lights from the cinema hall on the far side of the intersection.

Paluskar was a good-natured hefty policeman. When

they first met, he had looked at Pappu with open, cheerful curiosity—he had obviously heard of him from the Inspector.

Stanley had wanted to bring Pappu and the blind man—he owed them for reversing his suspension—plus it was only fair to bring the two who had put him on the right track for the letter, which they might find here. And he didn't think there would be any danger.

When Pappu had suggested bringing Scherezade, he said no. When Pappu told him that Scherezade was helping them against her father, he asked, 'How you know, men? She might be spying for her father.'

Pappu said, 'Trust me Inspector.'

Stanley looked at him oddly and said, 'Okay.'

Pande parked the jeep near Furtado's, the musical instrument shop on the ground floor of Jer Mahal. They walked along Jer Mahal, looking for Goan clubs. They couldn't find any.

'You never come here?' Paluskar asked Stanley in Marathi.

'No, men,' Stanley said guiltily. Stanley was his smart shaved self again, Inspector's cap at a dashing tilt on his head. But he seemed strangely nervous—almost awed.

Paluskar asked a passer-by. He pointed out what they'd missed: a narrow concrete path slicing into the building, lined with a gutter on one side and scaffolding on the other. This led them into the middle of the fat building, where a spacious musty staircase led up to three floors full of Goan clubs.

Stanley climbed up the stairs in a nervous daze, stepping gingerly as if he was afraid of disturbing the sleeping ghost of his father. On each floor there were huge wooden doors with signs saying Karkala Club, Raia Club, Chincholi Club …

'See those names?' Stanley whispered. 'Each name is the name of a village back in Goa, and each club has young men who've come to Mumbai from that village only.'

They finally stopped before one door. Stanley lifted his hand to knock, then put his hand to his mouth and cleared his throat … then knocked, gently. After a little while he lifted the crook of his knocking finger again, stopped to think, then knocked louder.

A few moments later, there was a slow grating sound from inside of the bolt being drawn, and the door slowly opened to reveal a small middle-aged man wearing only a pair of trunks hanging below a round beer belly. He was unshaved, and silver hair gleamed all over his dark skin in the dim neon light. He looked at them like a weasel who'd just been brought out of his hole: onc of his eyes was half-closed, the other gleaming wide and roving, staring.

'Unrrgh?' he grunted.

'Uncle, I'm police,' Stanley said, even though since he was in uniform everyone could see that. 'I have a warrant for confiscating Michael Da Cunha's box.'

The unshaven man thought. Then he repeated: 'Unrrgh?'

Stanley spoke in a different language—Pappu thought

it was Konkani. The unshaven man nodded 'unrrgh,' and opened the door. Pappu remembered a National Geographic film with beautiful shots of otters playing in the sun: some bits of the unshaven man, when they wobbled, reminded him of those dark wet little otters darting silver in the sun.

They followed the man inside, and then waited as he stood unsteadily in the middle of a large, messy hall. There were two armchairs, two partly unrolled mattresses on the floor: a wooden altar with Mother Mary; and three long trunks, each longer than a man's height, covered in transparent plastic sheets.

The hall had a large window in one wall, and a door in another, leading into a second hall where they could see dozens of sets of clothes hanging on wooden bars, trunks lining the walls, and a few partly rolled mattresses on the floor.

As they stared at all this, a smooth-faced youth of about twenty came out of the second hall. When he saw Scherezade, he quickly jerked a curtain between the two rooms.

'Yes?'

'Unrrgh,' the middle-aged man explained.

'I'm police,' Stanley parroted, as if he couldn't even concentrate on simple things like he *was* wearing a uniform. He had even forgotten to take off his Inspector's cap, and normally he would never be so rude. 'I have a warrant for confiscating Michael Da Cunha's box.' His eyes swung from the youth to the middle-aged man and back.

'I'm Max,' the youth said, and introduced the middle-aged man. 'He's Robert, the Coor-dorm manager. He's drunk.'

Stanley's eyes were roving all over the hall. Without really looking at anyone, he introduced each one of his group to Max. This confused Max.

Stanley's eyes were now fixed on the boxes. Was he thinking of his father when he first came to Mumbai, with only one box?

'Michael not here for weeks,' Max said. 'Even before, Michael here very little, living-sleeping in other places mostly.'

'I know, men,' Stanley said. 'We need to confiscate his trunk.'

Max looked at Robert, and saw he was useless in his condition. 'I don't know which trunk,' he said. 'I ask inside. Please, you all have a seat.' He gestured to the trunk Stanley had been looking at and disappeared behind the curtain.

Stanley stood there, and they all looked at him. He became conscious of their looks, and reluctantly took a step towards the trunk. All the others sat on the trunk at once, Pappu leading the blind man. As if in a trance, Stanley joined them on it.

Robert sat in a chair opposite, looking surprised at the sudden rise in population in his Coor.

'Now-only-fourteen-boys-in-my-Coor,' blurted Robert to Stanley.

Stanley was surprised—he'd thought Robert couldn't speak English. He nodded.

Robert said nothing else for a while. Then again: 'Used-to-have-thirty-two!'

'I'm sorry?'

'Used-to-have-thirty-two-boys!'

Silence. 'Thirty-two ... when?'

'Forty-years-ago-men!' Robert said as if answering a stupid question.

'Oh,' said Stanley.

Silence. 'You were here?' he asked Robert.

'I-was-boy-not-manager-here.'

Silence.

'Three-hundred-and-fifty-clubs-in-Mumbai-then. Today-only-few.'

'Oh.'

'So-many-working-in-flim-orchestras-they-would-been-phut-without-Goans-men!'

'My father—'

'Back-home-men-people-no-work-no-land-no-jobs-Mumbai-save-thousand-families—'

'My father—'

'Half-all-Goans-in-Mumbai-in-Coors-then-just-run-away-from-Goa.'

Silence. Stanley was looking at Robert misty-eyed.

The blind man asked Pappu what had been said about the film orchestras, and nodded deeply when he heard.

Max came out. 'Michael trunk dabbaa number E-51,' he announced.

The blind man started when he heard 'E-51'—though he didn't know English he could recognise the number. He turned his unseeing face to the others. 'E-51 ... of course! To misguide his enemies … '

'E-51 … ' Max was thinking aloud. 'That dabbaa was stolen one night. Don't know how they stole such a large box without us knowing, men.'

'And where,' Stanley whispered, 'is dabbaa number E-52?'

Max was taken aback.

Robert spoke out abruptly: 'E-52-belong-to-Michael's-uncle-men.'

'Michael's uncle?' Stanley asked.

'Uncle-at-sea-was-supposed-to-come-but-never-came.'

Stanley looked at the others, his face shining with a kind of greed. 'And E-51 was stolen? In the name of the law, show us dabbaa number E-52?'

'There,' Robert pointed at the dabbaa they were sitting on.

Stanley, Pappu and then the blind man jumped up as if they suddenly felt hot coals below. Then Paluskar and Scherezade too got up in a second rising wave.

Max drew back from this mass movement. Robert said 'Unrrgh!'

Max said, 'Yes, now I remember … In his last days Michael open it even more than E-51.'

This had to be it! The others tried to see through the plastic around the trunk, and suddenly it looked like a piece of magic wrapped in a protecting mist.

'Open it!' Stanley said breathlessly.

Max went to a hook in one corner and took down the huge bunch of keys hanging on it. He peered at the smudged stamp on the trunk. Then, going through the bunch carefully, he finally picked out one, parted the plastic around the trunk, and inserted the key in the lock.

He turned it, shook it this way and that, but the trunk didn't open.

Max couldn't understand it. He peered at the smudged stamp again, looked closely at the key, then at the keyring. He took another key and tried that. It didn't work either.

He again peered and compared, and tried another key. And another … Miraculously, they heard a click and the lock opened.

A gasp went through the hall. Stanley took off the dangling lock, parted the plastic further with Paluskar's help, and they caught hold of the bolts.

Everybody held their breath as they lifted the lid.

And that was a good thing because when they breathed again, a burst of stale air hit them from the opened trunk.

The blind man leaned forward. 'This dabbaa was owned by a hashish-smoker,' he said.

'How—' Paluskar started. The blind man tapped his nose. Paluskar looked impressed.

In the trunk was a vagabond's world: Pappu could see that Michael had increasingly used his uncle's dabbaa as his own. There were crumpled clothes folded in one corner, a few metal plates, spoons and mugs in another. Toothpaste tube, a shaving brush, blade. Belts, an old umbrella, scissors, knife (and it didn't look like a butter knife!), a small metal box, a small wooden one, one transparent plastic folder with some bills and other boring-looking papers.

'Looks like dead end to me,' Paluskar said, his face curled in distaste.

'I think we should search it,' Pappu said.

'Could be nest for treasure, men,' Stanley said. He bent and picked up the folder, took out the papers and started flipping through them.

'Ah!' He lifted one sheet out, which curled slightly as though it had been rolled for a long time. It looked as boring as the others but was less smooth, more patchy in shading and it had writing on it that seemed to be in Urdu.

Stanley dropped the folder in the trunk. The letter bobbed in his hand as he slowly raised it higher, peering at it in the dim light. The others gathered around, the blind man with Pappu's hand in his.

'Ahh ... ' Stanley went. 'Paluskar, get Pande from the jeep and let's take the trunk down.' His eyes drank in the letter. In this moment of awe, he took off his cap and stuffed it in his pocket. 'Wonder what it says, men. It is in Urdu or Persian.'

'Hassan can read it for us!' said the blind man.

'We'll take it to Mr Hassan, Chacha,' the Inspector said to the blind man. Paluskar closed the trunk and looked at the precious letter in Stanley's hand.

'Unrrgh!' Robert was suddenly standing up, his wide-open eyes glaring at Stanley. 'Unrrgh!'

Stanley was too lost in the letter to notice Robert. He held the letter to his nose and sniffed it.

Paluskar moved to face Robert. Did he object to them taking the letter, or the trunk, away? 'I'm sorry, Mr Robert, we got to take the box. We have warrant.'

Robert, eye still fixed on Stanley, slowly and unsteadily moved toward him. Paluskar moved his hand toward his gun, but Robert ignored him and came up to Stanley.

'Ambrose?' said Robert.

Stanley slowly lowered the letter. His jaw dropped.

'Ambrose!' said Robert.

A low moan escaped Stanley's lips. Paluskar looked on in amazement.

The unshaven little man grabbed Stanley's arms. Paluskar immediately grabbed his.

'He just drunk, men. Harmless,' Max said. Paluskar let go.

'Ambrose!' Robert said. 'I didn't recognise you in your cap, men! Where you gone these forty years?'

Stanley seemed moved beyond words. He sat with a thump on the trunk. He tried to speak, but couldn't. Robert hugged him. Stanley, trapped in Robert's arms, helplessly waved the letter in the air.

'You knew my father Ambrose?' his muffled voice asked Robert from under his chest.

'Your father? Ambrose, how should I know your father, men? I only know you when you moved here. I miss you, I even miss your music lessons! Though I used to shout to keep your music lessons down—you and your friend Pyarelal and your music teacher—what his name? Anthony Gonsalves.'

Pappu felt the blind man's hand tighten around his. 'Pyarelal? Anthony Gonsalves? What about them?' he asked in Urdu.

Pappu whispered to him, 'They were musician friends of Stanley's father.'

The blind man's face shook with emotion. 'Your father,' he said, turning to Stanley, 'your father knew Pyarelal? He knew Anthony Gonsalves?'

'Eh?' Stanley's head twitched toward him from inside Robert's embrace.

'Yes,' Pappu said.

'Ambrose?' said Robert.

'I … I'm not Ambrose,' said Stanley.

Tears came to the blind man's eyes: he spoke as if in a dream: 'Pyarelal was one of Hindi flim's great composers … he was taught by a musician called Anthony Gonsalves … later, he put his guru's name in his hit song, "My name is Anthony Gonsalves …" Innispector sahb, Innispector Stanley, your father was a friend of these great musicians …'

'Eh?' said Stanley, not able to take it all in.

'What he on about your father, Ambrose?' asked Robert.

'No,' Stanley said. 'I'm not Ambrose …'

Robert stepped back suddenly: 'I knew it, men, that you not Ambrose! You look like him but you not him. You think you can fool me? Ambrose and I best friends!'

'But—'

'We look for jobs together, all over Mumbai!'

'But—'

'We both sending money back to families in Goa. I put him in touch with lots of music gigs, he put me in touch with catering companies!'

'But—'

'And so I know his family back in Goa have father passed away years ago, and you say your father alive? Go to hell, men, you not Ambrose!'

The blind man asked softly, 'This Ambrose person is who?'

There was a minute's confused silence, broken by an ear-splitting scream.

THE BASHFUL THUG

Scherezade screamed again. She was staring at the door. They all turned to look—the door was half-open, swinging emptily.

Stanley was too stunned by all that had happened to move quickly, but Paluskar reached for his gun.

From behind the door appeared a face wearing a hood, followed by a gun, followed by a tall body wearing jeans and a black T-shirt.

Robert slid back into his chair in a dead stupor. Everyone else froze—the blind man stood there with his head cocked, straining to listen. Max cowered behind the curtain in disbelief, and Scherezade, trembling, looked in horror at the hooded man, then the door, then back to the man.

Pointing his gun at Paluskar, the man walked up to him. Behind him, the door opened to reveal another gun, another hooded figure.

'Ai,' the first man said to Paluskar in a weak, hoarse voice, 'drop the pistol or I'll drop you.' Paluskar very carefully did as told.

The man looked at Stanley and jerked his own pistol. Stanley, carefully, pressing the letter in one hand to his side, used the other to drop his pistol next to Paluskar's. The man picked up the pistols and giving one to his companion, tucked the other into his jeans. Then, keeping his gun on Paluskar and Stanley, he looked around the room.

Everyone stood still, except for Scherezade, who was trembling as if in a fury. The hooded man looked at her for a long time. Then he seemed to tear his eyes away from her to speak to Stanley.

'Ai inshpector give me dat letthor,' he said.

'Men don't fool around with the law—'

The hooded man pointed his pistol at Stanley's face. 'Don't fool with me, inshpector.'

For a few moments Stanley just stood, sweating. Then he slowly raised the hand that held the letter—

'Don't give it Inspector!' Scherezade cried.

Stanley froze, the arm half raised. His eyes looked sideways at Scherezade.

'Give,' the hooded man said. Stanley's hand began to go up again, offering the letter.

Scherezade stood swiftly in front of the Inspector, facing the gun. 'Shoot me!' she challenged. 'Shoot me! Go ahead!'

'What are you doing, Sherry?' Pappu yelled.

'Go ahead, shoot me!'

'What you doing, girl? Move!' Stanley shouted, and to the hooded man, 'Don't worry, men, I'm giving letter to you, she just a child, don't—'

Stanley stopped. To his amazement, the man's gun-hand had faltered.

'Pull the trigger!' Scherezade screamed.

The hooded man began to move back, slowly.

'What—' said Stanley.

Both the men were creeping backwards toward the door. Max was still cowering at the curtain. Robert snored on his chair. Stanley turned to Scherezade.

'What—'

'Shoot me!' she shouted.

The men suddenly jumped, turned—one stumbled, the pistol in his belt falling out—and rushed to the door and out.

Scherezade burst into tears and flung herself on the trunk. Paluskar picked up the pistol and ran out the door after the goondas. Stanley stood looking at Scherezade.

They heard feet desperately clambering down the stairs, and Paluskar's voice shouting: 'Oi! Stop!' in Marathi.

Stanley and Pappu rushed to the window. Stanley called urgently, 'Pande! Pande, stop these people running out—'

No one came running out from below. The goondas and Paluskar had run out the other side of the building.

'What is happening?' the blind man sat down on the trunk. 'Someone tell me, brother.'

Pappu went to Scherezade and took her by the shoulder. 'What happened, Scherezade? Why did he … ' and then he stopped. He thought he understood.

She began to answer—and then she looked at Stanley and stopped.

Stanley scowled. 'Why you stopping, girl? Tell me! Why did he run away when you said to him to shoot you?'

Scherezade trembled even more.

'Girl, you knew him and he knew you.' Stanley said this gently. But when she didn't answer, he snapped, 'Admit it, girl!'

Suddenly, understanding dawned on his face, and he looked from Pappu to Scherezade and back again. He leaned forward and whispered in their faces: 'Kenilworth.'

Blood drained out of Scherezade's face. Her terrified eyes darted from Stanley to Pappu. She thinks I betrayed her secret, thought Pappu, trapped between her look and the Inspector's sharp gaze.

Paluskar came back panting. 'They had jeep waiting. It was gone even before I hit ground floor.'

The Inspector didn't remove his eyes from the two children. 'Paluskar, take trunk to police station. Also both these kids. And don't leave them alone for a second.'

Since most of the conversation had been in English, the blind man was still a little confused as they climbed down the stairs. Pappu explained some of the details, but he could not explain Kenilworth, and the blind man sensed there was much more happening than

Pappu was revealing.

'But Innispector sahb, it is wonderful to learn that your father played with Pyarelalji and Anthony Gonsalvesji.' Stanley nodded—and grunted, so the blind man could hear him—but he was very quiet and thoughtful.

When they reached the police station near Breach Candy, Inspector Stanley insisted on having the blind man dropped wherever he wanted to go. 'Uncle, I thank you for your help. We would not have this letter without you—and without Hassan MLA. I will be in touch.'

'Come on, children,' the blind man said, 'I am going to a friend's chawl near Mohammed Ali Road. The jeep can drop Pappu at Churchgate Station, and Scherezade at Cusrow Baug.'

Stanley looked at Pappu and shook his head. Pappu knew he owed Stanley for trusting him, and said: 'That's all right, Chacha. We'll stay here a little longer.'

The blind man stood still, sensing the unspoken tension all around him. What could it be about?

'Pappuji—'

'Chacha, don't worry,' Stanley said. 'All three of us will see you soon. We will soon show letter to Mr Hassan to read!'

'I've already spoken to Hassan; he can't wait to read letter!'

Baffled, the blind man accepted the goodbyes of the three and allowed himself to be taken to the car by the police driver.

'Paluskar,' the Inspector said grimly, 'Take these

children's cell phones.' Paluskar took Scherezade's—Pappu didn't have one.

The Inspector made Pappu and Scherezade sit in the chairs in front of his desk, and ordered two cups of tea.

Scherezade had stopped trembling, and was completely dry-eyed and calm. While she and Pappu sat, Inspector Stanley stood silent. They looked out the window, at him, at each other.

The tea came. Inspector took the two cups from the tray and put them in front of the children. Though they had absolutely no interest in tea, both took the cups to their lips and obediently drank. Both spilled some hot tea as they put the cups back in their little chipped government saucers. They couldn't look at each other.

The Inspector continued to look at them in silence. It was torture.

Scherezade took another sip, hands trembling again, spilled some more and jumped up to wipe her jeans and scalded legs. It gave her something to do—but when she sat again she felt even more stupid and guilty.

The Inspector stood still. Pappu could feel his eyes burning into them, but when he looked up he saw the Inspector's eyes were looking just a little above them, out of the window.

They stopped reaching out for the tea.

Finally, Stanley took pity on them and said: 'Look kids, we got the big thing—the Mumtaz letter. Scherezade, thank you for saving the letter for the country. Soon I'll give to my boss and get promotion. So now why are we sitting here so suspicious of each other? Hm? What is happening? Who was that man with the gun? You can tell me, we're all friends, men.'

They just sat dumb.

'Look Scherezade, I brought you to Jer Mahal. I trusted Pappu, and I trusted you. It is only fair you tell me who that hooded man was. Now no fooling, everyone knows you recognised him, and he recognised you.'

'You've got your precious letter, let me go. I … I don't know why he ran away. I wanted to save the letter for you, that's all that matters, isn't it?'

'And Kenilworth?'

'She—' Pappu began.

Stanley silenced him with a hand. 'Enough! Enough Pappu, I trusted you enough. Now let her answer.'

Scherezade was looking at Pappu. Had he told Stanley about her father and Kenilworth? Pappu wanted to shake his head so bad it hurt, but the Inspector was watching them like a hawk.

Scherezade looked down at her hands and stayed silent. She could not possibly tell the Inspector about her suspicions about her father …

The Inspector turned to Pappu. 'This is a very important matter, Pappu, I need to know. Her father is mixed up in many things I know. But Kenilworth!'

'What's so special about Kenilworth, Inspector?' Scherezade asked crisply.

'What's so special?' Stanley looked at her for a

moment, dumbstruck. 'Now *you* are going to question *me*? Without answering *my* questions?'

Scherezade flinched: tears came to her eyes again. She took out a hanky to dry her eyes, and hid her face behind it.

Stanley caught his hair in his fists: 'Christ sorry, am sorry men.' He turned to Pappu and yelled, 'But you talk! Talk!'

Pappu was shocked.

Stanley cried in despair, 'Sorry! I *don't* want you to betray your Papa, I *don't* want you Pappu to betray your friend, but you people are driving me mad—you don't know how *important* this matter is.' He sank in his chair 'Christ! Girl, stop crying.'

After some time, Scherezade did. Stanley said, 'You two, go. I have no evidence against you, nothing to hold you.' Then, in a serious voice, 'If the matter goes out of my hands you won't be questioned like this, by a friend. Things will get ugly. You understand?' Pappu nodded.

The Inspector tossed Scherezade's phone to her and turned away. As she left the room, he pulled Pappu back: 'I trust you, boy. Keep to what you promised me. It is not a small matter.' He looked steadily at Pappu and Pappu nodded. 'And *don't* tell her anything you might think about Kenilworth. Otherwise our deal is off.'

Outside, as soon as they were in a cab, Scherezade turned breathlessly to Pappu and asked: 'What did you tell him about my Kenilworth story?'

'Nothing, I promise!' It was on the tip of his tongue to tell her about his suspicion when she asked, 'What is so special about Kenilworth?'

He almost gagged, because her question reminded him how important the matter was, and he couldn't tell her!

She looked at him suspiciously. 'Tell me! What is Kenilworth all about?'

Pappu asked himself the same question: what was it all about? Why was Mr Screwvala involved in it *and* the Mumtaz letter? What was the connection? *Was* it a coincidence?

He felt his breath stop, his head spin. She took his collar in her fist and was shaking him: 'Tell me!'

He blurted out, 'Who was the hooded man? How did you know him?'

She moved back. 'I saw his face before he put his hood on at the door, for a split second. It was the man who met my father in my drawing room, with the scar.'

'Why does he terrify you so much?'

'He doesn't terrify me.'

'Of course he terrifies you. You screamed like that, didn't you? Even though you were with armed policemen. Why are you so scared of him?'

'I'm not terrified of *him*. I screamed because …' Scherezade thought, 'because I was terrified for my father. For myself. I was terrified of what I could see was happening to my family.' She turned away from him toward the window, and Pappu held her hand and looked out of his window, afraid.

Later, Scherezade told Pappu that her father, who was out of town on 'important business', had phoned her ayah to ask where Scherezade had been that evening.

'Oh! What did she say?'

'She told him I was home the whole evening.' Pappu looked surprised, and she explained: 'When I got home from Jer Mahal, I told Ayah everything. She was shocked, but not …' her voice shook, 'completely surprised. You see, she knows Papa, she has been with us for a long time. She is much closer to me. She knew Papa would call, and she had already thought of her answer.'

'What did your father say?'

'He simply disconnected. But before the line went dead Ayah heard him say to someone, "I told Rustom he had gone mad …"'

That must be the name of the hooded thug, Pappu thought. Rustom.

The Feast of Warm Memories

On the ground floor of a Marine Drive building, sitting by a large window that let in light from the setting sun. Hassan looked eagerly at his uncle's face as he tried hard to sing a ghazal. Hassan's deep voice did not have range, but he was obviously enjoying singing.

At the end, two toadies clapped loudly. His wife Mehurnissa (they had married just six months ago), Pappu, Scherezade, PP and the blind man also clapped. Stanley hadn't come (he had said, 'Uncle-nephew reuniting after years men, I would be like interfering bone-in-kebab').

'Mian, your *sincerity* in those notes was … wonderful,' said the blind man, sensing his nephew's eyes on him. They spoke in Urdu, and the children understood most of what they said.

Hassan's drawing room had two levels. They were sitting at the higher level by the window, where there was a divan and armchairs. Hassan, on the divan, looked pleased with his uncle's words. 'Chachajan, how can one who has learnt music at your feet go wrong?

Here's another—'

'Mian, that's enough of your singing,' Mehurnissa said. 'It might fill people's hearts but they have stomachs, too. It's time for dinner.'

'But Mehr, let Chachajan play one more song before dinner.'

Her face lit up. 'Certainly.' Hassan beamed at her eagerness and pressed her hand. The whole evening Hassan had been almost a little drunk with emotion.

The blind man played another haunting song on his musical instrument:

Aage bhi, jaane na tu.
Pichche bhi, jaane na tu.
Jo bhi hai, bas yahi ek pal hai.
(What's ahead, you do not know.
Even behind, you do not know.
All that you have is this very moment.)

The song was from the classic film *Waqt*, about a family scattered by an earthquake and reunited after decades. Pappu did not know if the blind man had consciously chosen the song for this reunion, but Hassan's eyes were moist.

'Chachajan, I cannot believe that I've been living on Marine Drive six months and I never saw you.'

'I used to see him, and whenever I heard his beautiful music I thought about *you*,' Mehurnissa said to Hassan. 'Here we were, living in this beautiful place, and you are too busy with your MLA-work to be by my side on moonlit nights on famous Marine Drive.'

Hassan shook his head, doubly abashed, and got up and hugged the blind man again.

Dinner was finally announced, and everyone enjoyed the lavish North Indian meal, with servants offering dishes like naan, shahi paneer and tandoori chicken.

After dinner, Hassan sent his toadies away and said to the blind man: 'Tell your story, now there is only family to listen.'

He had sat his uncle on the divan, at the centre of the gathering. The blind man began his story: 'You know that after your late father fought with the family, he brought you to Mumbai twenty years ago. I continued to live with my sister's family till ten years ago when her husband passed away'—here the blind man and Hassan and his wife recited in unison 'Inna lillahi wa inna ilahi raji'un' (which means 'What belongs to Allah returns to Him'). 'His company paid your aunt some pension, but it was not enough. To help for their daily bread, I came to Mumbai. I had heard that there was a lot of money in Mumbai and mian, with my music I made enough to ensure that Salim was educated well enough so that—here, look at this letter.' The blind man took out a letter from his pocket. 'I got it just yesterday, it's from Salim! He has been called for an interview for the post of engineer by a good company. Inshallah, he will soon start earning!'

Hassan took the letter, read it, and gave a laugh that jerkily tripped over a sigh. 'I remember my little brother Salim, he used to drive me mad! Chachajan, I think the time to see him again is coming … '

'Yes, son, yes it is.' There was a silence.

Hassan said: 'Now tell me the story of the other letter—the one Inspector Stanley says is a national treasure. He is going to show it to me tomorrow.'

The blind man continued his story, from the night he heard Michael's murder on Marine Drive. Mehurnissa listened excitedly, but Hassan was calm. When the blind man came to his kidnapping of Pappu he began by saying, 'I committed a great sin—' but Pappu interrupted him to say, 'A goonda took me from the school with a gun and Chacha saved me from him with his empty gun.'

The blind man smiled secretly and said, 'My great sin was not to save him sooner. But anyway …'

Mehurnissa was on the edge of her seat by the time the story came to Inspector Malhotra knocking at the door—and the doorbell rang. Mehurnissa jumped, and Hassan bellowed, 'Ai? Who could it be at this time?'

At the other end of the drawing room was a curtain, hiding the corridor to the main door.

One of the toadies parted the curtain. 'Gopinathanbhai has come.'

'Laholvillakuvath!' Hassan cursed. The tall dark man they had seen with him at Worli chawl pushed aside the toady and appeared.

'Hassanbhai, it is urgent,' he said. His voice still gave Pappu a chill, even in that friendly drawing room.

Hassan did not get up from the divan. 'Gopinathanbhai, I apologise I can't get up because

I'm busy with family matters.'

Below Gopinathan's cold eyes appeared a frighteningly sweet smile. 'That's all right, Hassanbhai. I just came to deliver this.' He held up a little sealed paper, put it on a table near him, did a salaam and bowed out.

When they heard the door shut, Hassan called out, 'Has he gone?' A voice answered that he had.

Hassan apologised to the blind man and begged him to continue.

When the blind man came to the events on Akash Ganga's terrace, Pappu couldn't help asking: 'Chacha, how did you get past that rude watchman?'

'Beta, I stood outside the gate and played flim songs in which great beauties are singing adoringly about their man, to flatter the two watchmen.'

'Which songs?' Mehurnissa asked, fascinated.

In answer, the blind man took up his musical case and played a tune where Pappu could almost hear the words:

Yeh dil aur unki nigahon ke saaye:
Mujhe gher lete hai baahon ke saaye.
(This heart and the shade of his eyes:
I'm sheltered by his arms on all sides.)

'This is in Raag Pahari, which exactly suits my music box. And I also played "*Aapki nazaron ne samjha pyar ke kabil mujhe*".'

'Wah!' Pappu said.

'You recognise the songs?' Mehurnissa asked, surprised.

'Aaji, my grandmother, used to listen to them on the radio,' Pappu said. Pigface grunted-snorted, and of course they knew he didn't have any idea.

'Pappuji, you are *proof* that these great songs will live forever,' the blind man said forcefully. 'Anyway, both watchmen listened with eyes closed, enjoying clouds of sweet dreams. After I finished they thanked me …' his listeners laughed at the thought, 'and invited me to lunch. Afterwards, they even allowed me to practise my music somewhere far from the noise of the city—on their terrace!'

Mehurnissa, Scherezade, Pappu and PP clapped their hands in delight: the blind man bowed in acknowledgement. Hassan shook his head from side to side in appreciation of his uncle's charm.

The blind man continued his story. Hassan sat silently and shook his head after he had finished, his beard brushing the white material of his kurta.

'Chachajan, my assistant has found out that your Inspector Stanley seems to be an honest officer, but high-ups are interfering with his work. This Inspector Stanley is bringing me this Taj letter tomorrow and don't worry, I will see what I can do to help him.' He asked the blind man to repeat some of the names he had mentioned, and noted them down.

'Who was that tall dark man who just came?' Pappu blurted out.

Hassan was surprised. 'Hunh, son?'

Pappu was embarrassed but now he had to go on: 'He was there at the Worli chawl too, when we met you …'

'Pappuji …' the blind man began, but Hassan smiled and said, 'No, no, Chachajan, it's all right. Son, his name is Gopinathan. He is an MLA with the Hind Zindabad party, which is fighting my party. They are not my friends, but on one bill his party and mine are acting together. Otherwise you will not see me with them. Why do you ask?'

'That Mr Gopinathan, I …' Pappu didn't know how he could say it, when he wasn't even sure why he felt that dark, menacing chill when he heard Gopinathan's voice.

'Gopinathan is dangerous,' said Hassan, seeming to read his thoughts. 'Hind Zindabad is supposed to be patriotic. Actually, it is … more sinister. In fact, these are the people who like playing with the police and robbers—and worse.'

He turned to the blind man. 'It is a dangerous world, Chachajan. That is why you must come live with us. This is your own house. You must move into this house tonight.'

The blind man's face strained with emotion—happiness mixed with worry. 'Son—'

'Truth to tell, I'm not really saying this because you are being searched by goondas. I'm saying it because now we have found each other in this big city, it is the only way. You have to live with us.'

'Yes, Chachajan, it will make Hassan and me very

happy,' Mehurnissa said.

The blind man's face cleared into his most delighted, secret smile. 'Son, what you have just said gives my heart more happiness than it has known for years. I cannot accept your offer, but thank you, son. I hope you will understand.'

Hassan scowled. 'What, Chachajan, you do not think of me as family any more?'

'Hassan ...' Mehurnissa said in a warning tone.

He snapped at her: 'You keep quiet Mehr, this is between me and my uncle. Why, Chachajan, you would not feel comfortable living in my house?'

The blind man was taken aback by his anger. 'Son, you are my Hassan. But now you have a life of your own. I have a life of my own. Just because I don't live in your house does not mean—'

'Chachajan! If you consider I have any rights over you, as your family, then you will stay with us!'

The blind man's face became serious for a moment. Then he laughed gently: 'All right.'

Hassan's face cleared. Mehurnissa smiled too, through an exasperated look at Hassan.

'And you are welcome in my house always,' Hassan beamed at the children, 'Friends of my beloved uncle, any time you want to shelter anywhere, remember my house.'

Mehurnissa hugged all of them delightedly. 'And you can teach me English when you're here!' she said to Scherezade, and they all laughed.

But there was a shadow to Scherezade's laugh, and

Pappu knew it was the shadow of Kenilworth.

The following day, when Hassan received the letter from Stanley, he was ecstatic. Soon he was on the phone speaking to Commissioner Talwar, the chief minister and others. The Inspector was surprised at how smoothly the credit for the recovery of the letter suddenly belonged to Hassan.

'Typical politician,' he thought at first. But when he thought some more, he had to admit that Hassan, at the very least, was responsible for revoking his suspension. And if he hadn't, Stanley might not have been able to get the letter for a long time.

'Yes, yes … don't worry sir,' Hassan was saying to the chief minister. 'I will organise a press conference. Just tell me what evening you're free.'

THE ANCIENT LOVE LETTER

At 6 pm on Thursday evening in the mini-theatre at the Mantralaya, Mumbai's seat of government, all the seats were taken. The aisles were crowded with reporters from the major Indian news channels, and the big newspapers. There were foreign reporters from National Geographic, the History Channel and BBC—the cameramen's lights and wires snarled up the whole space. There were officials from the ministry of culture, Ahmed Khan, who had just directed a Bollywood film on the Taj Mahal, and Gurdev and Javed Rehman, the famous Bollywood lyricists, scriptwriters and poets (each was all three). Security guards were all over the place, adding to the confusion.

In the seats in the front row sat Pappu, Ayah, the blind man, Pigface and Inspector Stanley. The blind man was saying to Stanley, 'It made me so happy to learn that your father was a musician in the company of people like Pyarelalji and Gonsalvesji. And what a worthy son!'

Ayah's face was shining, her scrupulously oiled and cleaned hair were gleaming, as was the zari on her best sari, tied in the style of her fishing village. Pappu, too, was looking more scrubbed than he'd like to—Ayah had forced him to have a long bath for the big day, and then insisted on combing his hair till it hurt. Stanley was dressed at his rakish best, and Pigface, too, was vaguely well-dressed.

On the stage were Hassan, the chief minister, and Thakur Dev Yadav, the chief of the Social Reform Party.

Hassan had sent out a press release so that now people all over India—and the world—were watching on their TV sets to hear more about the dramatic new find from the Taj Mahal's history.

'Thank you, chief minister sa'ab, for your support, and your friendly words,' Hassan said in Hindustani. 'At the beginning, I must tell you that this historic moment is made possible by Inspector Stanley Coelho of the Mumbai police, my uncle Mian Hafiz, and my young friend Pappu.' He indicated them. 'I thank them …'

As all those cameras swivelled towards them and people applauded, Pappu and his friends ducked in alarm at this kind of attention. But then a novel warm sensation of comfort filled Pappu at the thought of so many people cheering them. Stanley managed a cool wave. Ayah blushed as she nudged Pappu and whispered, 'Ai Deva Chotu, people all over the world see you, baby. Get up and bow.' Pappu got up unwillingly and Pigface with him. Their four knees knocking with self-consciousness they bowed and sat down—or at least Pappu did. Pigface kept standing and lapping up all the attention until he realised that everyone was tired of clapping and wanted him to sit.

In Moscow, in a conference room of an exclusive hotel, the dozen businessmen who had been negotiating big deals broke for a late lunch.

As Pappu's father went to help himself from the lavish buffet, he chatted with a pretty Georgian fashion designer. His eye fell on the TV screen in a corner which was turned to the National Geographic Channel, and was showing a press conference in India. The caption at the bottom of the screen said: 'HISTORIC DOCUMENT FROM TAJ FOUND.' He went over and leaned forward to catch the low words: 'This historic moment is made possible by Inspector Stanley Coelho of the Mumbai police, my uncle Mian Hafiz, and my young friend Pappu ...' As the cameras turned on the nervous Pappu, Ayah and others, Pappu's father nodded grimly to himself.

Hassan continued: 'The national treasure they have helped uncover is a letter to Mumtaz Mahal, for whom the Taj Mahal was built! Written by Shah Jahan, its builder!'

There was a gasp in the Mantralaya mini-theatre, then loud applause. The little Hassan on TV held up a tiny pipe-shaped box, gleaming unevenly.

As Pappu's father watched, a voice in his ear said, 'Wow! Zat is vonderfull, ze letters of Taz Mahaal! Must be ze greatest love letters in 'istory, nyet?' The pretty fashion designer had followed him to the TV screen and was staring at it excitedly.

'Yes, interesting, isn't it?' he said politely. Just then Yevgeny Shamraev, the man he wanted to do business with, waved at him. 'Yev is calling, excuse me.' He rushed off, and she shook her head in disbelief at him before turning eagerly back to the TV.

'And now, the letter,' Hassan said, dramatically opening the pipe-shaped box and taking out a single sheet. 'I present to the nation a note, written by the Emperor Shah Jahan to his beautiful Mumtaz Mahal, just before she gave birth to their fourteenth child and passed away.' The camera flashes went off in a continuous flutter all over the room as he held up the little note.

'I shall read out the Persian,' he said, and he read out from the note as if he were reading out a love poem: just a line or two, and the poets Gurdev and Javed Rehman applauded enthusiastically. Some others clapped too, though they didn't understand.

'I shall now read a translation.

'"My dearest Mumtaz, I believe that Allah will keep you in my arms for many years to come. But if what you fear comes to pass, then I promise you this: just as your face has lain on my bosom like a piece of the moon, and bathed every day of my life in your silver beauty, so shall I immortalise your love by building a monument that will be like a piece of moon on the bosom of Hindustan, and that will bathe the world in a silver reflection of your beauty and love. I will meet you in a few hours. Till then, your adoring slave, Shah Jahan.'"

Pappu heard Ayah sniff loudly,. She looked at him and hugged him again. She was *so* proud! He wished she wouldn't hug him again.

In the Moscow hotel, the Georgian fashion designer wiped her eyes too. Behind her in the hall, Pappu's father was busy discussing a deal with Yevgeny Shamraev.

When they came out of Mantralaya they were surprised to find even more reporters. Bright lights flashed and half-a-dozen mikes were pushed into Pappu's face. People he would normally be calling uncle and aunty were pushing past each other, asking him questions. 'How did you get involved in the Taj Letters?' 'How old are you really?' He had no idea what to say to them, and he was glad when Stanley put himself between the cameras and his face and, saying 'No further comments, men!' bundled him, Ayah and Pigface into a police van. Pappu looked around toward the blind man and was glad to see that he, too, was entering a car with Hassan who was jovially waving at the crowd.

They were soon at Stanley's police station. Once there, Stanley pulled out his bike—Pappu had booked a pillion-ride to Bandra with him, and Ayah wagged her finger: 'You think riding on Inspector's motorbike is fun, but in the train I will reach home before you!'

Pigface and Ayah took a cab to nearby Churchgate station. Stanley and Pappu quickly made off on the bike before the reporters got to the police station.

The bike made quick work of the heavy peak hour traffic. In fifty minutes, they reached Green Park.

Pappu's house was not too far away, and Stanley rode toward it through the seaside lanes of Chimbai village. Sitting behind Stanley, Pappu tilted his body so that he could taste the sea air—some of the freshest in Mumbai. He kept thinking about the fabulous success with the Taj letter, the press conference. His whole school must have seen it, his relatives … Would he be a hero? He didn't know …

And he also kept thinking, Kenilworth-Kenilworth-Kenilworth. That remained a mystery.

Should he be cool and say, 'Inspector, if you tell me what you know about Kenilworth, I'll tell you what I know …' But that would be betraying Scherezade. But if he never mentioned it—was he betraying Inspector Stanley? Betraying the law—the country? If he *had* heard Inspector right that day …

The bike reached his gate. As he got off, Inspector Stanley looked at him in the streetlight with an expression Pappu could not quite make out.

'You take care, men,' he said solemnly, and raised his hand. Pappu too raised his hand and the Inspector clasped his tightly. He then revved his bike, and as he began to draw away the dark spoke, in the astrologer's voice:

'Kenilworth …'

Pappu went breathless for a moment. Stanley's bike swerved and crashed, and the Inspector went sprawling in the grass.

'Stanley!' In the dim light, Pappu could make out his face slowly screwing up in confusion as he squatted by the Inspector. 'Stanley! Are you all right?'

He *looked* all right, though his face seemed to be rediscovering itself in the shadows. 'Ai men, first time you call me by name.' With Pappu's help, he slowly sat up. 'How's my bike, men?'

'It looks okay.' Pappu looked into the dark row of trees on both sides of his bungalow, searching for that astrologer—was he an astrologer? He ran a bit in both directions, but there was no one there.

Stanley staggered up with his bike and made kicking motions as if he was going to start it again.

'What … what's happening?' He was in a daze.

Gopal came out of the bungalow and helped them inside. Ayah came out fluttering with worry: she *had* reached before them. She helped Pappu deposit the dazed Inspector in the long sofa in the drawing room, and soon she was pressing ice packs on his bruises. 'What happened?'

'Just a small accident, Ayah,' the Inspector answered.

'These boy-people!' she shook her head and said—

that was the phrase in her language for both children, as well as the male sex. The Inspector sat there under her ice-pressing, looking at Pappu and stroking his scratched cheeks slowly.

'You heard the voice, men.'

'Yes.'

Stanley looked at him, wincing as Ayah touched a sore spot. His face was screwed up again in a kind of slow confusion.

'You can't keep still what?' Ayah scolded Stanley in Mumbaiya.

Stanley froze and looked at Pappu. Pappu felt he was burning under the Inspector's look, and realised his breathing had become jerky.

'I can detain you for questioning. Last time I let you go, but how long can I? This is matter of national security, men.'

Pappu remembered the kick. 'It's also a matter of your promotion!' he blurted out.

Stanley looked shocked. 'You don't know how important Kenilworth case is—' He stopped.

'So I *did* hear you say that! Nuclear reactor parts.'

Stanley flinched and said, 'I didn't say that, men!'

Ayah got up exasperatedly: 'I'll bring some hot tea, it will be good.' Stanley thanked her as she went out.

Pappu thought about Screwvala stealing nuclear reactor parts. And his poor honest daughter.

'Whose voice that was?' the Inspector asked aggressively.

Pappu told him about the astrologer.

'What else you know about this astrologer?'

Pappu shook his head. Stanley again stroked his scratched cheeks in slow confusion.

'I'll detain you, Pappu. No jokes. Tell me what you know about Kenilworth.'

'I want to Inspector. But I … '

The phone rang. Pappu jumped up and answered it. 'Hello?'

'Hello Pappu, how are you?' It was Nandani, a girl in his class—he was amazed that she had called, she was a really shy girl. She said: 'It was really nice to see you on TV, Pappu. You know my favourite subject is history, and I love the chapter on Taj Mahal … Could you please tell me what this Taj case is about?'

Pappu was glad of the excuse to avoid Stanley, and so he told her a little about it. He could feel Stanley's eyes boring into his back, but luckily Ayah came between them to give Stanley tea.

But soon Ayah was back in the kitchen, and he was back with Stanley.

'The time has come to detain you, Pappu. Answer me! *What do you know about Kenilworth*?'

There was another long silence. Pappu didn't look at the Inspector. He could feel his face burning.

The phone rang again. He jumped even higher this time.

It was Scherezade.

'Hello?'

Pappu looked at Stanley—then looked away. What should he do? Should he just disconnect? Or …

'Hi Amita,' Pappu said.

'I'm sorry?' Scherezade didn't get it.

'I can't talk for long, Amita, I have a … a guest.' There was a silence.

'Inspector Stanley?'

'Yes, Amita. We can talk for a minute.' He could hear Stanley slurping the tea: the pressure was off a bit. He heard Scherezade take a deep breath.

'I've got a big lead, Pappu. An hour ago someone who resembles the scarred man—you know, the hooded thug, came to my house to meet my father. My father's out of town so the man gave me a paper for him. He said, "I don't know why Mr Screwvala and my brother are fighting, Rustom won't tell me, he is hot-headed. But please request Mr Screwvala to forgive my brother and come to our grandfather's funeral." After he went, I read the paper, it was a funeral notice. It said that a Mr A.L. Patrawala had passed away this morning in Kenya. The body is being brought to India and will be taken to the Towers of Silence tomorrow.'

Pappu was confused about where she was going with this. He knew that the Towers of Silence were the Zoroastrians' unique place for putting their dead to rest.

'Pappu, I'm sure Rustom is the hooded thug and he'll be there at his grandfather's funeral. If we find him there, we could question him.'

'Question him? How? And …' He lowered his voice but Stanley was deep in the tea, 'you're a Parsi but I'm not. They won't allow me in.'

'I have an idea,' she said.

When he kept the phone down, the Inspector had finished his tea. He put his cup down smartly.

'You're a good boy, Pappu, but I warn you, you are in dangerous waters. I give you a little more time, but if you don't tell me what you know about Kenilworth soon, the matter will be out of my hands and that could be big trouble for you, Pappu.'

He got up and went to the kitchen to thank Ayah. Then he walked straight to the front door, stopped and looked grimly at Pappu: 'Another warning—do not mention the word nuclear to anyone. I'm not saying it is a nuclear matter—but for your own good, do *not* mention that word.'

Pappu swallowed and nodded, and Stanley left.

Ayah surprised him with a new cell phone she had bought for him. 'Your daddy don't even think about such things. I don't like cell phones, but Chotu, you need it now, you're grown up, you're moving around, you're keeping all the time *me* worried!'

It was a basic model, and he sighed for all those kids whose parents fondly bought them sets with advanced functions. He didn't blame Ayah, he knew that she didn't even know what an advanced function meant.

As he sat on the bench in their garden to try out the controls of the phone, he had an idea: he went to his room and googled 'Kenilworth + Mumbai + Nuclear'.

1,830 links came up, and when he clicked on the second one his screen suddenly filled up with giant lettering:

NUCLEAR INDIA

Published by the Department of Atomic Energy, Government of India

An Outburst at the Towers of Silence

As he read and searched, Pappu's excitement evaporated. The webpage was a collection of articles about nuclear power projects in India. One article described how in 1945 Dr Homi Bhabha and J.R.D. Tata, both members of India's tiny Parsi community, started the Tata Institute of Fundamental Research from Kenilworth. Kenilworth was then a bungalow on Peddar Road—it was Dr Bhabha's ancestral home. But Kenilworth today was a huge, tall building on Peddar road—and anyway, the Tata Institute had moved out of there in 1949 according to the article. It didn't make any sense.

When he googled Homi Bhabha, he found that he was the father of the Indian nuclear programme. But he also found that he had passed away long ago, in 1966. He found that Tata Institute of Fundamental Research too had a large role to play in India's nuclear programme. But if they had moved out of Kenilworth the bungalow more than fifty years ago ... Nowhere on the net could he find any connection between the

Kenilworth building of today and the nuclear programme.

He looked up the Parsis and found that they were Zoroastrians, followers of Zarathustra of Persia. Today they were mostly in Mumbai—but of Mumbai's total population of fifteen million, only 40,000 were Parsis. These 40,000 were roughly half the Parsis there were in the whole world!

By now he was sleepy, so he went back to the nuclear webpage to try to make sense of it. But he couldn't. His head began to ache, and he went to the garden for some fresh air.

And he saw in the streetlight, near the paan-wallah, a man standing at the corner of the lane outside. He was wearing black trousers, black shirt, dark glasses, and reading a little book. He didn't look well-off, but he didn't look poor either. He didn't look respectable, but he didn't look like a good-for-nothing. And it crossed Pappu's mind that maybe he was a man sent by Inspector Stanley to try and catch the astrologer.

And also catch Pappu on Kenilworth …

The honks and roar of the traffic flooding Kemps Corner seemed to magically fade away as the large gates of Doongerwadi shut behind them. As they climbed up Doongerwadi's winding lane toward the green heights of Malabar Hill, they passed a tiny yellow cottage a little way up.

'This is where the Khandiyas rest,' Scherezade said.

'The Khandiyas?'

'They are the people who take the body into the Towers. Nobody else is allowed into the Towers of Silence except for the Khandiyas.'

'Oh,' Pappu said. He looked up toward the green forests where the Towers of Silence were. He had heard about the strange Parsi way of dealing with their dead. But he didn't know how much to ask or say, because for every community these things are sacred.

As they climbed, whenever a guard asked a question he kept silent while she answered in Parsi Gujarati and they would be let in. Pappu looked behind a few times to see if they were being followed: earlier, he had caught the man in black from last night trailing him. Pappu had frantically hopped off and on buses and trains so that soon he was sure he had shaken his pursuer. Even so, it was a relief to see no one.

At the top of the path they reached a car park behind which there were two open-air halls the size of cottages. They had neon lights in their rafters, very clean wooden park benches inside, and little else. Scherezade explained that here the bereaved relatives and friends sat, including non-Parsis.

The light outside was fading as they joined the two dozen people there—they looked a little ragged, their clothes clean but worn. They didn't look like most Parsis Pappu had seen, who were the elite and rich of the country. This looked like a funeral in a poorer Parsi family.

The departed man's family and friends looked at the

two children coming in, not accompanied by any adults. Scherezade looked searchingly back at them.

'He's not there,' she whispered.

Opposite them was a small cottage, from where there was the sound of praying.

'What's that?'

'That's a bunglee. Prayers are being said for the departed soul as the body is bathed, dressed and put on an iron stretcher. In the morning the body will be carried by the Khandiyas towards the Towers of Silence. On the way, the Khandiyas will show the face of the departed for the last time to family and friends, and then the Khandiyas only, no one else, will take the body inside the Towers of Silence.'

Scherezade looked at Pappu's face for a moment, then said sharply: 'Oh, come on, Pappu, ask it!'

'What?'

'You've been dying to ask me what it's all about, but you haven't out of politeness. Don't worry, it's normal for you to wonder about it. Go on, ask what you want.'

'Well, I've heard the body is laid inside the Towers so that vultures can eat it? Is there some sort of … reason for that?'

'There are many good reasons for that.' Scherezade stopped searching every newcomer's face for a moment, and explained: 'You see, our prophet, Zarathustra, was one of the world's first great ecologists. Three thousand and five hundred years ago he taught that the elements of nature—earth, fire, water—are sacred. He taught that when we die, we shouldn't pollute nature by either cremation or burial. Giving our dead bodies to the vultures is the most eco-friendly way in the world of dealing with death. Our bodies are cleanly put back into the cycle of life, into the ecosystem, through the Towers of Silence.'

'That's wonderful,' Pappu said. 'I never thought about it that way. Where are the Towers?'

Scherezade pointed at a path. 'That way. Though each tower is as wide as a building it's only one storey high, so you can't see it above the trees—there he is! Don't look now!' She dropped her voice and ducked.

'He's seen me,' she said.

Pappu, turning, saw a tall man with a face that was strangely young and old at the same time—Pappu couldn't tell how old he was. There was a scar below his left eye. He was looking with round, frightened eyes at Scherezade. When he saw Pappu, his eyes grew even more terrified.

'Beware the boss's daughter,' Scherezade whispered bitterly. 'Come,' and she got up, looking straight at the man with the scar. He reared back.

'What're you doing, Scherezade?'

'Follow me, Pappu,' she said in clipped tones, and started walking forward.

'Rustom!' an elderly lady suddenly cried out, for he was stumbling back as if he'd seen a ghost. 'Rustom? Where are you going?'

'I … I'll be back, Auntthy,' he said, giving a sickened polite smile over his shoulder as he hurried out of the open cottage.

Pappu hurried after Scherezade as she followed Rustom towards the car park. But he wasn't running, he couldn't run away in front of his relatives. They would know something was seriously wrong if he did.

'Help me block him!' Scherezade whispered to Pappu.

They overtook him just as he reached the car park. Scherezade blocked his way. He tried to dodge her, eyes flicking back at his relatives—his Aunty was still peering in their direction. Pappu too blocked him. He tried to dodge Pappu, too, without jumping or running but then Scherezade simply caught hold of his wrist.

'Whatth are you doing? Letth me go chhild!' He put his other hand in his pocket. 'I 'ave a gun in my poketth. Ith ish pointed at hyou.' Pappu could make that out.

But Scherezade just laughed. 'Oh yes, Rustom, you're going to shoot me here, in front of all your family, even though you didn't dare to at Jer Mahal.'

He took his hand out of his pocket and looked around desperately. 'Whatth do you wantth fhrom me, girl?'

'I'll tell you. But if you don't do as I say, I'll shout to your family that you're a criminal.'

'Firstt you make tthrouble between me and your fahther, now you mhake trouble between me and my fhamily?' Rustom's voice was a pathetic whine.

'I didn't make any trouble—'

'You told him you were not at Jher Mahal so he's saying I'm seeing things, he's notth tthalking to me and calling me moron!'

'And all you really are is a criminal. A *Parsi* criminal!'

she said in disgust, for the Parsis are the most law-abiding people in India.

Rustom was stung and snapped back, 'Whatth about hyour—' He stopped.

Now Scherezade was stung. She blinked back the tears in her eyes. 'My father? You tell me, Rustom. What about my father?'

Rustom glanced fearfully in the direction of his family, and he suddenly looked very tired—Pappu realised he was not really old, but tired lines had become part of his skin, like wrinkles. Suddenly Pappu's heart went out to him.

'If you don't tell me, I'll call your family,' Scherezade said.

Rustom looked at Pappu. 'In fhront of himh?'

'I trust him.'

'Scherezade, I'm talkingh abhout hyour *papa*!'

Scherezade thought, then turned to Pappu. 'I'm so sorry, will you excuse us for a few minutes?' Still holding his hand firmly, she took Rustom a little way off.

Pappu felt guilty about not saying something like, 'No no, *I'll* leave so you can talk,' but then he wanted to know about her father's role. But if he had insisted on being there when Rustom spoke, would Rustom have talked? And it *would* have been rude …

He stood there, puzzling over his own feelings until she came back. Rustom was nowhere in sight, and her face was bloodless.

'What happened? What did he say?'

'Papa has an arrangement with somebody in the ministry of culture. He's bribed an official there. One Haribhai Kapadia.'

Pappu stopped breathing. He suddenly remembered the final moments of the press conference: Hassan rolling the letter carefully, putting it back in the pipe-shaped box and saying, 'And now I present this letter to the people it really belongs to, the people of Hindustan.'

A small bespectacled bureaucrat had come on stage and carefully taken the box from Hassan, who said, 'Thank you, Haribhai.'

Panic at the Prince of Wales

Pappu used his new cell phone to call the Inspector. When Stanley heard Haribhai had been bribed by someone he said, 'Oh Christ! Who? Tell who, Pappu, man?'

'I can't say.'

'Men! Ow!' Stanley sounded like he'd eaten hot chillies. 'Letter right now being taken by Haribhai with police escort to deposit in Prince of Wales Museum—Paluskar!—talk to you later, Pappu—' and he disconnected.

Pappu looked at Scherezade—he was surprised to see she looked even worse than she had a moment ago.

'I have to go talk to my father,' she said.

'What else did Rustom say?'

'None of your business!' she snapped. She turned sharply away towards the dark path that led down towards the city.

'Sherry! Sherry!'

People turned and looked at this boy making this

disgraceful racket in this sacred place.

She was running in the dark. He began to run.

Suddenly, a tall man in white robes and high white turban stepped in front of him—a dasturji, the Parsi priest. He said something in Gujarati, which Pappu couldn't understand.

Pappu pointed helplessly at Scherezade: 'She is a friend …'

'But your friend wants to be left alone? Sit down for a moment, my friend,' he pointed forbiddingly at a bench. Pappu sat down.

The dasturji nodded solemnly and continued on his way. Pappu dialled Stanley.

'Yes?' Stanley barked. In the background, Pappu could hear the engine of his jeep.

'Urr … what are you doing?' asked Pappu lamely.

'I'm going to Prince of Wales Museum. Pappu, can you tell me proof about Haribhai so I can act officially?'

'No—'

'Okay bye!' Stanley disconnected.

It began to drizzle. The dasturji was out of sight. He began running down the path where Scherezade had disappeared.

The drizzle became heavier and heavier as he ran. When he reached Kemps Corner, he searched through the glistening umbrellas and the shining traffic lights, but Scherezade was nowhere to be seen. So he stopped a cab and asked him to get to the museum fast.

It was seven. The peak-hour traffic was flooding from town towards the suburbs, but in the other direction the roads were relatively empty. He tried Scherezade's cell phone, though he felt stupid doing it. 'This phone is currently switched off,' said the impersonal voice.

When the cab reached Chowpatty Beach his cell rang: it was Stanley. 'Any other information you got, Pappu-boy? Haribhai not reached the museum yet.'

'No—' Stanley disconnected the line.

What could Scherezade be doing? She was probably at home. Should he tell the Inspector about Rustom and her father and the Kenilworth blueprint? Scherezade certainly did not pretend she was telling *him* everything. But he couldn't bear the thought of betraying her—was it betrayal? He couldn't do it.

The Prince of Wales Museum had recently been renamed the Chhatrapati Shivaji Maharaj Vastu Sangrahalaya. But after the renaming, since it failed to turn into a Maratha fort overnight, people continued calling it by its old name. It was a mixed-up building, like a boring brown Mughal-Victorian-Rajput castle topped by three heavenly sky-white-blue domes.

It was after visiting hours. Behind the museum's gardens, the necklace-shaped driveway gleamed with rotating red and blue lights on police cars. One of them was the Inspector's jeep, and Pande waved him in.

The high vault of the museum's large central hall was dimly lit. In the centre there was a patch of bright neon light dense with people and uniforms and radio sets swarming around an empty glass case.

The Inspector perked up with irritated excitement when he saw him. 'Pappu-boy?'

'Where's Haribhai Kapadia?'

The Inspector put a finger over his moustache and took Pappu to a corner, so that they were almost leaning against a sculpture from the Harappan period. 'Because we don't have anything official on him we have to be careful. They were supposed to be here half an hour ago, but supposedly Haribhai asked his police escort to stop on the way to go to the bathroom—it's only ten minute journey man, he couldn't wait? Then they stayed at this restaurant for tea! I'm not liking this.'

'I'm getting tired of your games, Pappu-boy,' the Inspector's eyes suddenly gleamed hard and nasty in the dark. '*Who's side are you on*?' His harsh whisper rasped against the walls of the museum.

'Inspector!' a policeman shouted from the entrance, where there was the sound of a car entering the driveway. 'The police party with Kapadia is here!'

Inspector Stanley froze. 'Careful, don't say anything suspicious,' he said to Pappu. Pappu tried to sink into the shadows.

A small, thin Haribhai, dressed in a small brown safari suit and dwarfed by three hefty gun-wielding policemen, walked into the central hall. He had in his hand the small pipe-shaped box.

He walked towards the empty glass case in the centre, put the pipe-shaped box down, and opened the glass case with a key. He then took the letter out of the box, placed it on one little velvet-topped stand, and the box on another velvet-topped stand next to it. He swung the glass door of the case shut.

'That letter is fake!' a strange voice rang out from the shadows.

In broken Hindi, it was a girl's voice speaking from the shadows. 'Wait! That letter is a forgery!'

In sharp English, Stanley's voice rang out: 'Who is that?'

Someone snapped in Marathi: 'Who is asking? *I'm* in charge here—that's *my* question!' This was from an officer behind Haribhai's three guards.

Haribhai asked in Gujarati: 'Arre, what is all this happening, brothers?'

'Inspector Stanley Coelho,' Stanley answered the other officer.

Scherezade stepped out of the shadows, and the other officer asked in amazement, 'Who *is* this little girl? How did she get in?' He too stepped out of the shadows: he had an impressive, body-builder's body.

Haribhai was still holding the glass door of the case half-open, adjusting his spectacles with a trembling hand.

'Kakodkar!' Stanley said cheerily to the officer with the body.

'Coelho,' the officer with the body returned grimly. 'This is my turf. Don't butt in.'

The guard who had brought Scherezade in said to Stanley, 'Sir, she had asked to see you. So—'

Stanley was angry. 'Yes yes, bring in any more kids who take my name. Oh!' he remembered something awkward. 'Kakodkar, this is Pappu.' Kakodkar's jaw dropped as he saw Pappu in the shadows. Yet another kid!

'Girl,' Stanley went on before Kakodkar could say any more, 'you say that letter is fake? How do you know? *Tell me!*'

'My father bribed Mr Kapadia to switch it.' Scherezade said sharply.

After a while, Stanley said, 'Oh.'

Everyone was looking at Haribhai, whose hand was trembling so much the keys were clattering against the glass door. The Inspector moved towards him.

'Stop, Coelho!' Kakodkar ordered. 'Who *is* this girl?'

'She is an important source on this case, Kakodkar,' the Inspector answered. He again moved toward Haribhai.

'Stop!' repeated Kakodkar. 'We first have to find the person who has seen the genuine letter most closely.'

'Yes, that's true. And the person who last saw the letter so closely was … me!'

Kakodkar looked at him sourly, then motioned him forward. 'Okay.'

Stanley moved forward, leaned into the glass case and peered at the letter. It looked real. He picked it up to look closer.

There was a strange grating, buzzing sound. All the policemen reached for their guns, including Stanley.

The policeman next to Scherezade jumped back from her. 'It's from her!'

In Scherezade's hand her mobile phone glowed red.

'Quick, Inspector, we have to go!' she cried. 'Or the real letter will be transported somewhere no one can find it!'

Stanley leapt toward her with the letter in his hand—he stepped back and took the pipe-shaped box out. He said to Pappu, 'Come, Pappu!'

'Stop! Put that letter back!' Kakodkar snapped.

'Kakodkar, I have NX3 authorisation!'

'NX3 . . .' Kakodkar was speechless. He stepped back like a helpless giant. The team of policemen watched as Stanley and two children walked out with the thing that the government was spending lakhs to protect.

It had stopped raining. They hopped into the jeep and Stanley looked at Scherezade. 'Cusraw Baug,' she said, and Stanley nodded to Pande. 'Fast!'

The jeep got stuck in traffic at once and Stanley began studying the letter with a torch. A thought suddenly struck him.

'You sure this is fake, girl?' he asked suspiciously. 'You haven't just got Stanley Coelho to pinch the country's hottest national treasure?'

'Inspector Coelho, the last time it was being stolen *I* was the one who saved it for you, remember?'

'Sorry.' He went back to studying the letter. 'It's fake! I remember there was a mark in the corner here—and the whole letter is a different colour. I'm sorry, Scherezade, you keep so many secrets I got into the habit of not trusting you. But today—tell me all.'

Scherezade opened her mouth to speak. But a strangled sob came out instead. Stanley and Pappu waited for her to find her voice, and she explained with difficulty how she found the Kenilworth blueprint in her dustbin, how she spotted the man with the scar at Jer Mahal, and how she and Pappu found him at the Towers of Silence today.

'What did this Rustom tell you?' Stanley asked her.

Scherezade paused and swallowed. 'He told me that he was a small-time goonda, and he had started working for my father recently. He told me that he had been the one to burgle the Kenilworth apartment. He had been ordered to by … by Papa. Papa had given him the plan of the place, and Papa had already done homework on the security there.'

'What did he steal?'

'A large steel safe, there must have been paintings inside. The safe was locked.' She paused, and they could see she was again struggling to go on.

'Inspector, if it wasn't for a national treasure I would have protected Papa, even if he was a … a … thief!'

'I understand, girl. And appreciate.'

'After Rustom, I went home, and—I have a key. As soon as I entered, I overheard Papa saying to someone on the phone, "Right now Kapadia is at the Prince of Wales. I will get the letter in a few minutes, and we can bury it at Elephant's Kennel till we need it again—no one will find it there." I immediately stepped out of the house and tried to phone you, Inspector, but I got a network busy signal. I realised that I needed to get help at once if I wanted to stop them. So I took a cab and rushed to the Prince of Wales.'

'You did good, Scherezade. What was that signal you received in the museum?'

'It wasn't a signal, it was just an alarm I had set on my mobile, to remind me to hurry back. We're almost there,' she added sadly. They could see the big yellow arch that was the entrance of Cusrow Baug half a furlong away.

Pappu trembled to think what it must be like for her—in a few minutes her father would be arrested, and her family marked for life.

'Pande, stop the jeep,' Stanley said. Pande pulled over to the side of the road. 'Scherezade, we are not going to arrest your father for the Taj letter. There is a much bigger matter he is involved in.'

Scherezade was stunned.

'Much bigger matter? What could be bigger than the Taj letter?'

Pappu thought he knew the answer to that question, but he kept silent.

'Can't tell you now, it is top secret —'

'Is that what the NX3 authorisation is about?' Scherezade asked.

Stanley was taken aback. 'Er, I can't tell you. So we do not want to tip your papa off now, so we can keep following him and get to the bottom of the … larger matter.'

Scherezade was struggling to understand that her father was in even deeper trouble than she had thought.

'We walk from here,' Stanley hopped off the jeep and held out his hand to help Pappu. Then he held out his hand to Scherezade, but she didn't notice.

'Scherezade, we need your help in doing this.' She looked up, dazed. Stanley gave her a little smile, and nodded at her encouragingly. She took his hand and got off. The Inspector asked Pande to park inside a lane.

They started walking toward Cusrow Baug when suddenly Stanley stopped. 'Oh! I have my police uniform on! I can't go inside Cusrow Baug, it might tip Screwvala off—' Scherezade winced. 'Let me find some civvies.'

'But Inspector,' Scherezade said, 'we can't lose any time.'

'You go on kids.' He handed Scherezade the fake Taj letter, and the golden box. 'See if you can do a swap—but don't take any risk. I'll try to catch up soon.'

So only Scherezade and Pappu walked out of the hard noisy electric chaos of Mumbai into the great yellow gate of Cusrow Baug.

A few elderly people were sitting on benches, enjoying the air of the peaceful green enclosure that is Cusrow Baug, and some were strolling around. There was magic about such a space in the heart of clattering Mumbai. The buildings were all painted yellow, like government houses. Pappu followed the silent Scherezade.

Scherezade stopped before a building and looked uncertainly around. 'That's my house, on the third floor. Should we wait for Inspector …'

'You know best, Sherry, what we should do now,' Pappu said. She looked at him—or rather though him. After her talk with Rustom, she had seemed to be in a trance. Pappu wiped the sweat off his face—the weather was very sultry, but there was also something frightening about Scherezade's gaze. But he couldn't blame her. Her entire world was coming down, and she and Pappu were the ones who were helping the Inspector pull it down.

There were no lifts in Cusrow Baug, so they climbed the stairs. At the top, she turned the key in the door with 'Screwvalas' on it.

It was dark inside. They were in a balcony. On their right, a thin wooden wall separated the balcony from the drawing room. On either side of the central door were semi-transparent windows which were dewed from the air conditioning inside.

Scherezade motioned Pappu to crouch under a ledge with plants on the far corner of the balcony. She put her ear to the door, and he put his ear to the wall.

Someone inside was sniffing.

Screwvala rolled the ice in his drink and sniffed. He had a cold—he knew he was lucky it wasn't a bad cold. He had overdone the air conditioning and the ice, and now he was paying the price he had known he would pay. But he couldn't help himself.

Sitting in his favourite armchair, legs stretched out so that his feet were on his favourite footstool, he looked at the back of a tall, lanky, dark brahmin.

'You know, Unni, I have done many rum things in life. But never anything that was this risky.'

'It is all for something that is worthwhile,' Unnikrishnan said.

Screwvala sighed and took a deep sip. 'It's easy for you to say. You don't have kids. Half the time I'm going mad thinking what would happen to my Scherezade if things went wrong.'

'Keep calm, Screwvala-bhai. We have to take such risk. Think, I am being MLA taking such risk.'

Screwvala got up and stood by Unnikrishnan, who was gazing at a table set against the wooden wall. On the table was a flat wooden jewel box that held the Taj letter.

Screwvala shook his head. 'Such a little letter. We'll keep it buried in the Elephant's Kennel until the American comes.'

'The paper is so old. But so beautiful it is,' Unnikrishnan said, still gazing at it.

'That Inspector Stanley, such a crook he is—' Screwvala was interrupted by a man's voice calling from deeper inside the house. 'The internet is connected. Come, let us see what messages the American is sending.' They left the drawing room and went inside.

In the balcony, Scherezadc began to weep silently. 'Scherezade!' Pappu whispered, alarmed.

'My computer, my *home* … is a den of criminals.' She was leaning against the door tiredly—he knew the AC inside would drown out most outside sounds, but he helped her into a chair on the other side of the balcony, so that her voice would not carry. Pappu suddenly thought of his father's betrayal of him on the phone—who *had* he been talking to? What was he doing now—was *he* involved in all this?

Pappu remembered what guys did in Hollywood films and TV shows, and gave her his handkerchief—luckily it was clean. 'You know,' she whispered tearfully, wiping her eyes and tear-stained hands, 'Papa catches colds even in summer, because he can't resist taking his drinks really cold, and putting the AC on really high, even though he knows it's not good for him. He can never resist pampering himself. Once I tried to put him on a diet—it was no good. He's like a child, he couldn't resist good food. But now, that thing he couldn't resist isn't good for him, it isn't good for me, and it isn't good for the country …' She wept some more.

Pappu stood awkwardly with his arm around her shoulder.

Scherezade suddenly got up: 'There's no one in the drawing room. Please go back to your place,' she said in clipped tones, pointing at the shadow beneath the ledge. Pappu was surprised, but obeyed.

She gave him his hanky, took out the forged letter from her pocket and quietly opened the door. Pappu saw her arm go in and come out with a paper that she put in the gold box.

He followed her out of the house and silently down the stairs, knowing that she was in a turmoil.

When they reached the bottom, he said to her, 'You

know, when you were asking those questions, I was thinking, what are the answers for *my* father?' His voice caught and he, too, felt like crying. But he didn't, he looked into her face and saw his own fear mirrored there, only more strongly. And it was she who took his hand and squeezed it reassuringly.

'Hey! Hey kids!' Someone was whispering out loudly to them. There was a cab parked a little further, against the side of the path. Stanley was in it, in civvies.

'I have the original letter,' Scherezade told him as they got inside the cab. The cab took off, and outside Cusrow Baug they switched to the jeep.

Stanley studied the letter Scherezade had got with his torch and nodded. 'This is it.'

At the central hall of the Prince of Wales, Kakodkar got up and asked abruptly, in Marathi, 'Well?'

Stanley looked at Haribhai sitting miserably in a corner. 'We've got the original letter. Though we have to bring the government expert to check it asap.'

He went to the display case in the middle, and put the letter and box inside. Kakodkar gestured a constable towards Haribhai, who handcuffed him.

'Haribhai, you are under arrest for stealing the Taj letter. And *you,*' he turned around, 'Coelho, how do you come with the letter but without its thief?'

Stanley looked at Kakodkar: Kakodkar looked at Stanley. It was obvious there was no love lost here.

There was a long silence.

Someone's cell phone rang.

It was one of those thin little ringtones, high-pitched

but not too sharp, that seem to everyone to come from somewhere close to them, but are difficult to pin-point. Everyone patted their pockets and looked at their neighbours. The annoying ring continued.

'It's mine,' Haribhai said miserably.

'Well, take it out—' Kakodkar began sharply but realised Haribhai was handcuffed. He gestured to the constable, who in one movement opened the cuffs.

Haribhai, trembling, took out his cell—a little, plain one. Kakodkar snatched the phone, looked at the name on it, and returned it to Haribhai with a curt gesture asking him to get on with the conversation. Haribhai hesitated, and Kakodkar took out his pistol and held it to his head.

Haribhai wilted. 'Mr … Mr Screwvala! Yessir, I can talk … I'm in Prince of Wales, sir … no, sir, I have not put the letter in the case … I'm under arrest, sir, right now I'm surrounded by full one dozen policemen, sir … yes sir … they're listening to us—'

The Flight of Screwvala

The 'full dozen policemen' awoke from their trance and jumped on Haribhai. Kakodkar was the most surprised of all—and the angriest. He hit Haribhai with his pistol and switched his phone off. Haribhai cowered as a constable put the cuffs back on.

'That was a mad thing to do just for a little money,' Kakodkar said, looking at the cowering Haribhai.

'Don't accuse me!' Haribhai shouted, and suddenly pointed a finger at Stanley. 'HE IS THE ONE! He is the traitor and the people above him!'

Stanley staggered back. No one knew what to make of Haribhai. He seemed to be unbalanced. 'Keep quiet!' a constable snapped at him.

'Now Screwvala will run,' Stanley said. 'Now he knows that we know that he is involved in the Taj letter matter.'

'Yes. We should arrest him.'

'But—' Stanley stopped. 'Tell your men to step into next room, with Haribhai. I have something top-secret to say to you.'

'Go,' Kakodkar said to everybody. But Stanley pointed to the children and shook his head. Looking displeased, Kakodkar let them stay.

'Now tell me, what is this top-secret matter that my men can't know but these children can?'

'Kakodkar, they already know. Now this is NX3.'

At the mention of that code, Kakodkar stiffened to attention.

'Kakodkar, we already have a police team of more than a *dozen* behind Screwvala's building. But they won't arrest him, they are there only to follow him.'

'Why—?'

'Screwvala has many irons in the fire. He is involved in another matter, of NX3 importance. We don't want to arrest him before he leads us to … the big evidence. But now, because of Haribhai—and your bungling—Screwvala knows we know he is involved in the Taj letter matter. So if we don't arrest him, he will guess we are waiting for him to make his move in the NX3 matter.'

'So what do we do now?' Kakodkar asked.

'There is only one thing we can do. We have to *pretend* to chase him. Make him believe we are trying to catch him. But we have to make sure he escapes every time we get close. This way, he'll think it is about the Taj letter. All this time NX3 police team keeps on his heels, and catches him only when he leads us to the big evidence.'

'Oh,' Kakodkar was trying to understand.

'Kakodkar, under NX3 authorisation I appoint you

as assistant in-charge of the police search party for Screwvala.'

'And who is chief in-charge?'

'Me.'

Kakodkar was not pleased with this answer.

The plainsclothes team who were shadowing Screwvala quietly followed when he, Unnikrishnan and a short dark man hopped into his white Mercedes and drove out of Cusrow Baug at top speed. At the same time, Stanley, Pande, Pappu and Scherezade climbed into a jeep and, siren screaming, headed for Cusrow Baug. It was 8.45 pm.

Pappu could see that with each passing moment, Scherezade seemed to be shrinking into herself, the lines on her face growing more strained. When they reached Regal Cinema, Scherezade suddenly leaned toward Stanley.

'Let me down Inspector!' she said briskly. For a moment she seemed her usual self.

'Let you ...'

'I ... I can't stand it any more, I *can't* be riding in the jeep that's going to *arrest* my father ... *please* let me *down!*'

Though she didn't mean it to, it sounded like a sharp order. Stanley studied her face and told Pande to stop the jeep. She jumped off efficiently.

'Where're you going, girl?' Stanley asked.

'Home, I ... I suppose?' She suddenly sounded like a little lost girl.

'We'll be in touch, girl, don't worry.'

Pappu looked at Scherezade standing lonely on the road, not looking at them as they pulled away. She looked more lost with every extra metre between them.

'Stop the jeep!' Pappu shouted to Pande. Pande did. Stanley looked at him as Pappu jumped off too.

'Pappu?'

'I can't leave her alone now, Inspector.'

Stanley nodded, and Pande started the jeep again.

Pappu was thirty feet from her, and she wasn't looking towards him or the jeep or her home. Like a good Mumbai-wallah, her eyes looked everywhere except the place where she wanted to, so that no one could think she was weak.

Pappu walked toward her. She took a deep breath and turned her back to the jeep, and to her house, and looked at the big posters of the movies showing at Regal Cinema.

The jeep had to stop at the next red light, even though its siren was screaming, because there were four cars in front of it with no place to move. Stanley looked at the cars stopped in the opposite direction—there was a white Mercedes with tinted windows, it might be Screwvala. He looked away, but then thought that if he didn't look carefully at a white Mercedes only five minutes away from Cusrow Baug and Screwvala was in it, Screwvala would get suspicious. So he looked at it again—and this time the people inside got nervous, the Merc revved up, used its horn to blast a car and a bike out of its way, and jumped the red light.

This was it! Stanley couldn't pretend he didn't know any more.

'Pande! U-turn and chase that white Mercedes!'

Even though her back was to him he could make out that she was wiping her eyes again, carefully, with the edges of her sleeves so that people couldn't make out easily.

'Have you seen *Harry Potter and the Philosopher's Stone*?'

Scherezade jumped and turned. 'You?'

Pappu shrugged. He hoped she wouldn't mind, his having got off the jeep to be with her.

She didn't. She suddenly took his hand very firmly, looked him directly in the eye and asked: 'Have you?'

'Yes,' he said, shyly.

'I haven't. Come, we're just in time for the nine-o' clock show. My treat.'

Pande was able to just in time see the Merc turn left, towards Mantralaya. He followed. The Merc took a right. They took a right—they had managed to hop quite a few cars, they were closing in!

'Careful Pande, careful not to catch up!' Stanley gritted his teeth.

Pande slowed down.

'Pande not *so* slow!'

Now it was Pande's turn to grit his teeth. 'Sahb, this is more difficult than a real chase!'

Ahead of them the Mercedes disappeared in the traffic!

'Look what you've done, Pande!' yelled Stanley. This upset Pande so he tore through the traffic, siren screaming. People in other cars looked at them as if they were barbarians.

Suddenly Stanley remembered.

'Oh, it's all right, Pande, you can relax! We needed to lose them anyway.'

Pande was so angry that he slammed the brake, and was quite pleased when Stanley was thrown and hit his head against the jeep bar.

The jeep was once again near Regal. But luckily for Scherezade, she didn't hear the siren because she and Pappu were already inside the cinema hall.

When the movie started he could see she was really enjoying herself, losing herself in Harry's tragedies and amazing new friendships. After thirty minutes, even he was lost in Hogwarts—when he suddenly felt a tap on his shoulder.

'Let's go,' she whispered.

'The movie—'

But she looked at him, and he got up at once.

Outside she said, 'Do you think your Chacha will be awake? It would be nice to see him and Mehurnissa and Hassan uncle again.'

Pappu understood that she didn't want to go to *her* home, it would be empty and it would make her sad. So he phoned Hassan's home number on his new cell—Hassan was out, but Mehurnissa was delighted to hear from him. They got into a bus to Marine Drive.

In the bus, his phone rang. It was Ayah. She asked him when he was coming, and scolded him for being so far away from home when his dinner was waiting for him.

Soon he and Scherezade were in the cool Marine Drive drawing room, being served juice. Mehurnissa and the blind man listened to their story raptly. Mehurnissa sat next to Scherezade with an arm around her.

When they had finished Mehurnissa said, 'Come, dinner is ready.'

'Dinner?' said Pappu. 'But my ayah has made dinner at home …'

'No, children, not only will you have dinner, but you will sleep here. We have many rooms. Scherezade, tonight I will sleep with you and we can gossip like sisters! The house will be so bright with guests like you!'

'But—' said Pappu.

Mehurnissa took him aside and asked, 'Do you want to leave your friend alone? Do you know how hard this night is for her?'

Mehurnissa called Ayah, and explained to her that there were very special reasons why Pappu would not be coming home.

Late in the night, Pappu was woken up by the sound of Hassan coming home with someone. Except for a word or two, he couldn't hear what Hassan was saying but he could make out that Hassan was furious. And then Hassan raised his voice angrily and Pappu heard: 'Arre, that crook Screwvala has run away! He is a *very* dangerous man!'

Pappu prayed that Scherezade hadn't heard.

The morning after the recovery of the Taj letter, Stanley held a press conference. Journalists filled the Prince of Wales Museum gardens. A bad photo of Screwvala was flashed all over the world, and Stanley announced that the Taj letter had been stolen by this man, Keki Screwvala. The photo had been worked on to make it blurred and confusing. Stanley did not want anyone to capture Screwvala just yet.

Immediately after the press conference Stanley had a meeting for top policemen, the topic of which was 'How (not) to catch Keki Screwvala'.

'Gentlemen,' he said. 'This matter is top priority, NX3. My plan is simple. One, we *have* to warn the whole of Mumbai police force to catch Screwvala—Screwvala has spies in the force, and he will be suspicious if they haven't been alerted. Two, we distribute these blurry photos of Screwvala to whole force. Three, all searches by police teams of places Screwvala really might turn up in—like his cousin's house in Dadar, or the race course where he never misses a big race—will be done by special police parties who can be trusted to know that if they see Screwvala, their mission is to chase him but let him run away. Four, if anyone captures Screwvala he is to report at once to me, so that I can let him escape again as soon as possible. Now what I need from you gentlemen is, *more* ideas how to make it *more* difficult for police force to catch Screwvala …'

Stanley's plan was so good that it totally confused the police officers. Unluckily for Stanley, there was a disaster in the afternoon—the undercover police party that was following Screwvala lost him. And so his fantastic plan came back to confuse *him*.

'Don't worry, sir,' the chief of his undercover team said, 'we'll catch up with him in a few hours, I'm sure of it.' But as the hours passed and it didn't happen, Stanley cursed.

Soon the madness began. First there was a report from Kakodkar's constable at Jogeshwari's Parsi Colony that they had caught the mastermind behind the Taj letter case, and he rushed there. But when he arrived he found that they had arrested Keki Soonavala—the police control room had purposely broadcast a misspelled name.

'Why didn't you tell me it was Keki *Soonavala*?' Stanley hissed at Kakodkar.

'Oh, didn't my constable tell you?' Kakodkar asked innocently.

Stanley was about to give Kakodkar a not-so-innocent reply when he received a radio message from Mumbai police headquarters, near Crawford Market, that they had the Berlin police chief on a tele-conference link, saying that his men had the Taj letter mastermind in Germany. Stanley thought, Holy Mother of God! He must have spotted my police team, and he has fled the country. But what about the special policemen at the airport? They have his real photograph.

Stanley rushed to headquarters by train (faster than by road, clogged with office traffic). The large tele-conference screen was filled with the large Berlin chief, Hans Kruger, who first showed Stanley the bad photo that Stanley had released to Interpol.

'*I* said to my boys, let us help the great Indian police, *ja*? And *ve* ran your photo through *our* computer enhancement software—an Indian here runs it, Raj. *I* said to *Raj*, the Indians don't have you, *ve* have. So let *us* help them, *ja*? Ha! Ha! Ha!' Then Hans showed the blurred photo going through the computer-enhancement, and it was as if it were moving into focus, till it finally showed in sharp focus a man who might have been a distant cousin of Screwvala.

'And meet—Keki Screwvala!' Hans, with a magician's flourish, waved to the curtain behind him which dropped—and Stanley's jaw dropped as he saw, *live,* a real face like the one the computer had created from the blurred photo—like a distant cousin of Screwvala. The big fat man said 'Oi! Am *not* Screwvala–Shoovala, please to taell them! These Germans are crazy! Oi Screwvala on the loose kya, *they* have a screw loose! Myself Bhatia from J'llunder. Not Screwvala-Shoovala!'

After Stanley had gotten over the shock, he explained to Hans that there was a mistake, and the Germans let Bhatia go—but reluctantly.

Stanley really knew he was in over his head when a policeman in Andheri and a policeman in Thane both reported that they had arrested Screwvala.

Then he received a report from a senior officer of a white Mercedes parked outside Taj Mahal Hotel. 'I tell you, Stanley,' he said on the radio, 'that number plate is doctored. It is expertly done, but I have thirty years of experience in the force … '

Stanley sent men to Andheri and Thane, and joined the officer at the spot where he was watching the Merc through binoculars.

Almost at once, a man he recognised as Screwvala with a false beard came out of Taj Hotel with Unnikrishnan and a short dark man, got into the car, and drove away. Stanley jumped from surprise that it really *was* Screwvala, and the senior officer was pleased. Stanley jumped into his jeep, parked near by, and ordered Pande to follow the Merc with his siren on.

Pande did so. 'Sahb, do we really want to catch them?'

'Eh? No, no. But they should *think* we do?' And he barked into his radio to his undercover team: 'Men! Have found the real Screwvala! He's near Taj Hotel, speeding toward boat club!'

The Merc suddenly did a sharp u-turn—Screwvala had seen them in his rear-view mirror!

That evening Pappu and the blind man went to Scherezade's house, to keep her and her ayah company.

Scherezade's ayah's name was Janaki-bai, and at first she had looked at the blind man doubtfully.

'Hafiz Chacha is a friend, Janaki-bai,' Scherezade had to say pointedly, and only then Janaki-bai put aside her doubts and called him 'Hafiz-bhai'. The blind man just smiled his sad, secret smile.

Janaki-bai seemed to be shattered by what was happening to the family. She kept muttering to herself, 'Poor Keki, poor Keki.'

Janaki-bai reminded Pappu of his own ayah—or rather, she made him see how Ayah would be in thirty years, for she was double his ayah's age. She, too, was from a Maharashtrian-Konkan fishing village, and had been with the Screwvala family for decades. Seeing her pain for the family gave Pappu a horrible feeling.

Pappu was horrified to find that though he was there to be with Scherezade, a part of him was curious about what kind of man Mr Screwvala was, and how he lived. He thought he saw—in the too-plush drawing room, crammed with wall hangings and expensive pieces of art, with a big bar stuffed with costly bottles in a corner—Screwvala's over-the-top, pretentious nature. Deeper inside, the home was quite modest—the walls were in the cream-yellow colour of the Parsi colony's outer walls, and the furnishing was simple and tasteful. Here, Pappu saw the difference between Screwvala and his daughter.

A central corridor connected the drawing room and

the inner rooms. Here, Scherezade pottered around with her laptop while Janaki-bai served the blind man and Pappu dhansak, a delicious Parsi dal. He took a bite, and the flavours in it amazed him, and he almost said 'Wow!'—but stopped himself just in time. How could he say 'Wow!' in this sad house?

'Wah,' the blind man said in Urdu, gently, as he ate the dhansak. 'This is excellent.' As he continued eating with a gentle concentration, Janaki-bai said, 'Thank you, Hafizbhai' from the door.

Scherezade gave Pappu a sad smile and then a nod, as if to say, 'You too can go ahead and enjoy it.' But he stopped. And he was glad to see, in her sad eyes, a stern twinkle of mischief appear. Her chin pushed forward and she pushed the plate towards him in a determined, almost playful manner. And then Pappu ate, relishing not only the dhansak but also the knowledge that every bite he took was also feeding the little twinkle of cheerfulness flickering in her eye.

But as the blind man tried to cheer up the gloomy Janaki-bai by discussing cooking, Scherezade gave another sigh and went back to her laptop. She suddenly stiffened.

'What's the matter?' Pappu asked.

'My laptop—somebody's been tampering with it.'

'*Tampering* with it?'

'Some of my settings have changed … Christ!' She jumped back as if stung.

'What?'

'Arre what happened, child?' the blind man asked.

'He was—' she began in English, then tried to complete the sentence in Hindi: 'My father was using my laptop to exchange messages with the American! Suppose they are still on the hard disk ...?'

She looked at Pappu and went into the recycle bin. She shook her head. 'The recycle bin was cleared yesterday. It's obvious that they first deleted the records, then emptied the recycle bin.' Pappu could sense that she was partly glad.

Pappu put aside his plate. 'There is a chance ...'

'How can you say that Pappu, they've even deleted the files in the recycle bin?' Her voice started crisply, but ended in almost a whine.

'Sherry, deleting a file doesn't mean it's wiped out from the hard disk. Only the file's label and location are deleted so that the computer can't find it. The file remains on the hard disk until it is overwritten by some new file.'

Pappu took a pen drive out of his pocket and plugged it into the laptop. He downloaded a file undelete software into the computer. To the blind man he said: 'Chacha, we are trying to get the messages that are hidden in this computer.'

'Pappuji, you can try, but I don't think you will get them. Arre, those grown-ups must have hidden them well, how will you children just find it?'

In minutes, as Scherezade watched with emotions ranging from regret to fascination and a perverse excitement, Pappu found a 'Recorded Conversations' folder in the hard disk. Opening the folder, Pappu pointed at a file dated the day before: 'This looks like it.' He moved away from the keyboard and nodded to her. Scherezade took a deep breath and double clicked on the file.

It sprang open and suddenly they heard two voices: an uncertain, reedy American one and an Indian one.

AMERICAN: Where are the Kenilworth goods?

INDIAN: We don't have them, sir.

AMERICAN: You don't have them?

INDIAN: No, not right now. But Kenilworth goods in good hiding place. We will get them soon.

AMERICAN: You *keep* saying that—

INDIAN: And we have the Taj letter.

AMERICAN: Ah …

Silence.

INDIAN: Hello? You still there?

Silence.

INDIAN: Purfessor Dakkins? Hello?

AMERICAN: So when can we make the exchange?

INDIAN: We get Kenilworth goods out of very very safe hiding place. Then we come to you with that and Taj letter say, in a few days.

AMERICAN: Okay. But make it snappy, will you? I can't hang around in India's neighbouring waters forever.

INDIAN: We will be in touch. Bye.

AMERICAN: Yeah.

Pause. Click.

INDIAN: He has disconnected.

SCREWALA: We have to get the dog out of the Elephant's Kennel with Ramesh's help.

Pappu and Scherezade looked at each other. 'What can the Kenilworth goods mean?' Scherezade asked.

'And what does Elephant's Kennel mean?' Pappu replied, to avoid answering her question which he was sure he knew. 'We should tell Inspector Stanley.'

As he took out his cell, Scherezade began translating the conversation for the blind man.

Once again, the Merc drove back to the large circular traffic island in front of Regal Cinema, and the jeep followed, its siren screaming. Stanley's cell rang.

'Yes?'

'Inspector, the Kenilworth goods are now hidden in some place that Screwvala calls the Elephant's Kennel.'

There were many knots of traffic at the traffic island, each knot at a signal leading out of the circle. The white Mercedes was jumping the signals, making other cars turn away and bang against others.

'How do you know?' To Pande he said quickly, as the Merc banged into another car, 'Pande-don't-forget-we-still-don't-want-to-catch-him.'

Shouting to be heard over the traffic and some cursing drivers, Pappu told him as quickly as he could what he and Scherezade had found on her laptop.

'Scherezade is a good girl, men,' Stanley said admiringly. 'Any idea where this Elephant's Kennel could be? No? Anyway, thanks.'

Pande was jumping the signals more carefully than the Merc. The Merc turned towards Cusrow Baug, and the jeep was behind it, its siren screeching. … Stanley was muttering to himself, 'Elephant's Kennel? The dog's Kennel was Kenilworth. The elephant's kennel is?' The Merc turned back towards Mantralaya, then back toward Regal Cinema and its traffic island—then back again towards Cusrow Baug.

'Sir, last time also they were in this area. Why are they taking circles?'

Stanley slapped his forehead. 'Elephanta Caves! Elephant's Kennel! Elephanta Caves is near this coast—he badly wants to go to Elephanta Caves but he can't because we're chasing him!'

An empty cab was right next to them. Stanley hopped out of the jeep and into the cab, saying to the cabbie: 'Follow that big white Mercedes. And if you lose it, I'll arrest you!' He shouted at Pande: 'Pande! Slow down, disappear, let them think we lost them!' He turned back to the worried cabbie: 'But don't get too close to them.' The cabbie became even more worried.

As Stanley had expected, as soon as the police jeep with its screaming siren disappeared, the Mercedes did a full round of the Regal traffic circle, freed itself from the traffic knots and headed back towards Taj Mahal Hotel. It then stopped a little beyond the Gateway of India. The cab followed silently, and Stanley saw three men jump out. Unnikrishnan had what looked like a guitar case in his hand. They scrambled down a long slender diagonal of stone steps, on to a pier and into a motorboat.

The motorboat roared away into the night. Stanley got off the cab and watched after them from the top of the stone steps, looking rather like a hero in a film watching the love of his life going away on a long journey.

'Boat, sir?' The voice came from a small motorboat that was bobbing up and down in the shadows of the rampart.

'Yes!' said Stanley. 'Follow that boat!' He eagerly clambered down the steps and into the small rickety motorboat. 'Which direction is that boat going in?' he asked the boat man, who was a short plump fisherman, wearing a typical fisherman's lungi with large check patterns.

'Don't know, sir, could be Elephanta Island.'

The little boat started, its engine like a zipper loudly unzipping the waters in a spreading, white-toothed V. Stanley looked around him—the big boat was quite a way off, but they too were making good progress. He could see the huge pillars of the Gateway of India looking delicate in the clear moonlight, they had already left it behind. Beyond it the hundreds of windows of the Taj Mahal hotel gleamed in a rich cluster.

He took a deep breath—he was enjoying the boat ride. All he had to do now was talk to his team, and they should be able to catch both Screwvala and the goods hidden in the Elephant's Kennel. He pulled out of his pocket his radio set, and the boatman pulled out of his lungi a gun.

'Oh,' Stanley said, understanding.

'Yes. Screwvala sir will go that way, and we will go that way,' he pointed in the opposite direction. 'Come, come fishing in the open sea with fisherman Braganza.'

The Elephant's Kennel

In the moonlight, the silver smiles of the three gods in the Trimurti shone down with heavenly serenity on the three little mortals walking past. One of them suddenly stopped and looked back at the sculpture of the gods, his beard quivering with emotion.

'Look at that!' Screwvala's voice boomed against the centuries-old rock carvings. 'It is a masterly … er, masterpiece of a master of the Hindu universe!' He took off his false beard and put it in his pocket.

The short dark man called Ramesh suddenly jumped back.

'*What* has moved you to jump?' asked Screwvala with majestic irritation.

'Look! Bullet marks against the rock!'

'Everybody knows that the Portuguese used these … *magnificent* carvings as targets for target practice—a *barbaric* practice they indulged in because they thought the carvings were … uh, barbaric.'

'Screwvala-bhai, that was hundreds of years ago, I don't think bullet marks would last this long,'

Unnikrishnan said, leaning forward to look.

Screwvala peered at the marks, too. 'As an authority on culture and sculpture,' he boomed, 'and also, uh, gun-culture, I can, uh, assure you that these marks are at least a hundred years old. They are not relevant to our business proceedings. Let us proceed on our business.'

Screwvala walked majestically on, glancing around him as if he were enjoying the moonlit night as well as the carvings. He was followed by Unnikrishnan, glancing around him with nervous jerks of his tall body, and Ramesh, last of all, crouched and ready to duck if any trouble broke out anywhere.

'Isn't that our Elephant's Kennel?' Unnikrishnan pointed at a little rickety door near the three heads of Shiva, leading to a small room.

'Yes, but this time Rustom couldn't, uh, deposit the goods there. Restoration is being, uh, conducted in this cave, and our collaborators in the Elephanta Caves Department advised us to find a different spot for our own goods, uh, good.'

'So where did Rustom bury it?'

'I have a photograph of the spot on my mobile phone. It should be fairly straightforward to find the spot …'

Stanley saw they were passing some fishing boats, their sails fluttering with silver above the dark gold shadows of their old wood, polished by the storms of wind and sea. He could see a few fishermen in them—

'No use shouting to them, men, they all friends,' Braganza said shrewdly.

'I'm Inspector Stanley.' Speaking in Konkani, he politely held out a hand. Braganza looked at it and wrinkled his nose.

'Inspector, your hand reminds me of a dead fish I caught in my nets last week,' he answered in cosy Konkani. 'Please put your gun in it, backwards, then only I take your hand.'

Stanley chuckled and did so. Braganza took the gun without touching Stanley's hand.

'Hiding such a big gun in your lungi—how do you do that men?'

Braganza was pleased at this compliment. 'It is little like learning how to wear a sari, I think. You can only if you grown up learning to do it, men.'

'Like sari, how sweet. So Braganza, Screwvala is giving you ticket out of country or what? As reward for years of hard work smuggling?'

'You smart, Inspector Stanley. How you guess?'

'You not afraid to show your face to Inspector doing naughty things, I understand what that means.' Braganza smirked. 'But look, you're a fellow Goan, so let me give you really useful tip.'

'Anh?' said Braganza, cautiously.

'This matter with your Screwvala sir and me—it is not small matter. It is big big matter—smuggling of national treasure. And *even bigger matter than that.*'

'Bigger ... than national treasure?' Braganza was looking at him closely, but without being puzzled.

Stanley was impressed. The fisherman knew that more important than knowing what could be bigger than a national treasure, was knowing if Stanley was serious.

'You see in my face, Braganza—I not fooling. This matter so big, I promise, Interpol will look for you whether you in Australia or Antarctic or Sahara desert. Just because you leave tonight make no difference.'

In the moonlight, Braganza looked into Inspector Stanley's face, and the Inspector looked back ...

After zig-zagging over the island for forty minutes without success, 'straightforward' was not the word any of the three had in mind. As they took a break on a mountainside facing the sea, a panting Screwvala suddenly pointed at the horizon.

'Look! The energy of the atom, shining with the beauty of the moon ...'

Unnikrishnan and Ramesh looked: on the distant coast of Mumbai, the dome of a nuclear reactor shone in the moonlight, its outline sharp as a scythe. Around it a few towers rose like silver spears into the sky.

'What's that?' Ramesh asked.

'Bhabha Atomic Research Centre.' Screwvala rubbed his hands gleefully and jumped up. 'Come! This inspiring glimpse of nuclear energy, uh, inspires a clear new energy in me!' The other two groaned.

After another thirty minutes, they finally came to the slope of a hill near Cave 1 where a red stone tiger with curly hair had been carved resting on his haunches, gazing at the star-filled sky and surf-speckled sea.

Screwvala stopped thankfully. He took out his mobile phone and showed it to the others: it had a picture of Rustom and someone else close to the tiger.

'That is the exact spot!' Screwvala pointed. In a heroic effort, he bent and patted it. 'It's freshly dug up … but the ground is hard. Rustom, Rustom, what a stupid place to hide the safe … it's time to dig,' he boomed to the others. He snatched the long case from Unnikrishnan, took out three shovels, gave one each to the others and started digging.

Ramesh looked surprised at the shovel. 'Bhai, I am an expert at breaking into safes. It is not in my caste to break rocks.'

Screwvala stopped digging and, leaning against his shovel, said very sweetly: 'Oh. Tell me, Ramesh, is your caste a lying, cheating and robbing caste?'

'How dare you talk like that about my caste?' Ramesh spread his chest and drew up to his full little height to tower below Screwvala. 'I belong to the highest kshatriya family! For a thousand years we have been the trusted men of kings, and have even inter-married with brahmins.'

'Oh, do you? How nice … and what is it *you* do for a living Ramesh?'

'I'm India's top *expert* in breaking into the toughest lockers in the world—'

'Meaning,' Screwvala boomed, 'you lie, and cheat, and rob! If digging up other people's money is in keeping with your caste, then digging up dirt is in keeping with your caste!'

Ramesh began digging sulkily. For all his fine words it was Screwvala who found the digging the toughest, continuously wiping his large sweating face.

After a little while, they uncovered a small metal safe, knee-high and square.

Ramesh immediately pulled it out and greedily began to finger the numbered dials on it. 'It must have something special, for you to be paying me what you are paying.'

'No, no, it doesn't have anything much,' Unnikrishnan said in a bored voice.

'Just some parts for a water purification plant,' Screwvala said equally bored.

'Okay, okay, you don't want to tell me, don't. Aha!'

Ramesh put his ear to the locker's dials, and delicately turned it half-clockwise, quarter-counter-clockwise—and the door of the safe sprung open!

'Aha!' said Unnikrishnan.

'Aha!' boomed Screwvala.

'Aha!' came a voice from the other end of the slope.

The Inspector rose from behind a tree holding a gun to Screwvala, accompanied by five policemen who also had guns.

'You!' Screwvala hissed.

'Hands up!' said Stanley, and Screwvala and his cronies raised their hands.

'How did you get so many policemen here?' Screwvala asked angrily, as if Stanley had rudely disturbed him in his own home. 'I didn't hear any motorboat behind us!'

'Mr Screwvala, your fisherman Braganza very kindly told me you would be on *this* side of island. So he brought me to *other* side of island in his motorboat, so that you could not hear. Men! Put handcuffs on the other two, and empty their pockets. I will take care of this gentleman.'

Stanley moved to Mr Screwvala and handcuffed him.

'Christ, Mr Screwvala! Your fingers are trembling, why? Ai, empty the gentleman's pockets.'

He was surprised to see Screwvala was trembling with rage and glaring furiously at *him*. Stanley was confused—after all, *he* was the policeman and Screwvala was the thief. But he put it out of his mind and hurried to the slightly-open safe door.

He closed his eyes and, taking a deep breath, opened the door fully.

Screwvala, in spite of his anger, and even though a policeman was emptying his pockets, craned his neck to look inside the open door. Unnikrishnan, too, was eager to see what was in the safe even as he was being handcuffed. 'What's inside?' he asked.

Stanley didn't speak for a moment. He was staring with dropped jaw. His eyes kept roving the walls, the bottom, the top—but the safe was empty!

Empty, when he was expecting something that deserved NX3 authorisation!

'Inspector!' Screwvala boomed.

'Ai! You're not my boss that I answer you!' Stanley snarled.

'I am an MLA—' Unnikrishnan began.

'Ai! You're a criminal now, so better be careful!' Stanley snapped. He looked at Ramesh. 'You got any dialogues to say?' Ramesh merely shook his head.

'What did you think would be inside, sir?' one of the policemen asked in Hindi.

'Parts for a water purification plant.' Inspector Stanley shook his head and laughed sadly.

'Empty?' Screwvala couldn't believe his ears. He and Unnikrishnan looked at each other, aghast. 'Empty? How can that be?'

The Inspector saw Screwvala's face had drooped. He turned towards the policeman who had searched Screwvala—

'Hey!' Screwvala snapped.

The Inspector turned back to Screwvala, and saw him seething with anger and staring searchingly at him. 'So now you're going to put me in your jail, Stanley?'

'*My* jail?' the Inspector shook his head. He turned again to the policeman. 'Show me what you found in his pocket.'

There was a very small pistol, a cell phone, a Citibank platinum credit card, the key to the Mercedes, his home keys, and a wallet which had ten one-thousand-rupee notes, a letter in code, a photograph of Scherezade and an old photo of someone who looked like Scherezade's mother.

'*Your* jail, Stanley, will be easy for me,' Screwvala sneered. 'Everyone knows that if you have the money, your jail is like a five-star hotel. I have the money. And

I'll use it, Stanley.'

'You really have no respect for the law of this land, do you?'

'The truth is, in this land the law can be bought! I do it every day. People just quote their price.'

Stanley looked at Screwvala wonderingly. 'Well, too bad for you, I don't have a price.'

'That is only because someone else has *paid* your price!' Screwvala boomed angrily.

'Shut up!' Stanley turned and raised his hand.

'Hit me! Hit me, you thug!' Screwvala shouted.

Inspector Stanley had his hand up for a long time, his face working. Then he lowered his hand.

Screwvala's face brightened. 'Stanley? Stanley,' he whispered. 'I can pay more than them—'

'Shut your mouth! The only reason I didn't hit you was your daughter! How can someone like you have a daughter like that? Her mother must have been the opposite of you, men.'

'How dare you talk about my angel of a daughter, you *traitor*! You ... ' His voice shook. Suddenly, he turned his head and his body began to shake.

Stanley walked around to face him: Screwvala was crying! 'You are strange man, Screwvala,' he said. 'Just like a Parsi actually. Even when getting arrested you a little mad—'

Unnikrishnan was looking at Screwvala, shocked.

'You will not get away with this, Stanley ... '

Screwvala was still weeping when the police boat came to take them to jail.

The Man in the Egg-shaped Cell

Every morning, the jail superintendent of Mumbai's largest jail, Arthur Road Jail, stood in the corridor where there was a little window, and watched the shadows of the prison bars grow in the light of the rising sun. He enjoyed the artistic effect.

As he was doing this on the morning after Screwvala was caught, he heard a man yelling in Gujarati. The jail superintendent had a Gujarati mother, so he understood the words: 'No! No! No! Bapa, why are you driving your own family into the sea? Women, children, look they are drowning! Bapa, their blood will be on your hands! Nooo … '

The jail superintendent was sorry to hear the racket—he did not like being disturbed in the early hours of the morning. He called out to his assistant: 'Havaldar Sampat! Who is that yelling?'

'The new prisoner, sir. Screwvala, the man who has come with Unnikrishnan, the MLA.'

'The rich man who paid big money for a separate anda cell?' The anda cells were egg-shaped cells where the more dangerous or more famous—or more moneyed—prisoners were kept, away from the barracks where hundreds slept together on the floor. 'Why is he yelling?'

'Because, sir, he is having nightmares.'

The jail superintendent thought for a moment. 'Bring him to my office.'

Soon the superintendent was at his desk and Screwvala was brought in wearing handcuffs and a prison uniform. He was unshaven and without his smart glasses, and he looked quite helpless. The jail superintendent asked the guard to let him sit.

'Will you have some tea?' he asked Screwvala in Gujarati.

'All right,' Screwvala answered carefully, in Gujarati.

The superintendent asked for the tea. Two cups came in a minute, and the Superintendent signalled to the guard to leave them alone.

'What was that yelling, Screwvala?'

'I was having nightmares, chokra. You think I'll have sweet dreams in a place like this?'

'Tell the truth, Screwvala!' The jailor put down his tea and suddenly leaned forward. 'When did you see those people being pushed into the sea? How many of them drowned? Were you involved in their murders?'

Screwvala's jaw dropped and he put his teacup down. 'What in the world are you talking about, Mr Superintendent?'

The superintendent described to Screwvala how he had been shouting in his sleep to his grandfather. 'You were remembering a time in your life when many people were being murdered.'

Screwvala groaned. 'Oh no! And you think all this is something I remember from my life time? Actually it happened one thousand years ago!'

'One *thousand* years ago?'

'I was dreaming of how my people came to India, a thousand years ago. We Parsis came to India from Persia—today's Iran—in the tenth century AD.' They continued talking in Gujarati.

The jail superintendent took a sip of his tea. 'But all this drowning?'

'Persia was conquered by the Arabs then, and everybody had to convert to their religion or be killed. We were the followers of Zarathustra, and we chose to stick to our religion. So we were treated by our Arab rulers—and by our own people, converted to the new religion—like animals. We ran and first hid in the mountains of our land, then we had to run away to the sea.

'We sailed for years till we came to India, and we were given shelter here. For a thousand years, we have lived here, practicing our own religion without any interference—except once seven hundred years ago, when Alp Khan attacked us. A few hundred years ago, we came to Mumbai, and here the Parsis have become the richest people in this land! Oh, how good India has been to my people! How wonderful Mumbai has been to us!'

'I know that the Parsis are a good and honest people,

Screwvala. But you? How good and honest have you been?' The jailor finished his tea, and reached behind him and put on the TV.

The screen filled up with furious crowds shouting, 'Traitor! Thief of love!' For the hundredth time, the whole nation saw Screwvala under heavy police escort, being stoned by a crowd chanting, 'Screwvala dhoka-vala traitor!' Chased by reporters, Screwvala ducked and scurried into Arthur Road Jail. The news ticker at the bottom of the screen read, 'Taj Letter Mastermind Arrested.'

The show cut to a different scene: a press conference that the holy men of Screwvala's community were giving, some of them wearing their phetas, the high caps that went up backward like slanted ladders. One of them was speaking into the half-dozen mikes in front of him: 'Rarely has a Parsi brought so much disgrace to the Parsi community as Keki Screwvala. All Indians recognise that we have been one of the most progressive and patriotic communities—' The caption read: 'Parsi Panchayat Excommunicates Screwvala'.

'Put it off! Put it off!' Screwvala covered his face and shook his head. 'Please, please, I can't bear it … '

The jailor took pity on him, and putting the TV off, shouted: 'Guard! Take this prisoner back to his cell!'

As Pappu, Scherezade and the blind man sat in Hassan's drawing room with Mehurnissa, Pappu once again asked himself: is Screwvala, simply, mad?

Because whenever Screwvala saw Stanley, he would begin cursing and shouting, '*He* is guilty! *He* is the one who should be arrested!'

Pappu realised that he could hear someone sniffing. He looked up and saw the sounds were coming from behind a newspaper, which Scherezade was reading.

'Scherezade!' Mehurnissa hurried to her, and Pappu followed, slowly. The blind man sat where he was, his head moving to follow what was happening.

Tears in her eyes, Scherezade buried her face in Mehurnissa's arms, and shook with sobs. Pappu picked up the paper she had been reading and saw a photograph of her father with an article:

TAJ ACCUSED 'BUYS' SOLITARY CELL

Mumbai:

Keki Screwvala and Unnikrishnan, the main accused in the Taj letter case, are now housed in the anda barrack of Arthur Road Jail.

Jail sources said their cells are normally reserved for high-security or high-profile prisoners. The notorious D-Company's leading gangsters are their neighbours—as well as gangsters N.S. Rao and Farid Bandookwala, and smuggler Abu Malik.

Unnikrishnan and Screwvala's cells are well lit, but have no fan or TV. They get the same meals as other inmates: a breakfast of upma or poha, followed by a lunch of three chapattis, a plate of dal and vegetables. Dinner consists of two chapattis and a cup-sized mound of rice. Anda cell inmates are served their meals in their cells. The barrack is guarded round the clock by ten guards.

> Questions are being raised as to why Unnikrishnan and Screwvala have been allocated the scarce anda cells, instead of being put in one of the crowded barracks where, in a space meant for 800 people, 3,000 prisoners are housed. But it is common knowledge that prisoners with political or financial clout can get special treatment in Arthur Road Jail.

'Sorry!' Scherezade declared in a voice muffled by Mehurnissa's shoulder. Pappu didn't know where to look.

The blind man said 'Beta, let us go to the next room.' Relieved, Pappu followed him out of the drawing room.

They went to the kitchen, and sat at the little table. As the blind man shook his head sadly, the maid asked them if they wanted anything to drink.

After ten minutes, Mehurnissa looked into the kitchen and said, 'Chachajan, could both of you come here please? Scherezade wants to ask you a favour.'

Surprised, they returned to the drawing room where Scherezade was sitting, her eyes dried.

'Hafiz uncle, would you and Pappu take me to Arthur Road Jail? I want to … to talk to my father.'

'Of course, beta. That is an excellent thought. When would you like to go?'

The following day, after a short ride in one of Hassan's cars, Mehurnissa, Scherezade, Pappu and the blind man got off at Saat Rasta, in front of the huge metal gates of the huge complex of Arthur Road Jail.

'What a strange, busy silence,' said the blind man, facing in the direction of the gates.

Behind the gates, it looked almost like a small fairy-tale castle that had been painted in government colours: the facade even had two towers on the sides with flags on top. There were office windows rather than prison bars. They showed their pass at the gates (Mehurnissa had arranged for one) and were let inside. Because Mehurnissa was an MLA's wife, they had two guards with them. They walked past the clean compound that they could see had been swept again and again, to the visiting room. There, waiting on one side of the partition and looking worried and tired, was Screwvala.

He eagerly rose when he saw Scherezade—but when he saw the others, he tottered back as if he'd been slapped in the face.

Scherezade saw this—the tears sprang to her eyes, and she sprang into her father's arms. 'Papa!'

'Come, Mehurnissa, Pappuji,' the blind man said, 'there must be a canteen for visitors. Let us look for it.'

They waved to Scherezade, who waved back clearly relieved that they were leaving her alone with her father.

'We'll be back in half an hour,' Mehurnissa said.

When they came back, Mr Screwvala was talking to Scherezade in low, urgent tones. He looked up at them and said something to his daughter. She turned.

Pappu was shocked to see she was looking at him angrily.

'Go away!' she cried at them. 'I'll go back home myself! Go away!'

THE TURNING OF SCHEREZADE

'Scherezade?' he cried out, surprised and confused.

'Go *away*! I'll meet you later!' she said.

'Sherry … ' he started again, and though the frown on her face softened, his voice trailed off. Pappu felt his breath grow uneven. What was happening? He felt the blind man's hand on his shoulder.

'Beta,' the blind man said softly, 'don't worry. She says she will meet you later, so she *will*.'

Mehurnissa was looking at Scherezade and Scherezade waved to her.

'Bye, Hafiz uncle,' she added.

'Khuda hafiz, beta,' he said, and his hand still on Pappu's shoulder, he gently turned.

Pappu's mind was whirling—what had Screwvala said to Scherezade? Had he told her some lies about Pappu to make her hate him? As they walked away, the blind man said softly, 'Do not be hurt. It is not you she is angry at, it is herself, her own fear … She is angry at her own shattered destiny.'

When he reached home, Pappu tried to open his school books and study for his first-term exams which were a month away. But he kept thinking, has she got back home? Ayah was there … What had her father said to her? But she would phone …

Finally, he couldn't stand it any more. He snatched his cell phone and dialled her number.

The phone rang and rang and rang. Was she out of earshot? Or did she hear it and was coming toward it, slowed down by something? Or did she pick it up, see his name, and put it down … The line got disconnected.

No, it couldn't be … Soon she'll see I called and call back, he thought.

But she didn't. Pappu couldn't sleep properly at night—why didn't she call me back? Doesn't she know I'm her friend? He remembered the way she had looked at him angrily when she had said, 'Go away!'

The following morning, when he left for school, it seemed that the school bag was not the only load on him: his heart felt heavy with the fear that he had lost a friend who had become dear to him so quickly. Had he done something he shouldn't have? Of course not, she had changed only after her talk with her father.

In class, Pigface was surrounded by students lapping up his tale: 'And then, dude, I told them to arrest the big goonda—' he stopped when he saw Pappu, and almost blushed. 'Oh, hi, Pappu!'

'Pappu!' the others immediately left Pigface and surrounded Pappu. 'Oi, the minister congratulated *him*, not Pigface! Tell us, tell us!' But just then teacher came in, and all the students went back to their places.

In the break, Pigface asked him for the latest news. Pappu told him about the visit to Arthur Road Jail.

'Cool dude! What was it like?' and Pigface was surprised when Pappu's face tightened and he turned away.

That evening again, to make up for the last few days, he studied for his exams. At night, when Ayah turned out his bedroom light, Scherezade still hadn't called.

As he was dressing for school the following day, the phone rang. It was Scherezade.

'Hello?'

'Hi,' he said, not knowing what else to say.

'I ... I saw your call day before. Sorry I couldn't call before. There's a lot on my mind.'

'That's okay,' Pappu said, though he felt his heart sinking.

'How are you?' she asked, a little stiffly.

'Okay. How are you?'

'Okay.' There was a silence. 'Pappu, I had a favour to ask you.'

'Yes?' he said eagerly. He wanted to do something for her.

'You see, Pappu, my father's housed alone in a high-security solitary cell which has only one small window. He can't see anybody else. He's ... he's lonely, quite miserable ...' Pappu didn't know what to say. She continued, 'I want to visit him more often, meeting me cheers him up. I want to help him cope. But ...'

There was a silence. Pappu cleared his throat. 'But

what, Scherezade?'

'Every time I visit I have to pay somebody a bribe. And Pappu … I … '

'Tell me, Scherezade?'

'With my father in jail, I barely have enough money to run the house,' she said this with a suddenly crisp voice. 'So would it be possible for you to ask Stanley Uncle to give me a letter? If he, as Inspector, gave me a letter saying that I should be allowed to visit my father more often, I won't have to … to … pay … ' her crispness crumbled.

Pappu could hear in her voice the suffering of someone for whom the whole world was suddenly uncertain. He suddenly realised, with a shock, that she could understand his silence to mean 'No'.

'Of course! Of course!' he said quickly.

'Oh thank you, Pappu! Thank you so much.'

There was another silence. 'I'll talk to the Inspector right away. You have helped us so much, I'm sure he'll agree.'

Pappu phoned the Inspector at once, and he agreed at once. 'She has helped us so much men, of course.'

After school the following day, Pappu collected the letter from Stanley's police station, and then went straight to Scherezade's house to give it to her.

Her ayah opened the door, and her face brightened when she saw Pappu. She called Scherezade, and they sat at the dining table where Janaki-bai served them cold drinks.

Scherezade opened the letter and read it.

'Thank you. I'm enormously grateful!' she said. Her voice sounded strange to his ears again, like it had sounded when she had first come to his bungalow. He couldn't believe that was only a few days ago!

'Scherezade, is there any other way in which I can help you?'

'You already have, Pappu, thank you,' she held the letter up. 'This letter is so … precious. I have to go now, for something important. But we'll talk soon?'

Pappu realised their meeting had ended. At the door, she thanked him again, squeezed his hand, and he left feeling somehow cheated. Later, he was to remember that feeling …

·

A keening ambulance was speeding through Mumbai's roads with Scherezade in it, her face covered with an oxygen mask, her eyes wide and scared. But the traffic grew thicker, and suddenly the ambulance was hemmed in by huge trucks on all sides, unable to move forward. Inside, Scherezade's eyes grew wider … her breathing became harder, tighter, more and more difficult … The driver blew the horn again, and again—in fact, the horn blew in a regular beat—it sounded like a doorbell … it *was* a doorbell …

Pappu awoke from the nightmare in a panic. He looked at the clock: it was 8.15 am. He should have woken up an hour ago to get ready for school. He rubbed his eyes and remembered: it was Founder's Day holiday at school.

The doorbell rang again. 'Coming, coming,' he heard Ayah calling out. Suddenly he wasn't feeling sleepy any more. He rubbed his eyes some more, washed his face and went into the drawing room.

Ayah had let Stanley in. He was unshaved, and already looked exhausted though it was early morning.

When he saw Pappu he said: 'Screwvala's … Screwvala … ' He was panting.

'What? Tell me, Inspector!'

'He's run away!'

'What!'

'Escaped. This could be the end of my career, men.'

Pappu's heart suddenly filled with dread of a kind he had never felt before. 'Why?'

'Because of how he escaped.'

The dread deepened. 'How did he escape?' he asked.

Instead of answering, Stanley looked around the drawing room as if they might be hiding something.

'Where's Scherezade, men?'

Pappu felt his breath almost stop.

THE PRINCESS OF FORGERIES

'Where's Scherezade, men?' Stanley asked again.

'What you rushing early morning-morning like this and talking to Pappu like that?' Ayah said to Stanley in Mumbaiya.

'I don't know,' Pappu answered Stanley. 'She should be at her home?'

Stanley shook his head. 'My men have checked, only her ayah is home. Ai! Put on the TV!'

Pappu switched on the large set in the drawing room. At the bottom of the screen it said: 'FORGED LETTER HELPS BOTH TAJ ACCUSED ESCAPE!'

With pictures of Arthur Road Jail flashing on the screen, a reporter said: 'In a dramatic development Keki Screwvala, the alleged mastermind of the Taj letter theft, escaped with MLA Unnikrishnan, his accomplice, from his high-security Arthur Road Jail cell last night.

'Prison guards report that at 11.30 pm, three men in police uniforms reported to the assistant jail superintendent with a letter on official police letterhead, authorising the transfer of Mr Screwvala and Mr

Unnikrishnan to Pune Jail. The two prisoners were immediately handed into the custody of the three supposed policemen. Later, jail authorities realised that the letterhead was fake.' They showed a close-up of the letter, and Stanley groaned.

The reporter asked the jail superintendent: 'Sir, how could your men be so easily taken in by a forgery?'

'The letter had Inspector Stanley Coelho's signature who is the in-charge of the case,' the superintendent replied. 'But we will catch him soon. We are launching a nation-wide hunt.'

With another groan, Stanley sank into the long sofa. Ayah, who had been watching all this, now seemed to understand some more. 'I'll get some tea!' she said worriedly, and bustled away.

Inspector Stanley Coelho's signature! Pappu, too, sank into the sofa. Had Scherezade given the forgers the inspector's signature that she got from Pappu? It sounded like it. But ... they could have got that signature from someone else as well, even if she weren't involved. No ... he must not suspect her. It would be unfair. Or ...

'BREAKING NEWS!' the TV flashed. 'TAJ LETTER ON DISPLAY A COPY!'

A handsome newsreader appeared on the screen: 'While investigating an unrelated story, this channel has accidentally come across evidence that the famous Taj letter on display in the Prince of Wales Museum is a high-quality forgery, an exact replica of the original.' They showed some footage of the Taj letter. 'What's more, our investigative reporters have found that the government archaeologist who certified the letter as genuine was ordered by someone high-up in the government to falsify his report. In the meantime Keki Screwvala,' they showed some old footage of Mr Screwvala, 'the prime accused in the Taj letter case, is still on the run. This raises questions that perhaps someone at a senior level in the government might have also had a hand in Keki Screwvala's escape.'

Pappu's world began to swim around him. It was Scherezade who had got hold of Inspector Stanley's signature—with *Pappu's* help! It was Scherezade who had 'helped' him and Stanley get the 'genuine' Taj letter—now exposed as being a fake! It was Scherezade … he couldn't complete the thought. It kept going round and round in his head, strangling him …

'Christ!' he heard Stanley beside him breathe deeply. 'That Scherezade … was she planning to from the start? I can't believe it! But for some reason she changed. Pappu, you have any idea where Screwvala might be hiding? Tell me, men—' He put his hand on Pappu's shoulder and looked into his face, pleadingly.

And Pappu felt even more afraid, seeing so much fear in Inspector Stanley's strong face. 'I don't know, Inspector,' he managed to stutter. The Inspector's hand slid from his shoulder, and he looked away. 'Of course, you don't … '

The doorbell rang. Pappu jumped—he knocked one of his mother's precious crystal statuettes, and it shattered on the floor. They heard Ayah's cry from the kitchen: 'What broke? I'm just coming, the tea is boiling over!'

The blind man was at the door, wiping his wet sandals against the door mat. 'Pappuji,' he said, recognising his sound.

Pappu was surprised at how dark it was outside. The sky above was hidden in low clouds, and though it wasn't raining now Pappu could see it had been raining heavily through the night.

'Hafiz Chacha ...'

'Beta, early this morning Hassan came home very worried. He had some shocking news—' At that moment Stanley's cell phone rang.

'Yessir? Yessir!' His face turned grey, and he put his cell off with a final 'Yessir!'

'What happened?' Pappu asked.

Stanley got up and gave the blind man a tired, half-hearted wave. The blind man stood listening gravely.

'Commissioner Talwar has called me to a high-level meeting. They will ask me how I got the fake Taj letter. They will ask me how the forgers could have got my signature. I think it's all over for me, men. All finished.'

Pappu felt tears well up—he bent to gather up the shattered crystal. He was thinking, it can't be Scherezade! She can't have betrayed me! She can't have betrayed Stanley!

'There is someone high-up behind everything—the same people who suspended me at Akash Ganga. The Commissioner could even be involved,' Stanley shook his head helplessly. 'My head is just spinning.'

Ayah rushed in: 'What broke? What broke?' She shushed Pappu away from the broken crystal.

Stanley managed a 'Khuda hafiz, Chacha' to the blind man and rushed out. Ayah shook her head, clucking disapprovingly.

'Difficult times have come for him,' the blind man said sadly. 'He is the son of a superb musician …'

'I broke it, Ayah,' Pappu said. She looked at him, and without stopping her sweeping put his head to her bosom. 'Don't worry, Chotu, it happens. Chacha, good you come, just in time for tea.'

'Thank you, Aunty.' He turned to Pappu. 'So you have heard about Scherezade's father's escape?'

'Yes.' Pappu gave him the latest news, that the Taj letter in the museum was a fake, and there was someone in the government who was involved.

'Y'Allah!' the blind man breathed. 'Like a storm it goes round and round …'

Ayah served the blind man the tea she had prepared for Stanley.

'A storm is coming,' he said. 'I can feel it on my skin.' Pappu looked out of the window—it was still quite dark.

'Where is Scherezade?' the blind man asked.

Pappu shook his head. He found himself holding his breath as the blind man's eyes moved around as if looking at some terrifying secret only he could see. Scherezade! Where—who is Scherezade really, Pappu wondered.

'Perhaps you should phone Scherezade, beta,' the

blind man said.

Pappu stupidly dialled her, putting the TV on mute. It rang and rang and rang and got disconnected because no one answered. Out of respect for the blind man, Pappu switched the TV on to a Hindi news channel.

A weather lady was saying, 'An unusually large cloud formation has been spotted and should hit Mumbai in twenty-four hours. Heavy, abnormal rains are likely in the next twenty-four to forty-eight hours —'

His cell phone rang. He put the TV on mute and answered it unthinkingly. At first, he could only hear the hubbub of a busy, packed street—it was so early in the morning, his first thought was, it must be Daddy or Mummy from abroad. But then he heard people talking, loudly, in Hindi.

'Hello?' he said.

'How are you, Pappu?' asked Scherezade softly.

FATHER AND DAUGHTER

He didn't know what to say.

'Hello?' Scherezade asked again. 'Pappu?'

Pappu couldn't speak. Her voice suddenly filled him with a raging fury.

'Pappu?' her voice pleaded in his ear.

Pappu put the cell phone in the blind man's hand. 'It's Scherezade.' The blind man, taken aback, put the phone to his ear.

'Yes, Scherezade beti? … I am well, Scherezade beti, how are you? … hmm … Here, speak to him.' The blind man turned to Pappu. 'Beta, she wants to talk to you.'

Pappu put the TV off and took the phone.

She started off briskly: 'Pappu, I wanted to tell you … you might think that I've betrayed you. But I haven't, I promise. And I'll soon prove it.' Her voice grew gentler again. 'I wanted you to know, so I called you as soon as I could. I promise you, I haven't betrayed you. Or the Inspector.'

Pappu didn't know what to say.

'I've got to run. We'll meet again, soon. And you'll know that I didn't cheat you. Goodbye.' With the 'goodbye', her voice was suddenly brisk again.

He thought of remaining silent, but then some impulse of politeness—maybe of needing to hold on to the hope that there was still a chance that he hadn't been betrayed, forced him to answer 'Goodbye.'

And then he heard a voice behind her, in the middle of the street's hullabaloo: 'Scherezade, come upstairs.'

It was Screwvala's boom.

She disconnected. Pappu slowly put his phone down—and he saw that the blind man was listening to *him,* Pappu, and what he was doing.

There was a silence.

'Beta, it is possible that Scherezade is with her father now,' the blind man said.

After a while Pappu said, 'I heard her father calling her upstairs.'

There was another silence. Pappu thought, where could she be speaking from?

'Crawford Market,' the blind man said, as if reading his mind. 'You heard the voices of people behind her? It was the shopkeepers of Crawford Market, setting up their stalls of fruit and crockery.'

Crawford Market, of all places! The huge chaotic market for vegetables and fruit, and little electronic goods, and small exotic animals! What could she be doing there with her father?

'Upstairs could mean one of the municipality rooms in the Crawford Market building,' the blind man said.

'It is a strange place, for them to be.'

They both sat in silence for a few minutes.

'Shall we go, Pappuji? You and I? Perhaps they will still be there, perhaps not.'

'To Crawford Market?'

'Yes.'

Pappu tried to phone Stanley, but couldn't get through. The blind man asked Pappu to phone Hassan, but there was no answer from his phone. So they called Mehurnissa, and left a message with her for Hassan: that they had found Screwvala was somewhere 'upstairs' at Crawford Market, and they were going there.

After a quick wash, Pappu called for a taxi. The blind man rolled his unseeing eyes heavenward: 'Mian, why don't we take a bus? It won't take that much longer.'

'Chacha, we don't know how long they will be there. It will take time to catch a bus.'

Halfway through their journey, the blind man said, 'I was going to bring my umbrella but it was broken.' Pappu looked out: the grey clouds above were getting heavier and darker. In his shock, he had forgotten to bring his umbrella.

Crawford Market is a hundred-year-old, three-storey building with a central watch tower, two wings and a lot of bustle. It looks confused about whether it is a stone railway station, a medieval church, a Victorian university building, a fairy-tale castle—or just an old brown fort. It has some round windows with white and black stones around them, like cart wheels with white and black spokes. Especially on the ground floor, it bustles with a bazaar's confusion, filth and grime.

It had taken them over an hour to reach the market, it was 10.30. As they came closer Pappu smelt a giant dank sweet smell—was it the lowering dark clouds? No, the blind man said, that was hay and filth.

'They must be there—if they have not gone by now.' The blind man pointed, without looking up, at the big balconies and windows of the building's first floor.

As they entered the main lobby, it began to drizzle, but no one in the crowds seemed to notice. Pappu could see multi-storeyed stalls, rising in steps with tall piles of goods that you expected would fall any minute. The shopkeepers were comfortably perched, some on the third storey, some on the second, of their stalls. On the ground, their assistants were bargaining with shoppers secretly, with fingers hidden in a handshake. All the time there was noise, bustle, business and tumult.

'What is upstairs, Chacha?'

'Offices of Mumbai municipality's bazaar department. And the clock room. Come Pappuji, let us go up and look. There are so many people there, it will be safe. Take me to the door at the bottom of the clock tower, and we'll climb up the stairs.'

He led the blind man through the muck and clamour, avoiding the slow haughty servants of millionaires buying their masters' groceries for the week, the quick eager porters badgering shoppers to hire them, and even some hotel staff, in their shiny clean expensive uniforms, placing orders for their two hundred and fifty rooms of foreigners. The gas lamps on the sides made it seem that the Crawford building was still living in the 1800s. Some of the sounds were animal squeals—Pappu saw in one corner the meat market where animals had been cruelly squeezed into small cages. He quickly looked away.

They entered the large clock tower and walked up the dark stairs. Outside, the drizzle sounded heavier.

The stone stairs were soft with filth, and Pappu put his hand on his nose to protect himself from the bad air. But the blind man did not seem troubled. The racket outside had become a soft pleasant hubbub here.

On the first floor, there was a large roomy corridor, lined with a long wooden bench above which were windows, letting the grey rainy light in. It was crowded with people who seemed to be in some kind of queue for the office to their left. On the right was a door with a sign: 'Under Repair. BMC Bazaar Department.' In the middle, the spiral staircase went up; when Pappu described the scene to the blind man, he said that the stairs led up to the clock room.

They were wondering what to do when suddenly, the 'Under Repair' sign shook, the door opened and a peon came out who looked familiar. Pappu remembered: he was one of Hassan's men! The peon called someone, and Hassan appeared from the end of the corridor, wearing a white pathani kurta pajamas. He went to the 'Under Repair' door.

'Hassan uncle!' Pappu whispered to the blind man, and leading him through the crowd by the wrist touched Hassan on the shoulder.

Hassan stopped in his tracks. 'Chachajaan! Pappu!' he whispered. He gestured to them to follow as he went through the door, followed by two men. Both were tall and very hefty, and were dressed in dark clothes. The peon half-shut the door behind them, and Pappu and the blind man stood inside this half-shut door.

It was a large, dark room, dimly lit by partly boarded windows flickering with rain.

'Hassan!' the blind man said softly. 'Mehurnissa gave you our message?'

'Yes, I've got some plainclothes policemen with me,' he pointed at the two big men. He stood just inside the door, and his body prevented Pappu from looking inside. 'You should go back, it is not safe. I will take care of things here.'

'Hassan uncle, I have to meet Scherezade,' Pappu said firmly, though his heart was beating.

Hassan looked at him, and the blind man listened carefully to the silence between them. Pappu felt his cheeks burn but he looked back, up. He could see Hassan getting angry.

Then the blind man spoke: 'Hassan beta, this Pappuji is a very determined boy. And looking at it, you will have to admit that you and I reached here only because of him. How can we now force him to go?'

Hassan looked from Pappu to his uncle and back. He shook his head unhappily—and moved away, so that Pappu finally could see the room.

When his eyes got used to the dim light, he saw that it was a cross between a godown and a government office. Deep inside a scaffolding supported a high crumbling ceiling. Next to the scaffolding, though clear of it, were piles of boxes of 'Made in China' webcams reaching halfway to the ceiling. In another corner, there was an old office desk, with a battered executive chair behind it, and two smaller chairs in front. Behind the desk the partly-boarded windows were almost opaque with muck and bird shit. In one wall was a thin wooden door, on either side of which were an old almirah and divan. Everything smelt damp. Outside, they could hear the rain falling heavily. Though the room was large, it looked crowded.

'Where are we, Hassan my boy?' the blind man asked. 'We phone you, and when we reach you already have a room!'

'Chachajaan this is Screwvala's hideout. When I got your message from Mehurnissa I immediately called the BMC bazaar department in-charge here, who I know. I described Scherezade to him—he had noticed her already, it is very unusual for her kind of person to come and go from the first floor of Crawford Market. He told me on the phone that Screwvala and Scherezade had just left in an old Fiat car—this was thirty minutes ago.'

'So this is an ambush for Screwvala when he comes back?' asked the blind man.

Hassan hesitated: 'Yes. That is why, Chachajaan, it

is best for the child not to be here.'

The blind man sighed and turned toward Pappu. 'We must admit he is right, beta. This is no place—'

'Chachajaan!' Hassan whispered urgently.

Somebody was knocking at the outer door. He opened it carefully, put his head out to listen to someone outside and then asked, 'He's alone?' He shut the door and said, 'Screwvala is on his way up. Please you two, keep quiet and stand in this corner.' Hassan and a policeman flattened themselves against the wall behind the door.

Someone turned a key at the outer door, and the hubbub of the crowd outside wafted in as the door opened. And Screwvala came in.

He first saw Pappu and the blind man, and his jaw fell. The policeman and Hassan moved at once to hold him down.

Screwvala looked at Pappu and yelled: 'Help me boy! Don't you understand—' Hassan put his hand on his mouth, and the policemen took out a hanky and tied it on his mouth.

'I don't think anyone outside heard him, they're quite busy,' Hassan panted.

Screwvala struggled, but the policeman suddenly took out a pistol and pointed it at him. Pappu was shocked, and so was Screwvala—he stopped struggling. The policeman took Screwvala's cell phone.

Outside, the rain was drumming louder than ever.

They put Screwvala in one of the small chairs in front of the desk, and Hassan bent over him pleasantly.

'Where is the real Taj letter?'

Screwvala's whole body jumped, as if he was trying to spit through his gag.

One of the policemen made a warning sound. They looked at him, and he pointed to the door. There were knocking sounds, Pappu could tell they were coded: *Tock-[beat]-tock-[beat]-tock-tock-tick.*

Hassan opened the door quickly, allowing in the sound of the crowd and non-stop rain, and a small man shot in. Hassan shut the door quickly.

'Hassanbhai! How are you!' He was wiry, and dressed in yellow pants, dark glasses, a red cap and black leather jacket. His slightly wrinkled face had a thin pencil-line moustache, and he looked like an over-age film hero, like a younger Dev Anand.

'Commander!'

'Commander?' the blind man almost jumped at the name. Pappu remembered the blind man's story—Commander was the name of one of the two gang leaders who had first stolen the Taj letter!

Hassan looked at Pappu and winked. Pappu whispered to the blind man, 'Chacha, Hassan uncle is signalling that he's playing a game.'

'Let us go to the next room, Commander,' Hassan said, pointing at the door. Commander laughed and as they walked to the next room, he looked at Pappu and the blind man.

'They were the ones who found Screwvala?'

'Yes.'

'And have you got the Taj letter yet?'

'Not yet, but we will very soon, I guarantee you.' Hassan shut the door behind as he and Commander entered the next room. Commander gave a big laugh, and they could hear him shout in delight: 'Hahaha! They don't know the game we're playing is much bigger! So when are we meeting the American?'

Hassan said something in a low voice, they couldn't hear his answer. Commander stopped laughing: there were sounds of a scuffle in the next room, and then what seemed a muffled gunshot. One of the policemen ran toward the door as it opened and out came Hassan, carrying a gun with a silencer.

'Hassan!' the blind man cried out, as if he recognised him from the sound. 'What happened?'

'I killed him,' Hassan said to the policeman. The policeman nodded approvingly.

'This is the same Commander who first stole the Taj letter with Ikka? Who had his men kill Michael?' the blind man asked.

'Yes,' Hassan answered.

'Oh! And he tried to kill you? Good, you won.'

Hassan looked at the blind man in a strangely pitying way. 'Chachajaan—'

Just then the policeman by the door raised his arm, and Hassan became silent. He looked at the blind man, but he had heard the silence and nodded with his finger on his lips.

They again heard a key turn in the lock outside the door, and Scherezade opened the door. She was looking out to make sure no one had followed her, and carried a dripping umbrella in one hand and a packet in the other.

As she shut the door, she turned to see Hassan holding a gun to her father's head. She gasped sharply, her shoulders spiked in shock, and she dropped what she was holding.

'Both of you will keep quiet, or one of you will get hurt,' Hassan said to the father and daughter. Scherezade remained frozen.

'Understand?' Hassan asked again, and she nodded.

Pappu's heart sank. Just then Scherezade saw him and the blind man. She didn't show any reaction.

'Hassan,' the blind man said quietly. 'What is this happening?'

Hassan sighed. 'Chachajaan, let us go to the other room and talk.'

And he led the blind man to the thin wooden door.

The Secret of the Taj Letter

Pappu could hear their voices, but not what was being said—the rain was falling steadily, without any gaps, and the uncle and nephew spoke in low tones. One policeman took Scherezade's cell phone. Pappu looked at Scherezade: she was looking at him and slowly shaking her head, as if trying to tell him that no, she was not guilty. She then looked at Screwvala, and father and daughter exchanged a long, agonised look.

'How have you been, Pappu?' Scherezade asked him in a normal voice. Pappu realised she was pretending, being careful in front of the men with the gun.

'I am okay ...' Pappu answered casually, careful not to look at the policemen.

One was chewing paan, and both looked dully on at their English conversation, which they did not seem to understand.

'I did help my father escape with the Inspector's signature, Pappu,' she suddenly was quite crisp—Pappu could hear a quavering under it, but the policemen did not seem to notice. 'But I'm sure you'll *forgive* me when you learn why.' Her voice was gentle again. 'You see, my father is innocent. Or at least he did not do anything wrong. He did whatever he did out of love for our country, out of patriotism.'

Pappu looked at the gagged Mr Screwvala, who nodded slowly.

'How can it be?' Pappu asked, not looking at Mr Screwvala too long, so as not to attract the attention of the two men.

'It is true that my father is not a very honest man,' Scherezade said without looking at her father. 'He deals in shady art. And I was beginning to think he had become a traitor as well. So I helped you catch him. But when I met him in Arthur Road Jail, he told me his story.

'A year ago, in one of his shady deals he learnt that a scientist working at the Bhabha Atomic Research Centre had illegally got hold of some nucl—*nuke* parts,' she looked at the policemen. 'The scientist lived in Kenilworth Building—you know, Pappu, we were wondering about Kenilworth? Well, yesterday I saw it and it has a board saying, Residential Apartment of Government of India, Department of Atomic Energy. It is built on land donated to the government by Dr Homi Bhabha.'

So that's the connection! Pappu thought.

'Papa learnt that the scientist was planning with someone powerful in the government to smuggle the … *nuke* parts to a foreign country for a hundred crore rupees. Papa was worried. He discovered that he was a patriot after all. Especially when he learnt that these parts were going to be sold to … Persia, he knew he had to stop it. *Persia,*' she repeated, eyes flickering towards the two men, and Pappu understood she meant Iran but said Persia because it was a more difficult word to recognise.

'Why did he want to stop specially to Ira—uh, Persia?' he asked her. He looked at Mr Screwvala, who was looking straight at him. Pappu remembered reading about Iran's nuclear programme in the newspapers. He looked at their two guards and saw they were sharing the earphones of a cell phone, perhaps listening to FM—they had obviously decided that it was only children talking so it was all right. In the next room, too, they were talking. Pappu could not remember ever hearing rain that was so non-stop.

Scherezade sighed. 'You know I am a Parsi, Pappu. Our religion is Zoroastrianism. A thousand years ago, the Arabs conquered our homeland. They threatened to slaughter us unless we converted to their religion. We refused. Most … Persians did convert, and they treated us Zoroastrians like animals until we were forced to run away. We found shelter in this country, where we have lived and prospered without fear. Papa believes nuke power in the hands of such a people would be dangerous for the whole world.'

'But why didn't your father simply go to the police?'

'Remember what you told me about Akash Ganga, Pappu? My father knew that the police were involved, he even thought Inspector Stanley was involved.'

'They were involved in smuggling out stolen nucle—nuke parts?'

'Most of them thought they were involved in just helping to smuggle out the … the *letter*.' Now she was talking about the Taj letter. 'But the person they were helping, someone high-up in the government, knew that with the *letter* the American was also going to take out of the country the stolen nuke parts. You see, this powerful person in the government is the mastermind of the hundred-crore nuke deal. And he knew that to smuggle anything out of the country he had to bribe customs officials and policemen. But he also knew that nobody would take his bribes to help him smuggle out nuke parts, that would be too risky. So this powerful person was using the *letter* as a cover—and many policemen and customs people took bribes and helped him.

'Papa did everything he could to stop the smuggling of the nukes. He got hold of the Taj—the *letter*, from Haribhai. He also stole the safe from the scientist's house but he found it was empty, the nuke parts had already been stolen. But Papa knew that as long as he had the … letter, it would be difficult to smuggle out the nuke parts. Because so many people had taken bribes to help smuggle *only the letter* out. No letter to smuggle abroad, no help. So Papa made it difficult for the nuke thief to steal the letter from him by having one of his shady artists make two forgeries of it, and hiding the original. I innocently gave the Inspector a forgery—'

'Why did the government expert certify that the

forged letter was the original?'

'We think he was forced to by the nuke deal's mastermind, who is very senior in the government. He now wanted to keep the genuine letter a matter between himself and Papa. He knew that if the press found out the letter in the museum was a fake, there would be a national scandal—that would make it more difficult for him to play his game.'

'And this powerful person in government is …' asked Pappu.

Before she could answer, the voices in the next room grew louder. Pappu looked at the two policemen—were they policemen? The way they held their guns at Screwvala, the way they looked at Scherezade …

'Hassan!' he heard the blind man cry out, as if he were wounded. 'What are you saying!'

'Chachajaan, the American is coming for something more valuable than the Taj letter. He is coming for the nuclear parts!'

'What are you saying!'

'The babus in the government are helping me because they think I am smuggling only the Taj letter. They wouldn't help if they knew we were smuggling nuclear parts to Iran—that would be too big, too dangerous.'

'Nuclear parts to Iran? …' his next words were lost. Then his voice rose again. 'ARE YOU MAD? You are doing this for money?'

'Big money. *And* for the Jihaad, Chachajaan!'

'Laholvillakuvath!' they heard the blind man shout. There were sounds of something being hit—Pappu started up but a policeman pointed a gun at him.

'Chachajaan, give me your cane—aargh! STOP!' There was the sound of scuffling, and the blind man cursing.

Then the cursing stopped, the door opened, and Hassan came out holding the blind man on whose mouth he had tied a gag.

'Tie him up and tighten his gag,' Hassan told one of the policemen angrily. He was panting, and his face was flushed. The policeman took the blind man to one of the divans and did so.

Hassan sat down in the chair behind the desk, panting, angry, brooding. He did not seem to be aware of the others staring at him.

Finally, he burst out angrily: 'Why am I wasting my energy getting angry? Chachajaan, you are a beggar. You have not made anything of your life. Why? Because you are a man who does not know anything, but you feel everything. And you show whatever you feel. If I had been in your place just now, do you think I would have spoken my mind to Hassan'—he pointed at himself—'when he was holding a gun? No. I would have hidden my true feelings. I would have won the trust of the man with the gun, and then later escaped.'

The blind man made a scornful movement of his body but he was gagged. Hassan looked at him, and, shaking his head, laughed.

'You see, Chachajaan, I have been involved in this matter long before you entered the picture. It was I who contracted Commander and Ikka to get the Taj letter. If the two idiots hadn't fought, if that stupid Commander hadn't murdered Michael, I would have got the Taj letter the next day. It was I who had Inspector Stanley suspended on the terrace of Akash Ganga. It was I who spoke to Pappu's father to keep you out of his home.'

'Why should my father have listened to you?' Pappu asked, with a strange ring in his voice.

'I told him I would get his exporter's licence cancelled.'

Pappu was speechless.

Hassan turned to Screwvala: 'And you, mad bawa. It was I who had the nuclear parts stolen from Kenilworth.'

One of the policemen said, 'What a coincidence that uncle and nephew's paths should meet like that!'

'Coincidence? No, Mehfooz, not a coincidence. I have thought about it. Over twenty years I have become a big fish in this dirty pond that is Mumbai. Coincidences like this keep happening to me. I've realised this is because … the big fish moves and makes waves in the whole pond. The thrashing of its body makes the water one big water current leading to itself. So it is a law of nature that all things automatically come to the gullet of the big fish. Everyone who comes into Mumbai will get caught in the waves I make—and then, if they know me—like you do, Chachajaan—they will come to me for help because I have already made it impossible for these matters to move without me.' Hassan looked at his uncle for a little longer.

'Whatever we do for the Jihaad, Chachajaan, will count for us in Heaven. The bigger the sacrifice, the more Allah will be pleased. What bigger sacrifice can there be than family? And Chachajaan, *you* are *family* … ' His eyes gleamed with a love for his uncle—and with an even greater love for his *own* eternal reward!

He shook himself and turned to his policemen. 'We still need the real Taj letter. Take his gag off.' Hassan gestured to Mr Screwvala, and then pointed his silencer-mounted gun at Scherezade. 'Tell me where is the letter or right now I will make your daughter suffer.'

Screwvala slumped tiredly but didn't speak. Hassan shut one eye and looked through the sights of his gun as if he were carefully aiming at Scherezade's arm.

'Okay, okay, I'll tell,' Screwvala said in a tired voice.

The Great Mumbai Flood

The real Taj letter, Screwvala said, lay in the store room of a struggling artist in the faraway suburb of Andheri West. This was the same artist who had made the forgeries of the letter.

'Men,' Hassan said to his policemen, 'we will have to take this whole lot to Andheri.'

'Boss, why don't we leave them here and take only Screwvala?'

'Arre fool, Unnikrishnan escaped too, suppose he comes here and frees them? You, take the boy's phone.' A man went through Pappu's pockets and took his cell.

Hassan was dialling on his cell phone, but wasn't getting through. Finally, after much cursing at the mobile networks, he succeeded.

'Dawkins? Yes, I have letter and nuclears both.' He spoke a slow, careful English. 'It will take me some only few hours to collect nuclears from my godown … Okay, Dawkins, we meets at five o' clock at our same place—hain? From your man at Mahalaxmi Station? … Definitely, it's okay. ' He disconnected and turned to Mehfooz. 'Dawkins wants us to also bring him an envelope from his man at Mahalaxmi Station. You recognise him, no?'

Mehfooz nodded.

'Good! Good!' Hassan now sounded quite cheerful. 'Soon all the bribed policemen, crooked politicians, everyone will think that they helped in the sale of the Taj letter, never knowing that they were part of a hundred crore nuclear export to the faithful.'

'Bismillah, boss.'

At this, the blind man heaved and snorted under his gag. Pappu felt a chill in his bones, a breathlessness in his chest. Hassan obviously did not expect them to be alive to tell the tale.

Hassan ignored his uncle and, chuckling very loudly at Mehfooz, dialled another number. 'Ghani, good news,' he spoke in Hindustani. 'We are getting nuclears out today ... What?' He listened, and his face grew thoughtful. 'We will come at once.' He disconnected and looked at the window, darkened by rain and cloud.

'Brother, we need to go to the godown fast,' he said to his men. 'It is a few feet below the ground, and Ghani says that with this heavy rain, it might be drowned out in a few hours.'

'I have just heard on FM that trains are delayed,' one of the policemen said.

'What!' Hassan's forehead creased in angry thought. Every year, on the first day of heavy rains Mumbai's unrepaired old drains choked up, the roads flooded, and there were traffic jams and inconvenience all over.

But even on these days trains were seldom delayed.

'Ghani gets worried very easily,' another said. 'Even in heavy monsoon we had a little flooding, but we managed. This is not the heavy monsoon month.'

'True,' Hassan said, 'but Ghani is not such a fool. It has been raining non-stop since last night.' He looked at the windows again. 'Let us go *fast,* get the letter and get the nuclear parts out. Mehfooz …' Hassan jerked his chin at him, and Mehfooz took out some strips of cloth from his pocket and tied them to Pappu's and Scherezade's mouths.

His men stood all their prisoners in a line near the door and first tied each person's two hands together, and then all the prisoners together at the hands by a long rope. They took out from a bag some black hoods and two huge shiny badges—Pappu could see they were police badges.

'Now listen everyone,' Hassan said to them. 'You will walk in a straight line, behind each other. My men are going to walk with police badges, and if any of you becomes difficult, they will hurt you—and someone you care for. Concentrate on the heels of the person in front of you, you will be able to see that much.' He nodded to his men, who covered them with black hoods.

From below his hood Pappu could see the heels of the blind man, who was being held tightly by the arm by Hassan.

The door opened—a blast of wet wind came in, perhaps some windows had been opened. He sensed that the crowd of waiting people had thinned.

'Police! Make way, police taking arrested culprits,' Hassan called out as his prisoners were carefully hurried down the stairs and out of Crawford Market. 'Mehfooz don't wave your gun so much you idiot, *you* are the *police*!'

Downstairs, as the cold rain shocked them through their clothes, Pappu could see his feet walking through all kinds of other feet, until they came to some wheels. Hassan said:

'Take the girl and the blind man in the jeep.' Pappu felt the long rope connecting them being untied and he was led into a car and sat down awkwardly. The doors slammed shut and the air conditioner was put on.

'Remove their hoods,' Hassan said. 'If we get stuck in a traffic jam, I don't want people to see shapes of people with hoods. They are safely gagged anyway.'

When Pappu's hood was removed he saw they were in a Maruti Zen with tinted windows. He was sitting next to Mr Screwvala and the goonda called Mehfooz. Hassan's peon sat in the driver's seat, Hassan sat next to him, and over their shoulders Pappu could see a jeep in which he tried to make out the shapes of Scherezade and the blind man.

Behind Crawford Market is Mumbai's longest flyover. They soared past countless second-floor windows, a temple, schools and marketplaces on tyres hissing smoothly on rain water. It was normally a beautiful ride but today …

Pappu suddenly felt like he did in school when he was in big trouble … Only worse, because the trouble he was in was much bigger. His breathing become irregular, as if his heart were a small suffocating box. He looked at Mr Screwvala, but he was staring ahead impassively. He looked at Hassan, wondering what he was planning for all of them. Hassan was staring fixedly at his uncle's back in the jeep in front.

They made quick progress to Mahalaxmi Station—progress which struck terror in Pappu's heart: everything that Hassan did seemed to go so smoothly. The vehicles stopped at the station and Hassan said, 'Mehfooz, just go down and get the parcel.'

'Yes boss.'

Pappu blurted out: 'I need to go, too! To … to the bathroom.'

Hassan looked at him. 'Okay. But if you do anything funny, Pappu, my man here will *kill* you, and then we will just carry on. I promise. You understand?'

Pappu found it difficult to bear Hassan's face, which he had thought of as a friend's, looking at him with this cool, frightening rage. But he finally caught his breath and managed to nod. Hassan told Mehfooz to tie Pappu's hand to his own, and as he did so, Pappu tried to calm himself with his breath.

They set out holding hands with the rope hidden in Mehfooz's sleeve.

Even in the worst peak hour, Pappu had never seen a railway station as crowded as Mahalaxmi Station. From edge to edge, huge crowds stood densely, motionlessly, covering almost every square inch of the platform. As Mehfooz dragged him, he saw that according to the electronic signboard, the 'next' train was forty-five minutes ago.

Dawkins' man worked at Mahalaxmi Station's magazine stall: he asked Mehfooz to wait ten minutes. Mehfooz used the ten minutes to lead Pappu to the bathroom. Not a single train came to the platform in that time—something Pappu had never seen before. The packed crowds looked at the empty tracks, talking to each other aimlessly. It looked like the end of the world to Pappu: everyone crowded so close together no one could do anything, and everyone looking for somewhere to go but with nothing to take them …

At the magazine stall, Dawkins' man gave Mehfooz a small envelope.

Back in the deathly calm of the air-conditioned Zen, Pappu could see traffic running smoothly, even though there were some flooded patches near the corners of the pavements, where the drains led out.

In a minute, they had reached Tulsi Pipe road. On the sides of the road, people who would otherwise have taken trains were walking home. There was something pleasant, elegant about the non-stop, light rain. It was 12.30—at this speed they would reach Andheri West in about an hour, perhaps two if there were a few traffic snarls on the way.

Pappu tried not to think of what would happen when they reached …

Hassan made phone calls to the jeep in front—and to Dawkins, telling him that he had got his envelope. Then he received a call after which he announced,

'Gopinathan is going to catch Unnikrishnan, it is only a matter of one-two hours.' Under his gag, Screwvala moaned.

They slowed down about half a furlong in front of Dadar flyover, joining two long lines of vehicles. They could see flooding at the base of the flyover. Even where they were, the water on both sides rose to meet at the higher centre of the road.

There were some cabs stalled in the water on the sides of the road. The knot of traffic at the base of the flyover was getting bigger. Soon, they were moving forward but only a few feet at a time. Patter-patter-patter, the rain fell without stopping—Pappu found some little comfort in its busy, friendly sound. Office workers, secretaries, peons, walked past in a thickening stream. They would sometimes thump on the Zen, asking for a lift, but Hassan would shake his head. Again Pappu found an odd, sickly-sweet comfort in watching all these innocent people going honestly about their lives … some were alone, some were business executives in pairs. The office secretaries were in groups, huddled two or three under a shared umbrella, carefully protecting from the rain above *and* water below their suitcases, cell phones, purses—some even carried expensive shoes in their hands … More and more of them started walking in the centre of the road, which was higher than the sides and so the water was shallower.

After a while, there was only one almost motionless queue of vehicles on each side of the road. Pappu looked at the shapes of the blind man and Scherezade in the jeep in front: they were now moving only after every five minutes, only a few feet every time.

Hassan was fuming. 'These inefficient municipality wallahs! How many times have they been warned to clean the drains!'

With the Zen not moving, the air conditioning was beginning to suffocate. Hassan suddenly turned around to Pappu and Screwvala and made a little speech: 'Listen carefully: I am now going to wind the car windows down. We will undo your gags. But understand: if you shout or do anything like that, I will not have any choice but to hurt you and somebody you care for. Also understand, this car cannot be traced to me. My men can shoot anyone, and I can hop out and no one will remember me. Do you understand?'

Pappu looked at the gagged Screwvala, who moaned and nodded. Pappu, too, nodded. Hassan jerked his chin at his man, who untied the gags. The driver stopped the engine, and the car windows were wound down.

There were more stranded, abandoned vehicles now, like little marooned islands in a muddy stream. Every new sight of chaos warmed Pappu's heart. Normally, it would have taken them fifteen-twenty minutes from Mahalaxmi Station, but now it had taken an hour.

Every delay was a small blessing …

How was Unnikrishnan doing, being chased by Gopinathan? Pappu wondered. Unnikrishnan too knew Hassan's game. If he managed to escape, maybe he could—

His thoughts were interrupted by a commotion to their right. A housewife had suddenly sunk so that only her head showed above the water. She screamed and waved desperately—she had fallen into some kind of crater. People around her pulled frantically, finally managing to bring her up again. A shopkeeper called out, 'Aunty! Please come here and rest awhile.' He made her sit down and poured her some tea from his flask.

For Pappu, this sight was another small blessing …

'Boss!' Mehfooz cried. 'Water has come into the car—one inch!'

Pappu looked down and saw his shoes in water. Never had dirty water seemed so much like a friend … Next to him, Screwvala had his eyes closed, breathing heavily.

But then the jeep in front moved and Hassan nudged his driver, who turned the key in the ignition. The engine coughed—but wouldn't start.

'Boss, the engine has shut down.'

'Laholvillakuvath!' Hassan cursed. He phoned his jeep in front and gave them the news. Then he sat for five-ten minutes, steaming—the water outside was now two feet high, muddy.

Pappu breathed more easily. He suddenly felt that maybe—just maybe, the universe might come to their rescue … Anyway, as long as they were stranded here, Hassan could not harm them.

Just then, an eight-seater jeep drove up next to them and blew its horn repeatedly. Hassan turned to snap at the driver but when he saw who it was, his face broke into a wide smile.

He waved delightedly, speaking to someone sitting next to the driver who Pappu couldn't see. He then turned around: 'Mehfooz—take the boy and Screwvala to the back of this jeep.'

The eight-seater's driver stopped next to the Zen. Pappu and Screwvala's hands were tied, so Mehfooz carefully bundled them, one by one, across the chocolate waters swirling in between the two vehicles —the rain was still non-stop light—into the back of the jeep. He followed them and shut the door. Hassan waded ahead to check his other jeep.

The eight-seater, too, had tinted windows. The back had two rows of seats opposite each other, facing the back and front of the vehicle. As his eyes adjusted to the dimness inside, Pappu saw a huddled body in one corner. He couldn't see the face but there was something about the tall, dark body that made him feel a chill, as he did whenever he saw Gopinathan …

The person was trembling and moaning. As he turned, Pappu gasped to see it was the astrologer! His eyes were glazed, he looked drugged. And Pappu realised that the reason he had felt strange whenever he saw Gopinathan was, simply, that he reminded him of the astrologer. Suddenly, Pappu understood that this must be Gopinathan's brother.

The astrologer's glazed eyes lit up when they saw Screwvala. Screwvala shook his head sadly, muttering, 'Unni, Unni.' Mehfooz silenced him with a threatening gesture, and Unnikrishnan moaned and fell back into a faint.

Hassan climbed into the front seat. The man next to the driver turned and grinned at Pappu, his teeth very white in his black face.

'Gopinathan!' Pappu gasped.

Gopinathan chuckled. Every confident chuckle seemed to chop into Pappu's heart. Beside him, Pappu could feel Mr Screwvala flinch.

Hassan asked, 'How is it going, Gopinathan?'

'Good, with your blessings,' Gopinathan said. 'Behind is proof that now only you are my brother.'

'And what should I say? That in the jeep in front is proof that now you are my uncle?' Both Hassan and Gopinathan laughed.

The eight-seater jeep started, leaving behind the Zen with Hassan's peon-driver in it. But after ten feet, the traffic again forced them to a halt.

'Y'Allah!' Hassan groaned.

'You're giving Dawkins Kenilworth goods also today?' Gopinathan asked.

'Want to give but in this flood, how late will we be?'

They did a smart left turn before Dadar flyover into a lane leading to the main road, Senapati Bapat Marg.

Hassan tried his cell phone again and cursed. 'Anything happens and these mobile networks just crash!' He tried Gopinathan's cell phone, and then finally on Mehfooz's cell he managed to tell Dawkins that the flooding on the roads might delay them by an hour.

The water in the lane was cleaner than on the main road, and deeper. In the evenly-spread steel-grey light, the waters churned with the confusion of people and cars wading through, a fallen tree's emerald green fronds lying across, and reflections of huge dark billowing clouds, the light merciless rain. The jeeps waded on for about thirty feet, then Hassan's jeep ahead juddered to a stop. Hassan cursed and they stopped, too.

'I warn you, Screwvala, your daughter is sitting in a jeep with a bomb next to the petrol tank. I have the button for this bomb, and if you misbehave, I can press it.'

Hassan waded out to the other jeep: soon he, Scherezade and one of his men, up to their thighs in water, hair plastered to heads and clothes plastered to bodies, were pushing the jeep. Scherezade was thankfully in jeans, and Pappu could imagine her fear for her father's life as she pushed with all her might, feet groping at the pot-holed Mumbai road three feet under water … Every now and then, she would turn and look towards her father, and Hassan or his policeman would pat her smartly on the shoulder. Finally, the jeep started and Hassan was back in Gopinathan's eight-seater.

Now it was the turn of the eight-seater to cough, and stall.

Pappu looked at Screwvala. Mr Screwvala's face was frozen with fear, and he was looking in front of him where his daughter had been visible a minute ago.

Mehfooz undid Screwvala's and Pappu's ropes, and together with Gopinathan and Hassan, they pushed the jeep. But it wouldn't start. In the end, Hassan, leaving Unnikrishnan, Gopinathan and the driver inside their stalled vehicle, pushed Screwvala in front of him on the road while Mehfooz dragged Pappu. They kept in the lines of people wading on, to avoid falling into manholes.

They reached Senapati Bapat Marg after ten minutes, Hassan's other jeep keeping pace. It was more than two hours since since they had started from Mahalaxmi Station, normally a thirty-minute journey. One-and-a-half hours of grace period, Pappu thought. But how much longer would it last?

Just as they turned on Senapati Bapat Marg towards the suburbs, Gopinathan's sinister grinning face reappeared: he had managed to get his eight-seater started. Relieved, Hassan ordered Screwvala inside and climbed in himself. Pappu looked around: Mehfooz was glowering at him, his hand inside his pocket where Pappu knew was a gun.

Inside, as Mehfooz took the ropes out of his pockets and tied their hands again, Pappu felt as if he were being squeezed into a small box of fear by a world that would soon bury him and his friends, never to be found by anyone, while the nukes would spread, and spread the power of people like Hassan and Gopinathan over everybody else.

The jeeps took a lane leading to Hinduja Hospital, making frighteningly quick progress. They came to a halt at the rear of a massive block of traffic, frozen still at the Mahim Dargah road. Pappu breathed a little easier—but by now, he was exhausted with fear.

There was no conversation in the jeep; even Hassan and Gopinathan had stopped talking. Hassan's cell rang. It was Dawkins' man calling from a landline in Colaba: Dawkins hadn't been able to get through to Hassan after an hour of trying, even on a landline. Hassan told him to tell Dawkins they might be late by two-three hours ... Pappu saw it was 5.30 in Mehfooz's watch.

After a long time, when it seemed they would never move, the traffic slowly eased past Mahim's green mosque and spread onto the broader road. Past Mahim's Machimar village Pappu saw to his left ocean waves striking the concrete barriers and rearing up twelve feet high, like a gang of monster cobras attacking with hoods spread and throats inflamed from dirty blue venom. (He remembered the religious stories his grandmother used to tell, in which poisonous cobras were often described as saviours.) On the right, the polluted Mithi river had swollen so much it was only ten feet below the two pipelines that were normally forty feet above. On top of the pipelines, each as fat and tall as a man, he saw two long single queues of ordinary Mumbaikars balancing their way homeward. Beyond them he saw six long, unbroken, unbelievably straight rows of people walking home on the planks between the railway tracks.

Hassan was asking people in neighbouring vehicles about traffic and routes. Pappu wondered if he should yell for help. But then Hassan would just get back into the eight-seater and they would drive away—even if slowly, Pappu knew that Mumbaikars were not famous for their help to strangers in need. And then what?

Hassan turned to Gopinathan: 'They say the clearest route is the Lilavati Hospital road.'

It was getting darker. The two jeeps moved with terrifying speed on the flyovers towards Lilavati Hospital, but as soon as they touched down everything became dismal—comfortingly dismal to Pappu. It was like a ghost town in water that reached up to the tops of even the jeeps' wheels, and Pappu felt he could sit here and watch this fascinating scene forever. He suddenly knew what it must feel like to be an insect who loved miserable, dismal conditions because he lived and thrived in them. But slowly, in the middle of the muddy waters, a long single file of vehicles made it to the stretch of road leading directly to Lilavati Hospital. In the road's flooded corners, Pappu could see like coloured rocks in a stream, the rooftops of abandoned cars. In the centre of the road, where the water was always the shallowest, he would sometimes see a lonely figure walking, such as a gutsy middle-aged secretary making her way home.

After Lilavati Hospital, they turned back on to S.V. Road and then doubled back to Carter Road and turned right, on to the lane towards Pali Hill. As the lane rose clear of the waters they began to move quickly, and Pappu sensed the journey coming to an end. He felt he and his friends swiftly entering the shallows of the ocean of doom.

Near Pali Hill they paused as a jeep ahead with a Sikh family dropped some friends. 'Why don't you come up, refresh yourself for five minutes?' the friends asked them. 'No, our children are waiting at home in Andheri—we can't even talk to them on phone.' The friend said, 'It is 6.30, there is time.' But the Sikh family waved and drove off.

'Let us not take the Juhu route, it is too close to the sea,' Gopinathan suggested. Hassan nodded.

The jeeps went via Linking Road through the lane that turned into S.V. Road opposite Milan Subway … They were moving quickly, and Pappu felt a sickening sinking sensation.

When they turned left towards Juhu aerodrome, the sight that met Pappu's eyes struck him with an amazed numbness, as if he were a stranger in another world …

Anu and Sunita

This world was bathed in an evenly spread grey light. S.V. Road was four feet under grey water from end to end, with huge waves surging back and forth from buses that majestically moved through a mess of abandoned cars, taxis, autorickshaws, and even some buses. They rocked slowly in the huge waves, and some that had windows above the water still had people inside them. The Sikh family, just ahead of Pappu, knew at once that they would not see their children tonight.

Pappu was surprised to suddenly feel as if he was watching a movie from far away … A movie about someone like him, who he knew well, that would very soon have an interesting ending … It was a welcome feeling, after the hard gloom he had been feeling before.

On the sides of the roads two long, unbroken chains of people waded homeward, steadying each other against the unsettling waves. The homes lining S.V. Road too were flooded—they were dark, which meant power had gone out. People in them had begun burning candles, and there were torches on the road, too.

As Hassan's vehicles struggled slowly through the water—which came almost up to the windows, and was now flooding in from the cracks of the doors—Pappu began panting as his breath suddenly flowed free and strong, and his heart beat with a wild hope.

Hassan's plans could not work! At that very moment, Hassan turned and the sharp alarm in his eyes met the sudden hope in Pappu's. Both he and Pappu turned to Screwvala, and both caught an unmistakable spark in his eye—he couldn't disguise it. Pappu thought, in the other jeep Scherezade must be feeling the same—could she describe it to the blind man? Could he feel Mumbai's flooding through his feet?

Someone thumped the eight-seater jeep, and Hassan yelled out, 'No lift! Go—' But then he noticed that a boy stood holding a tray of snacks and cups above the water.

'Don't want lift, uncle, I live in that building. My mother thought you are on the road for hours and you would be wanting some tea and vada pav.'

Hassan looked open-mouthed at the young boy, holding the tray above the water which came almost up to his chest. A cricket cap sheltered his eyes from the rain. Hassan raised his hand to wave the boy away, then lowered it, ashamed. But he again raised his hand and shooed the boy away, his face wearing an ugly twisted expression. The boy stepped back with a hurt expression.

'Mother said you can use the bathroom if you want,' he added, but the eight-seater had slowly moved forward.

Pappu looked around: the other jeep was just behind, the windows were down so he could dimly see the shapes of Scherezade and the blind man. He noticed other people in the water going around with trays, and many stranded in vehicles as well as walking in the long lines were taking the tea and samosas gratefully. Nearby two women were standing in the water in their saris, holding a sign bobbing in the water: 'BEWARE CRATER HERE.' A man was shining a torch into the dark waters to guide passers-by around the crater; he was cracking jokes, and they were laughing.

There were more thumps on the jeep. Hassan flinched as if somebody was hitting him.

It was a group of teenage boys and girls. 'Uncle,' one of them said, 'If you tell us where you want to go to, we can guide you out. We know this area, we live here.' She was a short, eighteen-year-old tomboy peering through wet spectacles, her hair in short curls, wearing a red top and jeans rolled up to the knees.

Hassan looked at them all, open-mouthed. Some of the group were at Hassan's other jeep a few feet away, offering help and trays of biscuits, tea, water.

Before he knew it, Pappu was yelling to the tomboy in red: 'Help! Help us, they are kidnapping us!'

The girl couldn't believe her ears: she peered in the clear grey light into the eight-seater.

Hassan turned: Pappu heard his own words, and they sounded ridiculous. He had made a mistake. In this chaos, people would ignore one mad little boy and move on to save lives, their own and others. He should have stayed quiet—but then what? He had no choice.

As Mehfooz tried to decide whether to cover Pappu's face or hit him, Pappu yelled again at the top of his voice: 'HELP! Help that girl in the other jeep! HELP! HEL—'

Hassan angrily gestured to Mehfooz, and Mehfooz hit Pappu across the face. 'Quiet!'

Suddenly, from the other jeep, Scherezade's voice rang out: 'HELP US! WE'RE BEING KIDNAPPED!'

The group around the jeeps stepped back in the water, astonished. Hassan snarled to the driver: 'Just get out of here!'

The driver accelerated: the jeep moved a few feet. The other jeep revved up too, overtook them for a few feet—and sank into a pothole!

'HELP! HELP!' Pappu yelled.

'Children, call more help!' the blind man was also yelling, in the other jeep. Screwvala's boom sounded in Pappu's eardrums.

The tomboy, who seemed to be the leader of the teenagers, suddenly started shouting to passers-by: 'UNCLE, AUNTY, COME HERE! COME HERE! ANU, THESE PEOPLE ARE BEING KIDNAPPED!'

The unbroken line of passers-by paused. One of the women holding up the 'BEWARE CRATER HERE' sign asked, 'Are you sure, Sunita?'

'Anu, I'm sure!'

Anu turned to the line of passers-by. 'Those people are being kidnapped! Let us surround that jeep!' And at once, people who in a normal Mumbai day would ignore anything that would slow them down in their rat race, including cries for help, immediately turned and waded purposefully towards Hassan's jeeps.

By this time, water had entered the jeep, and was upto their shins. The water's cool sting cleared Pappu's mind. But, he could see, it enraged Hassan. As a circle of people gathered around the two jeeps, Gopinathan's driver stopped. Hassan looked at him: looked at the other jeep, which had stalled: and finally took out his gun.

'Mehfooz, Gopinathan, fire in the air,' he said. Opposite Pappu, Mehfooz was sweating as he took out his pistol.

The gunshots filled the eight-seater with hot sparks, deafening reports and smoke. Pappu put his hands to his ears and shut his eyes. When he opened them, the tomboy in red and her friends had fallen back—but still surrounded them.

Hassan got out of the jeep, wondering how he could get out of this situation, how he could get Screwvala to take him to the Taj letter in the artist's store room in Andheri. He pointed to Screwvala: 'See!' he shouted to the crowd, 'the Taj letter mastermind!'

Screwvala leaned forward—he was sitting at the central left window, behind Gopinathan at the eight-seater's far side from Hassan. In the even grey light, the interior of the eight-seater was excellently lit. 'MUMBAIKARS!' boomed Screwvala out of the right-hand window, on which side Hassan was. 'Take us to the police and see who—' Hassan motioned to Mehfooz to hit Screwala with his pistol, and Screwvala ducked and shut up—but he had made his point.

The crowd moved closer … Hassan waved his pistol, and the ones on his side paused: but the situation was so strange, and the day was so bizarre and there were so many in the crowd, that they didn't back off, they just looked at him.

Hassan walked up and down in the water, moving to the driver's side and waving his pistol. When he pointed it, people would crouch—that was easier in this water than backing off.

Splash!

Gopinathan had jumped out of the left front door. Hassan could only hear him, he was on the right of the eight-seater. The murky waters shook furiously as Gopinathan swam away underwater—he was obviously a good swimmer, and he had decided to take advantage of his skill.

'Gopinathan!' Hassan cried out in dismay. He trudged angrily and noisily in the high water past the front of the eight-seater in Gopinathan's direction. Pappu breathed deeply with a burning satisfaction at Hassan's distress. Mehfooz, sitting opposite him, turned to look at his boss with deep alarm. Hassan was lifting his gun in the direction that Gopinathan had swum …

Pappu suddenly felt a blow on the back of his head. He ducked, and was soon crushed by the weight of Screwvala's body. He couldn't see anything: Screwvala was moving violently, pressing on him unbearably—There was an ear-splitting explosion, and then another, less loud.

The weight lifted. Pappu looked up to see Mehfooz's unseeing eyes, slack mouth, and blood flowing from his neck. Screwvala snatched the gun from Mehfooz's twisted fingers, which he had forced to press the trigger.

Hassan was in front of the eight-seater on the left, and his gun too was smoking. He had just fired into the murky waters after Gopinathan. Another explosion split Pappu's ears as Screwvala shot Gopinathan's driver in the back of his head, and Unnikrishnan's body twitched violently at Pappu's left as Screwvala did a full turn in his seat towards Hassan: but Hassan had suddenly vanished.

Screwvala and Pappu peered into the grey rain. But there was no Hassan.

'Police!' Screwvala called out to the shocked crowd, looking carefully at the water for signs of Hassan. 'Someone call the police, fast!' He said this so the stunned crowd knew he was on their side. And he quickly pointed his pistol at the other jeep that had his daughter, the blind man, Hassan's policeman and driver.

The driver immediately put his hands up and cried: 'I'm only driver!'

'Not a threat,' Pappu heard Screwvala mutter.

Hassan's other goonda, next to Scherezade on the far side of the car from them, looked at the crowd and at Screwvala. He put his hands up, carefully placing his gun on the roof of the jeep, amongst the splinters of rain breaking on the metal. He then opened the door softly and slipped out into the water.

'Chokra,' said Screwvala, his eyes searching the water, 'keep looking and shout if Hassan comes above the water.'

'Yes sir.'

A few long moments passed. Pappu's eyes nervously scanned every direction. At a distance, he saw Hassan's goonda surface.

'Catch that man,' Screwvala boomed, eyes still scouring the water. 'The police will be wanting him.'

The crowd had been using ropes to help people around the crater, and they tied up the goonda.

Closer to the eight-seater, the rain-stung waters were eerily quiet. From the other jeep came the sound of someone stepping into the water.

'Beta Hassan? Where are you, beta …' The blind man was slowly treading in the water towards the eight-seater.

'Keep looking for the bastard,' Screwvala snapped tensely at Pappu.

'Beta?'

And then, in a violent eruption of heaving water right next to Screwvala's door, Hassan burst out gasping for air. Screwvala turned his gun on him but Hassan was too busy catching his breath to notice. Behind him, the blind man paused at the watery uproar.

Hassan didn't see his uncle. As he caught his breath he took in the scene in the eight-seater. 'Your hands … weren't …?' he asked Screwvala. He seemed strangely untroubled by Screwvala's gun. His right hand with his pistol hung by his side.

Screwvala's gun did not waver as he answered: 'The

rope became soft with water. I was able to tease the knot out.'

'Beta Hassan!'

Hassan turned in surprise. 'Chachajaan!' he said, with an almost innocent surprise. 'Where is …?'

'The man who was guarding me? Beta, I heard him slip into the water.'

'Your hands were tied, Chachajaan …'

'Beta, you have forgotten the magic your blind Chachajaan's fingers used to do for you?'

Hassan sighed. Now he remembered his uncle's magic fingers, made super-sensitive by blindness. 'I had forgotten …'

'It is a difficult situation, no beta?' His voice was loving, sympathetic.

'Mr Hafiz—stay where you are!' Screwvala shouted. 'I think I am going to shoot this man.'

'That gun is empty,' Hassan said to Screwvala. 'Mehfooz's gun was empty, I always count the bullets my men use up because they are too stupid to.'

Screwvala knew he was telling the truth, even before he pulled the trigger and nothing happened.

Hassan lifted his pistol towards Screwvala. 'Now you need to remember,' Hassan said, 'that I can press a button to set off the bomb in your daughter's jeep.'

'If the jeep explodes you will die too, you are so close.'

'I do not mind.'

Screwvala took a deep breath and answered, 'I do not mind too.' It was more difficult for him: Hassan was talking about his own life, but Screwvala was talking about his daughter's.

'Beta Hassan …'

'Chachajaan—stay where you are, stupid old man!'

'Beta, I cannot.' The blind man was slowly moving towards him. 'Shoot me if you want. But how can I leave you alone in this difficult time? Hassan beta, let me help you. Let me help you to make peace with yourself.'

'Chachajaan, you are siding with these people who lynched our people fifteen years ago …'

'No, not these children.'

'Well their people, their parents, their families!'

'Beta, they can say our people started the Mumbai killings … and we can say their people started it by destroying the Babri Mosque, and they can say our people first destroyed temples to make mosques … How far back should we go? If everyone goes on forever about the past, it will go on forever in the future … Beta, you will find peace only if you free yourself from this …'

The blind man wanted to embrace him, his voice ached with love for his little Hassan, which disgusted Hassan to the core.

'Stay back, Chachajaan …'

Screwvala swung the door into Hassan's midriff and grabbed hold of his right hand which held the gun. Hassan immediately reached with his other hand for his kurta pocket and Screwvala, without letting go of the gun hand, tried to stop his left hand.

'Mr Hafiz, catch hold of his arm or he will blow up the jeep!' Screwvala boomed.

The blind man was already reaching out for Hassan, and felt Screwvala's arm struggling against Hassan's left arm.

Hassan's pistol went off. There was a loud cry—Pappu looked, and saw the lady in the sari bend, her face screwed up in pain.

'Anu!' cried Sunita. She dived into the water and swam quickly to her friend.

Screwvala and the blind man struggled to trap Hassan's arms. Seeing their hero wounded, a dozen people waded angrily through the water towards them. Unnikrishnan began to stir and moan violently next to Pappu.

Hassan roared and struggled angrily, his left hand straining to reach his pocket.

'Dikra!' Screwvala called out to Scherezade. 'Get out of that jeep!'

'I'm out, Papa!' cried Scherezade.

By now the crowd was on them.

'He's a suicide bomber!' cried a terrified boy.

'I am holding his hand!' sobbed the blind man. 'I am holding his hand!'

Other people in the crowd helped the blind man hold Hassan's left hand, and others helped Mr Screwvala hold his right. But the crowd was in danger of letting Hassan go in the confusion.

Hassan struggled savagely: the terrified boy put his knee on Hassan's chest and others too put their weight on him till his face was below the water.

The blind man could feel Hassan's body sink below the water—but he couldn't see where Hassan's mouth and nose were. He moved his head, trying to listen to what was happening. 'Hassan? Hassan?' he cried desperately.

When there was no answer from Hassan, the blind man understood that his face must be below the water. Three or four people held Hassan down below the water, and they watched the blind man in astonishment.

'Hassan!' he wailed skyward, weeping for the little nephew he had once known, who he still loved. The terrified boy kept an eye on the blind man's grip of Hassan's right arm—and he saw that it did not loosen a bit, even as Hassan's body began to shudder below the water, below so many bodies.

'Hassan! ... Oh Hassan ...' the blind man's unseeing eyes rolled at the grey clouds rolling above, while his tears poured copiously into the flood waters that were drowning his nephew.

SANCTUARY

Screwvala let go of Hassan's arm. He hugged his daughter, still in shock, and untied her hands.

'Anu's leg is hit!' Sunita was supporting her friend. 'Come, we need to take her to Nanavati Hospital, fast!' A dozen hands rose to lift one of their heroes and carry her to Nanavati Hospital, half a furlong away.

'Oh,' Sunita added, turning back and pointing at the 'BEWARE CRATER HERE!' sign. 'Keep that sign up. And help those kidnapped people! Come, Anu.'

It was getting dark. Unnikrishnan was sitting, dumbly rubbing his eyes. A helpful stranger untied his hands, and Pappu's too.

Pappu waded out of the eight-seater towards the other jeep. The blind man was sitting in the back, weeping as he held his dead nephew's body. Scherezade was standing by him in the water, stroking his arm.

'Oh Pappu!' she hugged him with her other arm: and he, awkwardly, hugged her back.

Meanwhile Screwvala was taking charge. He asked Hassan's goonda where Ghani's godown with the nuclear parts was. He then gently urged the weeping blind man to leave Hassan's body in the jeep and took from Hassan's kurta his cell phone. Pulling the goonda with him, he put the Mumbaikars in charge of bringing his daughter, the blind man, Pappu, and Unnikrishnan to a place of shelter.

Pappu and Scherezade led the blind man gently into the middle-class drawing room of a house on the main road. As the kind family served tea, vada pav and samosas, Screwvala managed to get through to Inspector Stanley on his landline.

He greeted the Inspector cheerfully. But then he boomed angrily: 'Hello—hello—hello?' Screwvala turned to the kids. 'He's gone to have a trace put on the line, the idiot! Here Pappu, you talk to him, so that he knows I am not the enemy.'

When Stanley came back on the line, he was amazed to hear Pappu's voice! He was even more amazed by the story Pappu told, and kept interrupting with questions. When Pappu told him about Hassan being behind the whole nuclear theft, there was a long silence, and Pappu knew that Stanley was wondering if anything in his story was true. When he told him about Hassan's death, the Inspector went speechless with shock.

Screwvala impatiently grabbed the phone and gave Inspector Stanley the location of Ghani's godown. Then he told him they had Hassan's goonda with them, and he gave their present address. After this he listened silently for a very long while, and then said: 'Okay! We will wait here!'

He turned to the others. 'He will come in a helicopter to pick up Hassan's goonda and go to the godown with him.'

In an hour's time, a helicopter hovered over the terrace of the little building under a massive see-through umbrella of rain spray around its propellers. Screwvala and half-a-dozen Mumbaikars took Hassan's goonda to the terrace.

'Will be in touch!' Stanley shouted from inside the helicopter as he waved to his friends. As they took off, Paluskar too waved by his side, Hassan's goonda behind him safely handcuffed between two men.

Mr Screwvala got the crowd to get the jeep unstuck, and gently herded Scherezade, Pappu, the blind man and Unnikrishnan into it. They avoided looking at the eight-seater with the three bodies as Screwvala turned around and slowly drove them out of Vile Parle.

They turned back towards Pali Hill, where Unnikrishnan lived with his sister and her family.

By the time they reached, it was 10 pm, and Unnikrishnan had almost fully recovered from the effects of the drug. The blind man was weeping silently, ceaselessly as the rain. They were all drenched and tired.

There was electricity in the building—it was on high ground. Unnikrishnan's sister, Anuradha, was enormously relieved to see him and his friends. She soon had them despatched in turns to the three bathrooms for hot baths, and within twenty minutes they were all sitting in Anuradha's vast drawing room in front of the TV, wolfing down little steaming hot idlis in fragrant hot-*hot* sambar. Scherezade wore a salwar kameez of Anuradha's, Pappu wore a T-shirt and shorts belonging to her elder son, the blind man wore one of Unnikrishnan's kurta-pajamas, and Mr Screwvala—Anuradha was confused about what to dress him in, since he was so large. Finally, she gave him some of her husband's loosest pajamas—which fit him perfectly, like tight slacks—and also tied some bedsheets as robes.

'Where is brother-in-law? And the children?' asked Unnikrishnan. It turned out that Anuradha's husband was stranded in office. Her little one had gone to visit his grandparents in Andheri and was now spending the night with them. The elder one had gone to a movie with friends and now the whole gang were sleeping over at one friend's house.

'I wonder where Gopi is,' Anuradha sighed.

Unnikrishnan snapped, 'We agreed never to mention him in this house!'

'Please relax, brother' Anuradha said, taken aback by his strong reaction.

Pappu called Ayah. 'Chotu!' Ayah yelled with relief. 'You are okay! I went mad dialling-dialling your number whole day long! You don't know what I am thinking, not hearing your voice! On TV, what horrible-horrible things they are showing happening to Mumbai!'

After Pappu had explained to her that he was safe, he requested Anuradha to put on the TV. As they sat, safe and warm on the sofa watching TV, it was clear that the most tired and soul-weary was the blind man.

'Uncle, would you like to lie down?' Anuradha asked him.

The blind man did not answer, just shook his head in despair. Scherezade helped Anuradha prepare her little son's room for the blind man. Soon the blind man was in bed with the lights off. Pappu wondered: would he be able to forget his sorrow in sleep, or would he just lie in bed and weep?

On TV they were showing dramatic scenes from all over Mumbai. 'The floods are due to a simultaneous combination of peak high tide, record rains, and unrepaired drainage systems … ' The chief minister of Maharashtra was saying, 'Government declares two-day state holiday … ' Another channel was showing railway stations with platforms looking like piers by the sea waiting for ships. 'For a city that is often accused of being heartless, it is astonishing to see how people can also be helpful … these young boys are risking their own lives to rescue people stranded in trains and buses …'

Hassan's phone rang and Screwvala picked it up. 'You found the nuclear parts! Congratulations, Inspector Stanley Coelho! You deserve a promotion! And I deserve the dropping of all court cases … plus one Padamshree please!' He gave Unnikrishnan's address, and disconnected. 'The Inspector is coming soon. He is sending nuclear parts to headquarters with Paluskar.'

Anuradha couldn't believe her ears. '*What* parts? And how can he just come? All roads are flooded?'

On TV, a reporter was at Mahim where office-goers

were still dangerously balancing their way home on the pipelines above the Mithi river! 'Mumbai is paying the price for its heavy pollution of the Mithi river, which used to be Mumbai's giant drain for the extra water in times of heavy rain and high tide. But now the Mithi river is blocked with waste and the extra water and pollution is being dumped into Mumbai's streets … '

Another journalist reported, 'To feed the greed of builders, businessman and politicians, green zone rules have been violated, changing the pattern of tides and the absorption by the earth of the water … '

For dinner, Anuradha served them delicious home-made masala dosas, with the freshest, yummiest coconut and green chutneys they'd ever tasted. Pappu enjoyed his favourite combination of hot dosa with cold cola. Outside, it continued to rain gently but ceaselessly.

At around 11.30, as Unnikrishnan and Screwvala went to the bar near the dining table at the other end of the large room, the sound of the TV was suddenly drowned by a huge racket outside.

'Ah! Just in time, Time beats with the wings of a … a … flight that is about to land … in Time,' Screwvala said.

Unnikrishnan shook his head in wonder at what he could do with the English language.

'I can't believe it! Is that a heli …' The rest of Anuradha's words were drowned, as a helicopter landed in the park behind the building—and then, at once, was gone.

Screwvala filled a wine glass and, holding it elegantly by the stem, went to the main door. When a soaked Inspector Stanley entered, Screwvala solemnly offered him the wine: 'Just in time, Inspector.'

'Oh,' Stanley said, refusing the glass because he had got the habit of trying not to be too Goan with drinks. 'Oh well,' he then said, and took it.

'Stanley, Unni,' Mr Screwvala went to the table, raised his glass and boomed, 'Here's to the blind man!'

'Would he be approving,' asked Unnikrishnan, 'us drinking to his health with alcohol, as a Muslim?'

Screwvala put down his glass. 'Hmm … you're right.'

'Oh,' Stanley said, putting down his glass, disappointedly.

Mr Screwvala asked Anuradha: 'Do you have any fruit juice?'

She did. And Screwvala was soon booming: 'Gentlemen—to the blind man!'

'To the blind man, without whom we would not have made it!' The three men lifted their glasses. Stanley looked at his. 'Oh well,' he said and with a quick grimace, downed the juice.

Soon Unnikrishnan was laughing at the memory of how Stanley fell off his motorbike the night he whispered 'Kenilworth' near Pappu's house. Anuradha, Scherezade and Pappu had switched the TV off, and sat in chairs close by.

'But, men,' and Stanley's face screwed up in the familiar manner, '*how* did you know about Kenilworth? And why did Pappu think you were astrologer?'

Unnikrishnan told them how he had been with Screwvala from the beginning, and how Samrat Singh, the paan-spitting policeman in Stanley's police station, kept Unnikrishnan informed for a bribe, and how Unnikrishnan had followed Pappu at first just to warn him and his friends against being involved.

'Near your bungalow Pappu, I saw astrologer sitting. I thought, if I sit there with his big-big rings and brahmin-marks—*we* are Keralite brahmins also—I would do very very good astrologer. For fee, he let me sit in his place, wear his big rings .... I knew Stanley honest man. But Screwvala not sure, ordered me not to help Stanley—but I try to give him clue, even that night he ...' he began to laugh again 'falling from his motorbike ...'

Later, Mr Screwvala called Pappu to his side and hugged him warmly. 'Pappu, we are now family. Scherezade! From now on, I have *two* children!'

'What does that mean, Papa?' Scherezade walked up to him. 'That from now on, you're going to be out of the house *double* the time?'

Mr Screwvala gave a hearty laugh to cover up his confusion, letting Pappu go and turning back to the Inspector. Scherezade shook her head, took Pappu by the hand and led him to the sofa at the other end of the vast drawing room.

Pappu looked at the rain tapping on the large windows and savoured his own contentment. Then he thought, with a pang, that the sardars must still be stranded in the flooded streets, their children still waiting at home. He hoped the kids at least had electricity in their building …

President Abdus Sami, in a ceremony in Rashtrapati Bhavan's Durbar Hall, gave out medals of honour to the blind man, Mr Screwvala, Pappu, *Chief* Inspector Stanley Coelho and Scherezade.

The President had been one of the nation's leading nuclear scientists, and was also known for his love for children. So it was no surprise when he invited them all to tea after the public function.

In a room overlooking a garden, the President shooed away the maid and personally measured out the tea for his guests. He was a bachelor—but his sister's family had come to visit, and he told the guests that he had to join them in fifteen minutes.

He told his guests stories of the days when he had been head of the country's nuclear programme. Then the talk turned to larger issues.

'You see,' he said, pronouncing it 'seeyee' in his sing-song Tamilian accent, 'we are *not* a puhrfectly democratic country—far from puhrfect. But we *are* truly democratic. We are also not a puhrfectly secular country. Far from puhrfect. But even then, we *are* truly secular. You see … India is a great country, but it has great injustices also. But the yimportant thing about India is, we are moving forward—unlike some countries who blame us, who are moving *backward*! Slowly but steadily, India is moving towards greater democracy, greater secularism, less casteism and removal of poverty ... For me India, where it is headed, is one of mankind's most *sacred* ideals.'

Soon after, the President of India rose and joined his sister's family to perform namaz in the splendidly serene gardens of Rashtrapati Bhavan.

ACKNOWLEDGEMENTS

Thanks to Shruti Tandan, Leena Basrur, Ranjit Hoskote, Tejasvi Tandon, Dipalle Parmar, and Varkha and Maya Chulani for their invaluable feedback on this book.

Thanks to Naresh Fernandes for putting me on to Jer Mahal when we met in a Mumbai local: Nilufer Palia and Farrokh Nanavati for allowing me greater insight into the world of the Parsis: and Sandeep Vitekari for his guidance on Marathi and Maharashtrian cuisine.

Thanks to my editors at Scholastic, Anushka Ravishankar and Sayoni Basu, for believing in this book. Thanks to Himanjali Sankar for providing editorial input and suggestions that improved the book.

In my research, I would like to acknowledge my debt to Sooni Taraporevala's *Parsis: The Zoroastrians of India*; Naresh Fernandes' articles, 'Love and Longing in Mumbai's Jazz Age' and 'Remembering Anthony Gonsalves'; Olga Valladares' thesis *The Coor System: A Study of Goan Club Life in Bombay*; and Adil F. Rangoonwalla's *Zarathushtrianism*.

And last but certainly not least, I would like to thank my family for their invaluable support.

About the Author

Vivek Tandon has published a book of poems, *Climbing the Spiral.* He has written a play which was selected for Royal Court Theatre London's prestigious International Residency Programme, and has also acted on the Mumbai stage. His funny poetry will soon appear in a forthcoming Sahitya Akademi book of children's verse. He is at present working as a creative consultant in advertising in Mumbai.